Tourist Shopping Villages

Routledge Advances in Tourism

EDITED BY STEPHEN PAGE, *University of Stirling, Scotland*

Tourist Shopping Villages

Forms and Functions

**Laurie Murphy,
Pierre Benckendorff,
Gianna Moscardo and
Philip L. Pearce**

Routledge
Taylor & Francis Group
New York   London

First published 2011
by Routledge
711 Third Avenue, New York, NY 10017

Simultaneously published in the UK
by Routledge
2 Park Square, Milton Park, Abingdon, Oxon OX14 4RN

Routledge is an imprint of the Taylor & Francis Group, an informa business

First issued in paperback 2012

Typeset in Sabon by IBT Global.

Library of Congress Cataloging-in-Publication Data
Tourist shopping villages : forms and functions / by Laurie Murphy . . . [et al].
    p. cm. — (Routledge advances in tourism)
    Includes bibliographical references and index.
1. Tourism.   2. Shopping.   3. Tourism—Marketing.   I. Murphy, Laurie.
    G155.A1T5987 2010
    910.68—dc22
    2010025613

ISBN13: 978-0-415-96527-9 (hbk)
ISBN13: 978-0-203-83482-4 (ebk)
ISBN13: 978-0-415-81151-4 (pbk)

Contents

Figures

Tables

Case Studies

Preface

You do not have to like shopping to read this book. An enthusiasm for shopping may make some sections of this research work more interesting for you to read but in company with those people who dislike shopping (and there are certainly quite a few in the latter category) we ask you to set aside your personal views and view tourist shopping in small villages in two interrelated ways. First, we ask that you consider how this form of tourist shopping can be used as a tool to sustain rural or peripheral communities. In this context we also ask you to consider with us what factors or features of such villages, their settings and their practices might enhance their value to multiple interested parties.

A second perspective can accompany the first. On this occasion we seek to kindle your interest in viewing the contemporary village shopping practices and forms as a study in the experience economy. Here we are interested in seeing how experiences may be understood not just for the shopping context but for a broad range of leisure and entertainment settings.

The fact that you are reading this preface is at least a start (especially for those who dislike shopping). We have used a number of cases and illustrations throughout this book to maintain your interest and represent some of the core ideas. Most of you will live somewhere near a shopping village and if this book stimulates you to look at a familiar setting with fresh perspectives it will have achieved one purpose. A second goal lies in providing source material which can assist the creation of superior tourist shopping village settings which in turn support the experiences visitors find enchanting, purposeful and rich in positive story telling potential. This arm of the research program represents the functional and pragmatic arm of applied tourism studies, or at least provides the groundwork for creating useful applications. For those whose interests lie in developing the groundwork of academic ideas rather than seeking applications we also have a continuing organizing theme threading through the book. We argue for the applicability of a TSV Visitor Experience Model and by implication we suggest a broad role for this conceptual scheme in explaining the forces affecting people's experience.

All of the researchers contributing to this volume have family members who have shopped along with us in our travels and work. For Laurie

Murphy, Caitlin has endured shopping bravely and her mother Marion more enthusiastically; for Pierre Benckendorff, Kym and later Joel have been feisty shoppers and for Gianna Moscardo and Philip Pearce, Tom and Jack have been mostly welcome companions. We thank them all for their contributions. All members of this research team have been based at James Cook University for the preparation and writing of this book. We thank the Faculty of Law, Business and Creative Arts which provided some of the funds to support this research program.

Laurie Murphy
Pierre Benckendorff
Gianna Moscardo
Philip Pearce

Townsville, Australia, June 2010

1 Tourist Shopping Opportunities
Placing Tourist Shopping Villages in a Larger Context

INTRODUCTION

Shopping is the core of consumption and retailing the emblem of a consumer society (Timothy 2005). The primary goal of retailing is to encourage people to shop and purchase merchandise and services. As shopping is one of the oldest and most common activities associated with travel, it might be expected that the relationship between tourism, retailing and shopping should be of concern to tourism academics. Perhaps surprisingly, and however obvious the relationship would appear, an analysis of shopping has not been at the forefront of tourism research (Coles 2004b). While the existing tourism academic interest may be limited, shopping is becoming increasingly important to tourism both in terms of the actual consumption of goods purchased and as a source of enjoyment and satisfaction. Shopping stimulated by visitors outside of the local region has an important economic impact on host communities as well as being a key attraction for visitors (Asgary, et al. 1997; Jackson 1996).

The shopping districts of the world, which attract tourists and beguile locals, form an impressive array of high status locations. Guidebooks frequently highlight elite districts known for their shopping. The street names have the aroma of money. Rodeo Drive, Fifth Avenue, the Champs Elysees, Oxford Street, Via Veneto, Orchard Road and the Bund symbolise prestigious shopping opportunities in their respective cities. Many may gawk at their wares but only the affluent are truly at home inside the palaces of contemporary consumerism (Ritzer 1999). Importantly, shopping in many other forms also attracts tourists. There are duty free shops and there are outlet stores. For some tourists local markets are attractive while for a few others black markets appeal. Beyond the cities and the airports and reaching into the countryside a special form of tourist shopping can also be identified. High Street, Bridge Street, Gorge Road and Mountain Drive may not have quite the cache of the big city thoroughfares but the shop lined roads of many small villages are also a tourist attraction. These kinds of precincts, and the people who shop, work and live there, form the subject matter of this book.

In essence this volume seeks to examine in detail the phenomenon of Tourist Shopping Villages (TSVs), which are defined as:

> [S]mall towns and villages that base their tourist appeal on retailing, often in a pleasant setting marked by historical or natural amenities. They are found along touring routes, in destination areas and near urban centres, but are markedly different from urban business and shopping districts in terms of their small scale, speciality retailing and distinct ambience. (Getz 2000: 211)

Tourist shopping expenditure represents a source of funding for both the private and public sector and this income source can revitalise retail areas, townscapes and streetscapes (Turner and Reisinger 2001). Tourist shopping villages are places of entertainment and leisure and they can also be pathways for local communities to share in the economic benefits of tourism. There are many interest groups affected by, and keen to understand, tourist shopping villages. These groups include but extend beyond academics and tourism analysts to those keen to develop tourism. Government officials and civic leaders may wish to attend to the development of shopping villages as a consideration in their policy initiatives. Of course individual entrepreneurs and retailers seek satisfactory returns while local community residents may identify a suite of amenity benefits.

Tourist shopping villages are also a fertile academic ground for analysing the planning and delivery of contemporary tourist experiences. It can be argued that much tourism research and theory has been focussed on understanding the nature and outcomes of tourist experiences. Recent attention has been focussed on trying to map out conceptual models to explain the nature of tourist experiences (Moscardo 2008c; Uriely 2005).

The present book therefore has two main aims. The first is to use new research and existing literature to critically examine tourist shopping villages in order to understand how their performance can be enhanced for multiple stakeholders. The second aim is to use this context to examine in more detail key elements of tourist experiences and thus contribute to the growing interest, both within and outside tourism, in developing a theory of tourist experience. Figure 1.1 provides an overview of the structure of the book.

This first chapter will place tourist shopping villages in a wider context of tourist shopping opportunities and forms and introduce the concept of tourist shopping villages. Chapter 2 will examine tourist shopping villages in more detail with a focus on the sustainability issues they face in terms of impacts and changes to destinations and their residents. The third chapter will provide an overview of both recreational and tourist shopping and identify a number of concepts and theories that could be

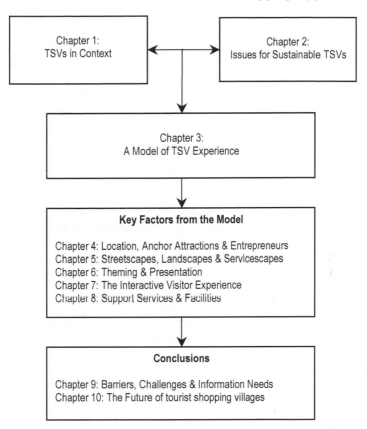

Figure 1.1   Overview of the book.

used to understand this phenomenon. This chapter will also introduce a TSV Visitor Experience Model. The detail in this chapter will provide an extensive rationale explaining the choice and selection of sets of factors to be considered in the subsequent chapters. At this point in the volume it is simplest to record the layout of the subsequent chapter structure and to await its justification at a later point in the sequence of work. Based on the model in Chapter 3, Chapters 4 to 8 will explore dimensions of this model in more detail using a variety of research evidence and literature to develop a more detailed understanding of the nature of tourist experiences in these shopping villages. In many instances these chapters will present case studies of villages drawn from a multi-country sample which the researchers have visited and studied. The penultimate chapter will highlight an array of research futures while the final chapter will reflect on the nature of the tourist shopping village experience and review likely trends into the future.

TOURIST SHOPPING: AN OVERVIEW

The current tourist interest in shopping can be explained by an increasing demand for leisure activities in general and the search for new experiences in particular. As a consequence, shopping areas are now being developed as a core element in many tourist products (Jansen-Verbeke 2000). Given this growing demand for shopping by tourists, destinations have begun initiating major shopping promotional campaigns and have often adopted retailing and tourist shopping as official policies in their tourism development efforts. In some cases, overall shopping policies have been altered considerably as a result of tourism. Extended trading hours in tourism areas is an example of such an influence (Timothy 2005).

The growing importance of shopping as a leisure and tourism activity results from an increasingly materialistic and consumption oriented society in which the act of shopping is not only utilitarian, with a focus on acquiring necessities for daily needs, but has become a part of the touristic experience in which clothing, souvenirs, artworks and handicrafts are purchased as reminders of travel experiences (Michalkó 2001; Timothy 2005; Timothy and Butler 1995). Although the tourism marketing literature discusses the importance of tourist retail expenditures to local economies, few studies are actually concerned with retailing to the tourist segment (Heung and Cheng 2000). Turner and Reisinger (2001) argue that tourists form a different retailing segment. In this view tourists place importance on different products and product attributes to those sought by other groups. Shopping may have its own inherent promotional power for tourist destinations since items purchased during travel, as well as photos and videos, may entice other visitors (Kim and Littrell 2001). Backstrom (2006) argues that research must acknowledge recreational shopping as a multifaceted activity since it may be performed in different ways in various settings and embody different types of consumer meanings. She also emphasises that the multiplicity of the individuals engaged in recreational shopping needs to be studied in more refined terms. The core theme, which integrates many of these studies, is that tourist shopping is an important but understudied phenomenon which is somewhat different from other forms of retail activity.

THE IMPORTANCE OF SHOPPING
AS A TOURIST ACTIVITY

The importance of shopping as a tourist activity can be seen in several statistical indicators. A consideration of expenditure, levels of participation by tourists and day-trippers and ratings of shopping as a reason for travel and/ or destination choice all attest to the importance of shopping in multiple destinations. Tourism Australia, for example, provides statistics for 2009 indicating that expenditure on shopping, gifts and souvenirs for domestic day visitors was more than $3 million, which is the highest expenditure of any category. A further $2.5 million was spent by domestic visitors on overnight trips (Tourism Research Australia 2009b). The average shopping expenditure for international visitors was $312 per trip (Tourism Research Australia 2009a). Statistics provided by other tourism marketing organisations provide a similar picture. In Poland the figure is 24 per cent reflecting higher levels of cross-border shopping from neighbouring countries for cheaper goods, while the figure for the United Kingdom is 20 per cent (Institute of Tourism Poland 2008). In New Zealand gifts, souvenirs and other shopping make up 14 per cent of domestic tourist expenditure and 30 per cent of day-tripper expenditure (Cooper and Hall 2005).

These expenditure figures are consistent with the levels of participation in shopping as an activity reported by tourists in various studies. In a survey of more than 1600 international and domestic tourists to the North Queensland region of Australia, 62 per cent reported engaging in general shopping and 48 per cent reported shopping for local arts and crafts (Moscardo 2004). Robertson and Fennell (2007) report that shopping is one of the United Kingdom's most popular leisure activities. From a tourism perspective, some 16 percent of day trips in the UK are to go on non-regular, non-convenience shopping trips, which is the third most frequent activity after eating out or visiting friends and relatives. The focus of Robertson and Fennell's (2007) research was on regional shopping centres and they reported that 42 percent of visitors to Essex were planning to visit shopping centres, making them nearly twice as popular as seaside attractions which were listed by 26 per cent of the sample.

A report from the Travel Industry Association (2001) indicates that shopping was the most popular activity among domestic travellers. Shopping was included in 30 per cent of domestic trips. Similarly, and based on an analysis of the Travel Activities and Motivations Survey, the Ontario Ministry of Tourism (2007c) in Canada reports that shopping and dining are Canadian travellers' most popular activities. A further detailed component of the report reveals that shopping at the destination, although not usually a trip-motivator, is an important activity for 66 per cent of travellers from the U.S. and 70 per cent from Ontario (Ontario Ministry of Tourism 2007b). In both cases shopping or browsing in clothing, shoe and jewellery stores was the most popular style of behaviour reported.

Overall, 16 per cent of American travellers and 15 per cent of Ontario travellers rated "great shopping opportunities" as a highly important condition when choosing a pleasure destination (Ontario Ministry of Tourism 2007d). The Ontario Ministry of Tourism (2007b), conclude that, while shopping is not frequently a trip-motivator, even for those who engage in shopping, it remains an important activity that many travellers expect to engage in while travelling. As such, it is not only the actual shopping opportunities that a destination offers, but also the perception of a destination's shopping opportunities that is important to travellers. According to more academic analyses shopping is among the most common and enjoyable activities undertaken by people on holiday and, in many cases, it provides a major attraction and basic motivation for travel (Jansen-Verbeke 2000; Timothy 2005). The core of this view is that tourists search for unique shopping and leisure experiences to define and structure their day trips. This brief review of evidence on the extent and economic importance of shopping indicates not only that this is a substantial component of tourism, but that there are also different types of shopping within the overall category of tourist shopping.

TYPES OF TOURIST SHOPPING

One way to improve our understanding of tourist shopping is to develop a classification scheme for different types of shopping. In the reminder of this chapter a scheme is developed following Hall's (2005) approach to tourism systems. The scheme uses three dimensions of tourist shopping. The first component to be considered is a temporal dimension based on when in the holiday or travel experience the shopping takes place. Secondly, shopping has a spatial dimension and the incorporation of this component helps formulate the approach. The third and final dimension to be considered is psychological and here traveller motivation and interests are important.

TEMPORAL AND SPATIAL DIMENSIONS OF TOURIST SHOPPING

In terms of the temporal dimensions of travel Hall (2005), following Clawson and Knetsch (1966), describes five phases for tourism experiences—pre-departure, transit to the destination, time spent at the destination, transit to home and post-travel. It is possible to identify several different types of tourist shopping opportunity using these five time phases and combining them with the locations where shopping can take place. In the pre-departure phase tourists can shop for travel essentials—the things they need to take with them—including special clothing and equipment, luggage and medicines. If the travel involves visiting friends, family or work colleagues it may also be necessary to purchase gifts before departure. These shopping activities are most likely to take place in the tourist's home location at local stores and shopping malls. But it is also possible that shopping for gifts to present to friends, family and colleagues at the destination may take the tourists to places where souvenirs and local arts, crafts or food products are available such as souvenir stores near local tourist attractions, local markets or nearby shopping villages. Gifts purchased for others may also be acquired in the transit to the destination. Duty free shopping, which can serve the purposes of both buying for oneself and for others, is offered both in transport terminals and on transport vehicles, especially aircraft and ships.

The number of shopping opportunities expands considerably when tourists are in their destination. In this phase tourists may shop for many different reasons and typically there are multiple venues to acquire necessary and desired goods. Such venues include gift shops in and around major attractions, shopping precincts or areas in cities and towns, markets, shopping malls and shopping villages.

Shopping is also a possible component of the post-travel phase with tourists purchasing items from websites and mail order catalogues, specialist outlets and other stores in their home locations. In this instance it may be that the travel experience has stimulated an interest in, or awareness of some product that is purchased on return to the traveller's home base. One of the arguments made for offering wine tasting tours, for example, is that it may not only generate cellar door sales to visitors, but may also increase brand recognition when returning travellers shop for wine in their local stores (Hall, et al. 2000).

PSYCHOLOGICAL DIMENSIONS OF TOURIST SHOPPING

Inherent in this discussion of the temporal and spatial locations of tourist shopping is recognition of the existence of different motives for shopping. For example, it was noted that some shopping may be driven by necessity, a need to buy gifts and a desire to extend the experience of the destination. A survey of travellers in the United States conducted by the Travel Industry Association (2001) asked about reasons for shopping on the respondent's most recent trip. The most common responses for this general query were "something to do, wanted to buy something for other people, wanted a souvenir of the trip, like to shop or always shop on trips, lower prices/saves money, wanted to buy items unique to the destination and a different selection of stores to those at home" (2001: 5–8).

These kinds of reasons represent the third or psychological dimension of the tourist shopping classification scheme which incorporates motivation, attitudes and actual behaviours. There have been three main areas of research into the psychological aspects of tourist shopping that are directly relevant to the present discussion—segmentation studies seeking to identify and describe different types of tourist shoppers, research into souvenir and gift purchase and analyses of cross-border shopping. These three areas of interest will be succinctly considered since the goal of this volume is to study intensively these psychological components of tourist shopping and their operation in tourist shopping villages.

Tourist Shopping Segmentation Studies

Table 1.1 provides a summary of the most commonly cited tourist shopping segmentation studies. These segmentation studies have used a range of different segmentation techniques and variables to analyse a variety of tourist samples. Despite these differences, consistent patterns can be identified across the various studies. Firstly, many of the studies included some form of involvement or interest in shopping as a segmentation variable and where this was the case all studies found a group not interested in shopping. This

Table 1.1   Summary of Tourist Shopping Segmentation Studies

Author/s	Type of Tourist	Segmentation Variables	Segments Identified
Hu and Yu (2007)	Out of state tourists in US Midwest	Attitudes to products (crafts only) Shopping involvement	• **Shopping enthusiasts** – high involvement and high importance for craftsmanship and cultural linkage • **Shopping lovers** – medium involvement • **Indifferent shoppers** – low involvement and highest importance for ease of handling of crafts
Josiam, Kinley and Kim (2005)	Out of town tourists to large shopping malls in four US cities	Shopping involvement (profiled on motivations, demographics and desired mall features)	• **Low involvement** – more likely to be driven by social obligation and functional needs • **Medium involvement** – moderate on all variables • **High involvement** – focussed most on socialising, and entertainment/ novelty features of shopping experiences, less interested in souvenirs/gifts for others
Carmichael and Smith (2004)	Domestic tourists who reported shopping while visiting rural areas in Canada	Tourist activity preferences	• **Shopping vacation only** – focus of the trip is on shopping for pleasure often on a day trip • **Short vacation** – shopping is part of an experience focussed on the region visited • **Getaway and visit friends/ relatives** – shopping is one activity • **Outdoors and sports** • **Long -vacation** – - shopping is part of an experience focussed on the region visited
Littrell, Paige and Song (2004)	U.S. travellers aged 50 and older	Travel activity participation Shopping activity participation	• **Active outdoor/cultural tourists** – ambivalent about shopping, but like to experience local culture through food and crafts • **Cultural tourists** – shopping was important, use tourist shops, malls and craft stores and seek authenticity • **Moderate tourists** – limited interest on most variables

(continued)

Table 1.1   (continued)

Author/s	Type of Tourist	Segmentation Variables	Segments Identified
Moscardo (2004)	Tourists to a non-urban region in Australia	Importance of shopping in destination choice and actual participation in different shopping activities	• **Non-shoppers** – low levels of interest and participation • **Serious shoppers** – high levels of importance for destination choice and participation • **Regional art and crafts shoppers** – focus on regionally distinctive shopping opportunities • **Not-so-serious shoppers** – low levels of interest but participation especially in utilitarian options
Geuens, Vantomme and Brengman (2004)	Travellers in Brussels Airport	Shopping motivation	• **Mood shoppers** – the experience of shopping is central • **Apathetic/indifferent shoppers** – not interested in shopping • **Shopping lovers** – all aspects of shopping are important

group represented one end of a spectrum, which had a contrasting group of serious shopping enthusiasts. In those studies that supplemented a measure of involvement or participation with other variables such as place of shopping and attitudes related to shopping, more complex patterns emerged. More specifically it seems that there can be a link between general travel motivation and shopping behaviours. Some tourist shoppers use shopping as either a means to achieve their motivation or as an adjunct to their motives. For example, several of the studies in Table 1.1 describe a segment or type of shopping focussed on using shopping to access the local destination and/or to develop a better understanding of the destination culture. These links between travel motivation and shopping behaviours are also described by Fairhurst et al. (2007). Overall these segmentation studies suggest that for those who do seek and enjoy shopping while travelling there may be two different motives for shopping—as an activity in its own right and as a way to experience or access the local destination and its culture. In the former case shopping while travelling seems to be an extension of shopping behaviour conducted at home as part of a general leisure profile.

Souvenir and Gift Buying

A second topic which extends the psychological inquiry into tourist shopping focuses on souvenir and gift purchasing. Two reviews of tourist shopping literature (Hu and Yu 2007; Moscardo 2004) concluded that research into souvenir production and consumption has dominated the published literature on tourist shopping. A common focus of this research has been on shopping for souvenirs or gifts for others and much of this research has analysed specific cultural groups and the social obligations related to travel in these cultures. Park (2000) summarises much of this work in a discussion of the Japanese tradition of *Omiyage* and Korean tradition of *Sunmul*, both cultural norms prescribing the need to maintain important relationships through the presentation of gifts.

Buying gifts for others while travelling is not just restricted to those cultures with a clear set of cultural traditions related to obligatory gift-giving. Kim and Littrell (2001) suggest that as many as 70 per cent of U.S. tourists buy souvenirs for friends and relatives. This suggests an additional or third motivation for shopping which extends the previously mentioned objectives of extending one's home-based leisure activity and developing local insights. This third dimension can be summarised as the need to maintain positive social relationships through gift-giving.

Kim and Littrell's (2001) paper also analysed the purchase of souvenirs or gifts for oneself. Their findings develop further the range of key motivations involved in shopping. Four main types of shopping behaviour and experience associated with the purchase of items for oneself were identified by Kim and Littrell from previous research and the results of their own study into tourist attitudes towards souvenir purchase.

The first of these shopping for self-motives was the purchase of souvenirs that act as memories or markers of the place or holiday experience (Hitchcock 2000; Kim and Littrell 2001). According to Timothy (2005) a key reason people purchase keepsakes, or souvenirs, is to remind them of the place they have visited. In the post-trip period, usually referred to as the recollection phase of travel, memories may change and experiences are altered by time, and souvenirs can help keep the memory of the experience alive (Timothy 2005).

The second reason tourists may purchase souvenirs or local products is that of connecting to or accessing the local place or culture (Kim and Littrell 2001). This reason reinforces rather than extends the theme previously noted in the tourist shopper segmentation studies. Carmichael and Smith (2004), Moscardo (2004) and Littrell and colleagues (2004) all identified a group whose shopping behaviour and attitudes reflected a desire to meet and mix with locals, to gain an understanding of local culture and to appreciate the distinctive features of the visited place. In this case items purchased on holiday are associated with the travel experience and are linked to a generalized image of a culture or even a specific town or village. Smith and Olson (2001) argue that shopping creates a significant opportunity for visitors to become exposed to the host culture. Through the familiar form of social consumption, shopping activities allow the tourist to access select aspects of the local culture, assimilating local customs and norms. The shopping activity associated with these purchases can also require significant social interaction on the part of the tourist. The local market place can thus afford tourists the opportunity to unobtrusively observe the customs, habits and language of local people as well as engage in basic forms of social interaction (Smith and Olson 2001).

The third reason provided by Kim and Littrell (2001) is partially related to the social interactions mentioned previously. In this case shopping while on holidays is an extension of a general interest in shopping as a recreational or leisure activity (Fairhurst, et al. 2007). Here the focus is on the shopping experience itself rather than the destination and this tourist shopping behaviour can have a range of dimensions including the opportunity for social interaction with others (Fairhurst, et al. 2007), the ability to meet novelty-seeking needs (Kim and Littrell 2001), the provision of an activity to fill in time and a diversion to avoid boredom (Fairhurst, et al. 2007), an adaptive response to bad weather (Timothy 2005) or the means to achieve various self-development goals related to developing collecting and bargaining skills (Fairhurst, et al. 2007).

[handwritten margin note: leisure experience]

Finally the fourth reason for buying local products while on holidays is related to the nature of the products themselves. In this case the primary motive for buying souvenirs or local products is to demonstrate an appreciation of the workmanship and aesthetic qualities of the items. As part of the destination encounter, some tourists find pleasure in watching artisans demonstrate their skills (Kim and Littrell 2001). According to Evans (2000), useful and appealing handicrafts can be an interesting attraction and effective form of guest entertainment while they become a source of income for local artisans. The authenticity of these crafts and other retail products in relation to the local area is one of the most important elements in purchasing pursuits, as tourist shoppers are specifically interested in locally made items that are typical or indigenous to the destination (Kim and Littrell 2001; Tosun, et al. 2007). The consumption of local products can also provide sensory stimulation (Fairhurst, et al. 2007) which is evident in food and beverage tourism. Tourist shopping based around the seeking and consumption of local food products and beverages such as wine, whisky, ale and tea is another way in which tourists shop for local products (Plummer, et al. 2005).

Taken together the four themes about tourist shopping for gifts reported by Kim and Littrell (2001) build a rich motivational pattern as to why tourists shop and contribute to the psychological profile of shopping being developed in this section to help construct a typology of shopping. Additional ideas are also revealed in some further types of shopping including cross-border transactions.

Cross-Border Shopping

Michalkó and Váradi's (2004) discussion of cross-border shopping in Europe and Timothy and Butler's (1995) analysis of the phenomenon in North America suggest another set of types of shopping motivation and connected behaviours.

In this case shopping activity centres on price differentials between the countries around the borders and differences in the range and options available. These analyses suggest that some tourist shopping can be driven by a desire to take advantage of cheaper prices in the visited destination. Additionally tourists may also shop in order to take advantage of a wider range and/or better quality of products (Michalkó and Váradi 2004; Timothy and Butler 1995). Finally it is suggested that this type of shopping can be driven by the opportunity to buy branded luxury goods at better prices than at home (Michalkó and Váradi 2004). Both these analyses also suggest that some tourist shopping is utilitarian in terms of tourists buying daily necessities such as groceries for those in self-catering accommodation, the purchase of items lost, damaged or left at home or the purchase of items required for activities at the destination such as sporting and recreational equipment. The distinction between shopping as a utilitarian or as a hedonic activity is a longstanding one in the broader literature on retail consumption (Babin, Darden and Griffin 1994).

Summary of Psychological Dimensions

In summary tourist shopping can be seen as meeting a range of motives including:

- Utilitarian shopping for necessities;
- Shopping to take advantage of price differentials and wider product availability;
- Shopping to buy gifts to fulfil cultural and social obligations;
- Shopping as a form of self-development or self-gratification in which tourists may be motivated by the aesthetic and sensory qualities of the products bought, the role that souvenirs can play in sustaining memories of the holiday experience and an interest in buying luxury branded goods that may not be available at home;
- Shopping as a way to access, connect to and understand the place and culture of the destination; and
- Shopping as a recreational activity in its own right with the ability to satisfy several more general needs including novelty-seeking, self-development and social interaction.

A NEW TYPOLOGY OF TOURIST SHOPPING

The three key dimensions of motivation, spatial location and phase of the travel experience can be used then to identify six main forms of tourist shopping—utilitarian, social obligation, value for money, self-indulgence, destination experience and extended leisure. These six forms are summarised in Table 1.2 and linked to aspects of the three dimensions.

Table 1.2   Summary of Main Forms of Shopping

Form of Shopping	Key Tourist Related Motivations	Link to Temporal Dimensions	Link to Places to Shop
Utilitarian			
Shopping for necessities	Meet basic needs in terms of food, medicine and equipment to support other travel motivations	At any time	More likely to be in non-tourism related stores or shopping areas
Social Obligation			
Shopping to buy for other people as part of social, family or cultural obligations and traditions	Meet social and cultural traditions associated with travel	At the destination, pre-departure and in transit	Souvenir stores in particular Tourist shopping precincts
Value for Money			
Shopping to take advantage of price differentials between home and the destination.	Shopping as a direct motive for travel.	At the destination and in transit	Cross-border shopping areas Outlet malls Markets
Self-Indulgence/Self-development			
Shopping to satisfy aspects of internal motivations such as indulging in sensory experiences, buying luxury branded items, buying souvenirs for oneself, and collecting.	A range of internal motives including meeting sensory needs, self-development through collecting and shopping associated with other activities and self-esteem through purchase of luxury items.	Mostly at the destination but also in transit	Different locations depending on the type of motive.For example, luxury brands are most likely to be purchased at duty free stores and urban shopping precincts.
Destination Experience			
Shopping as a way to experience a destination.	Motives related to learning about other places and peoples, and sensation/ novelty seeking	At the destination	A focus on shopping precincts, markets and shopping villages

(continued)

Table 1.2 (continued)

Form of Shopping	Key Tourist Related Motivations	Link to Temporal Dimensions	Link to Places to Shop
Extended Leisure			
Shopping while on holidays as an extension of shopping at home as a leisure activity. In this case tourists shop at a destination in the same way they shop in their leisure time at home.	A range of motivations including being social, novelty seeking, and development of identity.	Mostly at the destination	All locations

TOURIST SHOPPING VILLAGES

It can be suggested that TSVs are especially linked to shopping as a destination experience, shopping as extended leisure and shopping as self-indulgence and self-development. The position of tourist shopping villages within this typology can be justified with a brief overview of some of the features of these types of tourist settings. As noted previously, TSVs are places that offer tourist shopping as part of a larger destination experience. These shopping places are usually smaller in scale and typically located in rural areas peripheral to either an urban centre or tourist destination centre and often offer an opportunity to experience local cultural and/or natural heritage. According to Mitchell (2003), the emergence of shopping villages can be attributed to the twin forces of demand and supply, to the desire to purchase 'signposts' of the past and to their provision by enterprising entrepreneurs. As the demand for heritage products has emerged, so too have the landscapes that satisfy these desires. In the developed world, TSVs are often located near larger urban centres and benefit from suburbanization, which creates demand for people to get away into the country—but not too far.

Natural or cultural heritage themes, an attractive small town setting and the provision of amenities and services such as parking, toilets, eating areas, food services and interpretive signs are all an important part of the success of TSVs (Timothy 2005). Special events and festivals that appeal to the visiting public are also common, along with a variety of souvenir shops, craft markets and other speciality shops, together with generalized merchandise retailers and in some cases, factory outlet stores.

heritage settings in both rural and urban contexts engender a pleaseisure shopping environment (Timothy 2005). Many of these rural shopping villages have a main street appeal based on an existing heritage streetscape. Often the heritage streetscape is associated with a unique local history, like the historic gold mining town of Arrowtown New Zealand. In some cases the heritage streetscape is anchored by a key building, such as an old mill or a fort. While that may be sufficient to attract visitors, there are other elements which can add to their appeal. Some of the villages studied had a distinct ethnic or cultural history which served as a key drawcard, for example St. Jacobs Mennonite community in Ontario, Canada or the German heritage of Hahndorf in the Adelaide Hills region of Australia. Other villages are based on a tradition of local arts and crafts (e.g. Bayfield in Canada and Montville in Australia) which attract visitors to watch the artisans at work and to purchase unique products. The performing arts can also play a key attracting role, for example the rainforest village of Kuranda in North Queensland, Australia first gained in popularity as a result of the success of a local Aboriginal dance troupe that performed in a building on the main street. Towns such as Stratford and Niagara on the Lake in Ontario, Canada rely on summer theatre festivals, Shakespeare and George Bernard Shaw respectively, to attract many of their visitors. If the anchor attraction or draw card provides sufficient appeal, these villages may become destinations in their own right. Others are viable because they are situated on established touring routes such as Hokitika in New Zealand.

It must also be recognised that TSVs are varied in terms of their stage of development. Some may be stalled (started but limited in scale) while others may be at an incipient stage (possessing good resources but awaiting critical inputs). Others may be emerging (actually growing and beginning to prosper) and still others may have reached a stage of maturity or consolidation. Finally others may have stagnated, perhaps moving through a transition phase (changeover of images and products) to avoid decline.

These preliminary remarks about tourist shopping villages and their characteristics indicate some core themes worthy of more detailed investigation and intensive analysis. The pathway to undertake this examination is outlined in the following section of this introductory chapter.

THE TOURIST SHOPPING VILLAGE RESEARCH PROJECT

This book is informed by an ongoing research program which has analysed in detail shopping villages in a range of countries including Australia, New Zealand, the United Kingdom, Ireland, Canada and the United States. This research program has a number of components including:

- Detailed onsite case study analyses of more than 60 tourist shopping villages in eight countries, collecting and analysing information on layout, size, historical developments, themes, shopping styles and support services;

- Focus groups and interviews conducted with key stakeholders in villages in Australia and the United States (see Chapter 2 for method details);
- Expert analyses of the features that contribute to the success of TSVs as a tourist experience (see Chapter 3 for more details on this method);
- Content analysis of marketing materials (see Chapter 6 for more details); and
- Content analysis of web-based travel stories about the villages (see Chapter 6 for more details).

In addition to the variety of methods used to analyse TSVs in this research program, a particular value of the research to be presented in the remainder of this book is the range and detail of the analyses of a large sample of these tourist settings. The villages examined and presented in this book vary in terms of their development approach, key attractions and stages of development. Table 1.3 provides a list of the TSVs studied with some key details of each. This sample of villages is not intended to be comprehensive and reflects the opportunities and experiences of the authors. Within these constraints, we have attempted to maximise the variety of villages on a number of dimensions. We acknowledge that there are many other villages that exist that have not been identified or included in this analysis.

Table 1.3   A Summary of the Tourist Shopping Villages Studied

Country	Village Name	Main Themes
Australia	Blackheath	Mountain environment, history & heritage
	Castlemaine	History & heritage, crafts
	Daylesford	Health & wellness
	Eumundi	Local food & produce, crafts
	Gembrook	History & heritage
	Hahndorf	Ethnic culture, local food & produce
	Healesville	Environment
	Hepburn Springs	Health & wellness
	Kuranda	Rainforest environment, arts & crafts
	Kyneton	History & heritage, antiques, local food & produce
	Leura	Crafts, antiques
	Maldon	History & heritage
	Marysville	Environment, outdoor recreation
	Montville	Mountain environment, arts & crafts
	Mt Tamborine	Environment, arts & crafts, antiques
	Olinda	Environment, crafts
	Sassafrass	Environment, crafts
	Strathalbyn	History & heritage, antiques
	Woodend	Local food & produce
	Woodford	Music, local produce
	Yarra Glen	Food & wine
Canada	Bayfield	History & heritage, arts & crafts
	Elora	History & heritage, environment
	Niagara-on-the-Lake	History & heritage, arts & crafts, performing arts
	St. Jacobs	Crafts, ethnic culture
	Stratford	Performing arts

(continued)

Table 1.3   (continued)

Country	Village Name	Main Themes
Ireland	Adare	History & heritage, crafts
	Blarney	History & heritage, crafts
	Dingle	History & heritage, crafts, coastal environment
	Kinsale	History & heritage, food & dining
	Sneem	History & heritage, environment
New Zealand	Akaroa	Ethnic culture, crafts, environment, history & heritage
	Arrowtown	Mining history & heritage
	Cromwell	Local food & produce (emerging)
	Geraldine	Arts (emerging)
	Hokitika	Arts & crafts
United Kingdom	Broadway	History & heritage, crafts
	Bourton-on-the-Water	History & heritage, crafts
	Burford	History & heritage, crafts
	Cheddar	Local food & produce, history & heritage, environment
	Chipping Campden	History & heritage, crafts
	Hay-on-Wye	Books
	Shere	History & heritage, crafts
	Stow-on-the-Wold	History & heritage, crafts
	Windsor	History & heritage, crafts
United States	Agonquit	Coastal environment, arts & crafts
	Avoca	Crafts
	Bethel	Environment, history & heritage, crafts
	Bethlehem	History & heritage
	Brenham	Antiques, local food (emerging)
	Bridgeton	History & heritage, environment
	Cherokee	Ethnic culture, arts & crafts, environment
	Freeport	LL Bean
	Gatlinburg	Environment
	Johnson	Recreation (emerging)
	Naples	History & heritage
	North Conway	History & heritage, environment, recreation
	Salado	History & heritage, arts & crafts
	Sedona	Environment, ethnic culture, arts & crafts
	St. Albans	History & heritage
	Stowe	History & heritage, environment, recreation
	Williams	History & heritage
	Williamsburg	History & heritage, arts & crafts
Hong Kong	Ngong Ping	History religion & Chinese culture
The Netherlands	Volendam	History & Dutch culture

SUMMARY AND CONCLUSIONS

This introductory chapter has attempted to establish a background and context for the phenomenon of tourist shopping and then within that context locate the role and nature of tourist shopping villages or TSVs. There are several features of the broader context for tourist shopping that are worth highlighting. Firstly, shopping is a major activity, a key destination attraction feature and sometimes a primary travel motivation for tourists.

Secondly, shopping is also recognised by many destination marketing and management organisations as both an important part of the available tourist experiences and as a major source of revenue contributing to tourism's positive economic impact. The third feature to highlight is that tourist shopping has its own specific characteristics and types that make it different from shopping in general.

These distinctive characteristics support the need for specific tourist shopping research which to date has not been extensive. Analysing the temporal, spatial and psychological features of tourist shopping suggests six basic types of tourist shopping. A variety of tourist shopping styles exist and TSVs represent one of these shopping settings for visitors. It is argued here that TSVs are the places most likely to be used for shopping as a way to access the destination, as locations for shopping to express self-indulgence/self-development needs and as settings for shopping as a recreational experience. In addition to this complexity of tourist shopping types, a preliminary consideration of this sector suggests TSVs are also complex in terms of their development trajectories, their relationships to other attractions, the interactions between tourism and residents and the nature of the experience opportunities available for tourists. The next chapter will explore these complexities in more detail before examining the TSV experience and the results of TSV research project.

It is valuable here to finish by repeating the two main aims of this book. Our first aim is to examine tourist shopping villages in order to understand how their performance can be enhanced for multiple stakeholders. Both original research and existing literature will be used to pursue this aim. The second aim is to consider the tourist experiences in these settings so that an analysis of this context can assist in the growing interest, both within and outside tourism, of the nature of contemporary experience.

2 Issues for Sustainable Tourist Shopping Villages

INTRODUCTION

This second chapter seeks to enrich the approach taken in the previous chapter by examining the tourist shopping villages from a range of different perspectives. An array of impacts, issues and development strategies will be explored. Discussion in Chapter 1 reported the importance of shopping to the tourism industry. The chapter introduced the concept of a tourist shopping village and provided a typology of different styles of tourist shopping. A consideration of the typology and a discussion of some distinctive features of tourist shopping villages suggested a need to study this form of tourism in a comprehensive context of contemporary leisure and development concerns. The approach adopted in this volume and specifically in this chapter is to further the study of tourist shopping villages through an expansive and critical approach to sustainability and quality of life concerns (Costanza, et al. 2007).

Moscardo (2008b) argues that one of the limitations to developing a better understanding of sustainability and tourism is a tendency to examine tourism impacts solely from the perspective of the tourism industry. It would be very easy to suggest that the word sustainability has become a cliché in discussions of tourism and as such lacks any real meaning or power. It is important to remember though that the widespread adoption of the term in academic and government discussions of tourism reflects the concerns of people about the long term and overall balance of positive and negative outcomes from activities such as tourism development. When evaluating different forms of tourism development there has often been an almost exclusive focus on the potential of the proposed form of tourism to enhance visitor numbers and expenditure, with little attention paid to other impacts. Additionally, alternative options are frequently not fully considered. There is clearly a need to evaluate tourism activities and forms, including tourist shopping villages, in terms of their impacts and contributions to the quality of life of all involved (Moscardo 2009).

Coles (2004b) argues that much of the existing research attention in the area of tourist shopping has focussed on the spatial, temporal and purchasing behaviour of the shoppers and little attention has been paid to the supply side dimension or the relationship between tourism and retailing. Timothy (2005) also emphasises the need for residents of tourist shopping communities to be involved in the planning, development and management processes. He argues that community members should be afforded opportunities to learn about tourism, its benefits and its consequences so that they will be better prepared to make decisions and to be involved in preparing a local tourism strategy. A holistic and comprehensive approach to sustainability calls for a consideration of the needs and quality of life of all stakeholders. It also directs attention to the environmental and economic performance of the shopping villages.

Two studies examining the perspectives of residents, local government officials and business owners in tourist shopping villages in the New England region of the United States and in several rural areas of Australia will be considered. These studies, though small scale, provide some rich insights into the dominant concerns held by a range of people involved in these settings. The chapter will then review the literature on TSV development dynamics and impacts and formulate a set of issues relevant to the sustainability of TSVs. The sum of these processes will provide a sustainability context in which to analyse and understand the nature of the experience offered in TSVs for both residents and visitors.

SOME ALTERNATIVE PERSPECTIVES ON TSVS

Two studies conducted by the authors provide information on TSVs from the perspectives of residents, business owners and other stakeholders, one conducted in the New England region of the United States and one conducted in four TSVs in rural Australia. Together the studies build an understanding of some key concerns of those who provide the tourist shopping experiences. The New England study consisted of a series of semi-structured, in-depth interviews with 14 participants who lived or worked in or near one of the six TSVs listed in Table 2.1. Nine of the participants were long term residents of the destination, three were more recent residents running tourism businesses and two were medium term residents who worked in tourism.

The in-depth interviews in the New England study were organised around three questions:

- Did the participant see their village or others in the region as a TSV?
- How had tourism and/or the village developed or changed over time?
- What were/are some of the issues or challenges associated with tourism, especially tourist shopping?

In the case of the first question, it was interesting to note that most of the residents not closely involved in tourism tended not to see their village as a tourist shopping village, while participants more directly involved did

Table 2.1   Brief Description of the Six New England TSVs Studied

Village	Key Features
Agonquit, Maine	Coastal resort town, just south of Portland with the motto "beautiful place by the sea". A shopping precinct offers jewellery, clothing, arts and home wares. Summer holiday area with an increasing number of second homes. The village is close to a major shopping outlet area, Kittery.
Bethel, Maine	Small village on the Maine/New Hampshire border that promotes history and access to the region's mountain areas and parks.
Freeport, Maine	One of the largest villages examined in this study and one with a substantial number of outlet stores. The village is famous for being the original location of the L.L. Bean store which acts as a major anchor attraction.
North Conway, New Hampshire	Is an access point to the White Mountain National Forest and ski fields and has two shopping areas. One north of the station for the Conway Scenic Railroad in the historic part of the town, offering a range of speciality shops and boutiques. The other to the south is a major outlet shopping area.
Naples, Maine	Is a major summer mountain resort area located near several lakes with an emerging speciality shopping district.
Stowe, Vermont	Is a major ski and summer mountain resort area with two shopping precincts – one in the historic part of the village offering a range of speciality items and one a little out of town offering local produce including ice cream, cheese and apple cider products.

recognise and use the label. All participants, however, preferred that the village be marketed to tourists using some feature other than shopping. Emphases on historical features and access to natural environments were preferred directions compared to selling shopping. The answers to the second and third question often overlapped and together could be summarised around three main themes—discussion of amenity migrants and second home owners, the course of development including the move to outlet shopping and the impacts that shopping and its associated development had on the village and the region.

Three of the participants described themselves as amenity migrants or people who moved to the region in the last three to five years to escape high pressure stressful lifestyles in major urban centres. Each of these ran an accommodation business and one also provided crafts for a local shop. These participants and others noted that this change in population due to amenity migration created two forces that encouraged the development of specialist shops. Firstly, many amenity migrants sought employment and business opportunities in tourism and related shopping areas. They often ran tourism businesses or shops or provided the art, craft or specialist food and beverage for sale in local tourist shops. Secondly, these migrants offered a market for such shops.

The shops in the villages were also supported by people with second homes in the region. Several participants noted that the growth in speciality retail and even outlet retail was due not just to tourists but to changing local demand especially from second home owners. The participants who discussed second home owners were generally very negative, suggesting that this was a phenomenon associated with many problems. Some respondents stated that tourists created far fewer challenges for local residents than did second home owners. More detailed discussions of the sustainability issues associated with second home ownership can be found in Mottiar (2006) and Visser (2004).

Additionally, select participants suggested that amenity migration also presented challenges for local communities, particularly over the development of outlet shopping in or near their village. Longer term residents were positive about outlet shopping stating that it provided more employment and a greater volume of short term visitors to the area. The greater volume of visitors provided support for local farmers who needed higher product turnover for viable businesses. But this pro-development perspective created tensions with the newer amenity migrants who did not like the style of the outlet shops nor the type of tourist it brought. Similar tensions and development cycles have been noted elsewhere by Weaver (2005).

The cycle of retail development was the second major theme in the open-ended discussions. The topic of outlet shopping was again implicated in these discussions due to its high profile in the areas where the study was conducted. A relatively clear and common development cycle was identified for TSVs. Figure 2.1 provides an example of St. Jacobs in Canada. The success of a village in attracting tourists is initially due to its heritage or access to an environment. These rising visitor numbers support the development of, and are stimulated by, the existence of speciality retail stores especially selling local arts, crafts and produce. The speciality shops provide an incentive for tourists to stay longer in the region and this supports the further development of support services notably in accommodation and restaurants. This in turn supports greater numbers of tourists. For some retailers these successes increase the value of their business and make it attractive to sell. For some retailers the motivation to sell and move reflects a desire to maintain a relaxed and less stressful lifestyle. It also increases the potential value of the buildings in which the shops are located and often landlords increase shop rents. These two forces result in a turnover of retail businesses, with a move away from smaller and more specialised local retailers to larger operations which often begin to stock a wider range of more generic products. In some cases, such as Freeport (see Case Study 2.1), the shops become factory outlets, usually for more expensive brands.

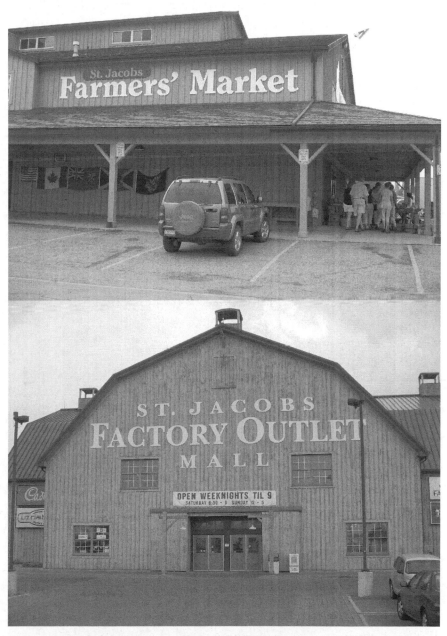

Figure 2.1   The move from farmers markets to factory outlets in St. Jacobs, Ontario.

Case Study 2.1   Freeport, Maine, U.S.

Freeport is located in Maine just a short distance (16 miles/26 kilometres) north of Portland and within two hours driving time from Boston (128 miles/ 206 kilometres). It has a resident population of approximately 7,000 and in the nineteenth century was a major port and ship building centre. In the early twentieth century it became a summer holiday destination with the development of amusement parks, attractions and lodging. In addition it became a centre for clothing manufacture and most notably in 1912 L.L. Bean's first hunting boot manufacturing centre and apparel store. This business grew into a significant mail order centre for outdoor clothing and became the main economic activity in the town. In the 1950s people began to visit the L.L. Bean retail store in Freeport as part of their vacation in the region and in 1951 demand was enough that the store began trading 24 hours a day.

Figure 2.2   Well-known brands can be found in historic Freeport buildings.

(continued)

Case Study 2.1   (continued)

This attraction encouraged the development of other stores catering for tourists and the 1980s a number of fast food chains and brand name stores were proposed. This created considerable tension between the developers and the community over the proposed changes to the historic architecture of the town. As a result a number of local planning ordinances were changed, meaning that new stores must be located within existing heritage buildings. In reality this means that many historic buildings have been preserved on the main street but there is clear evidence of the chains through signage and substantial development of new buildings in the surrounding blocks.

The village now has over 200 outlet shops in buildings on or near the main street, mostly for expensive brands such as Polo Ralph Lauren, Burberry and Coach. There are some local stores but these are mostly for gifts and souvenirs and there is little in the way of options for local produce, arts or crafts. The shops are supported by multiple restaurants (including many fast food chains) and accommodation. Although the history of village is often referred to in marketing literature there is little for tourists to experience other than the facades of historic buildings. Some outdoor recreational activities are also available in the region, but on the whole tourism to Freeport is about outlet shopping.

Case Study Sources:

http://en.wikipedia.org/wiki/freeport_Maine (accessed August 2009),
http://www.llbean.com/customerService/aboutLLBean/background.html
   (accessed August 2009).
Hogan, M. (2006). 'Thinking Outside the Big Box'. Preservation Online
http://www.preservationnation.org/magazine/story-of-the-week/2006/
   thinking-outside-the-big-box.html (accessed August 2009)
http://www.freeportusa.com/ (accessed August 2009)

A related and alternative growth pattern was identified. For some villages the growth in tourist numbers supports an interest by mall developers in building outlet malls in or near the villages. While the level of tourism is one factor supporting the development of factory outlets, it is important to remember that this type of development is usually stimulated by low land cost and state and local tax incentives (Lowry 1997). Over time the number of tourists continues to increase and this in turn supports the turnover required for more budget outlets and 'big-box' stores. Nearly all the participants described some variation of this development with several noting that it could only occur because of a lack of planning and building controls. The TSVs of North Conway and St. Jacobs are examples of this type of development pattern. Case Study 2.2 provides more detail and images of this TSV.

Case Study 2.2   North Conway, New Hampshire, U.S.

North Conway is one of a number of small villages located in the Mt. Washington valley on the border between Maine and New Hampshire and close to the White Mountain National Forest and ski-fields of Mt. Cranmore, Blackcat and Wildcat Mountain. It is within easy driving distance of Portland (63 miles/101 kilometres) and Boston (195 miles/314 kilometres). In the nineteenth century it became popular for outdoor recreation, especially hiking and climbing and artists. The artwork generated further tourist interest in the area with the addition of a rail service in 1874. The rail service in turn supported the development of skiing. The region is sometimes referred to as the home of North American skiing with some of the earliest developments of ski clubs, lodges and chairlifts in the 1930s.

In the 1950s and 1960s there was period of decline and the railroad closed. In the 1980s three Boston business partners who had travelled to the area in their youth bought the railway station and abandoned lines and began the Conway Scenic Railroad. Over the last 25 years this has expanded to become a major tourist attraction bringing visitors to the village and supporting the development of speciality shops, restaurants and local accommodation in the historic village centre immediately to the north of the railway station.

Figure 2.3   From historic buildings to factory outlets in North Conway.

(continued)

Case Study 2.2   (continued)

The 1980s also saw the development of a major factory outlet shopping mall, Settler's Green, located on the main highway on the southern entrance to the village. The outlet mall was stimulated by the lack of local and state taxes, the availability of cheap land and reasonable proximity to large residential and recreational populations. The growth in tourism supported the development of more outlets, chain restaurants and motels and over time there has been a move to cheaper brands and big-box stores such as WalMart.

The development has resulted in two very different precincts in North Conway – a historic downtown region north of the railway station and a more standard modern urban shopping precinct stretched along the high way on the southern entrance. Traffic congestion in this southern precinct prompted the development of a north-south bypass road allowing people to avoid the outlet malls and travel directly to the historic village.

Case Study Sources:

http://www.citytowninfo.com/places/new-hampshire/north-conway (accessed August 2009)
http://www.northconwaynh.com/ (accessed August 2009)
http://www.nhinns.com/direct.html (accessed August 2009)
Colclough, M. (2006) 'Fifty miles of track and ties.' New Hampshire To Do Magazine.
    http://www.thesilentforest.com/journalism/stories_html_csrr.html (accessed August 2009)
Lazar, D. (2009) 'Mountain of opportunity', New Hampshire Troubadour.
http://www.nhtroubadour.com/feature/mountain-of-opportunity/ (accessed August 2009).
Schoenherr, S.E. (2006) Evolution of the Shopping Center.
http://history.sandiego.edu/gen/soc/shoppingcenter.html (accessed August 2009)
http://www.settlersgreen.com/index.cfm?fuseaction=home.links (accessed August 2009)

Two conflicting or polemical social representations (Moscardo 2009) appeared in these discussions of the development patterns with some participants very positive about the directions of change and others very negative. Those that were positive tended to be longer term residents not so directly involved in tourism. For them the outlet shops provided opportunities to access goods and services not usually available in a small community. The new stores also offered a wider range of job opportunities for locals, especially younger residents, as well as creating more small business opportunities in areas servicing the stores. These participants also believed that the outlet shops increased customers for the more specialised local stores as they were essentially the same type of tourist.

The alternative social representation was that outlet shops attracted a different type of tourist. These new or additional tourists were often described as less desirable and not interested in the more speciality retail options or in supporting locally produced goods. While these new tourists existed in larger numbers they were seen as preferring budget meal and accommodation options. These preferences in turn supported an influx of franchise and fast food restaurants as well as cheaply built motels. The net effect of these new establishments was seen as creating problems for the visual landscape of the village. In addition a view was held that the new tourists were likely to spend less and that less of their expenditure was likely to stay in the region, thus meaning that their overall contribution to the region was likely to be limited. Those describing a negative social representation also argued that the outlet shops were disliked by the type of tourist who frequented the speciality shops and who were able and willing to pay more for locally owned, more upscale restaurants and accommodation. As a result these participants believed that the outlet malls displaced the customers needed to maintain the businesses that were more supportive of the local economy and more appropriate for the local architecture and lifestyle. These kinds of debates are associated with outlet and regional shopping malls in a number of locations (Jones 1995).

Regardless of which social representation was held there was considerable agreement over the negative impacts associated with any kind of tourism development in the area. The main negative issues involved traffic congestion and parking problems, increased litter and negative changes in architecture and landscapes. These were balanced against positive impacts including increased dining and shopping opportunities for local residents, less seasonality in tourism businesses and employment, support for local farmers, artists and craft producers and resources and motivation to preserve local heritage. In summary, this first group of interviews in one set of shopping villages raises important concerns for future studies and addresses some key sustainability issues to be pursued in this chapter and other sections of the research and analysis reported in this volume.

The second study consisted of four workshops held in Australia conducted with a computer supported focus group format. A total of 42 people participated in the workshops and they represented a range of local shop and business owners, representatives in local government, chamber of commerce staff and members of local and regional tourism marketing organisations. The four workshops were conducted in three TSVs, Daylesford in Victoria, Hahndorf in South Australia and Montville in Queensland and one was held in the Dandenong ranges region of Victoria where several TSVs are located (see Murphy, Pearce, Benekendorff and Moscardo. (2008) for more details on the method).

This study was more structured and explored in detail participants' views about ideal shopping village experiences, as well as the opportunities, threats and challenges to the villages. Any forms of assistance needed to manage tourist shopping and the future of the villages in more sustainable ways were also considered. There was consistency across the four regions in the issues and themes that emerged from the group discussions of these four topics. In describing an ideal TSV, participants felt that it should offer visitors and residents good product diversity, regionally distinctive merchandise and local produce and high quality products; and retain its heritage and architectural cohesiveness. In terms of the opportunities that tourist shopping offered, participants believed that tourist expenditure in local shops could support, and in turn be enhanced by, the development of more recreational and entertainment activities and could encourage a greater sense of community and town pride.

The participants also highlighted a number of challenges associated with tourist shopping including the difficulties in getting visitors to actually buy from local shops. Several participants noted that many tourists may walk through the shopping precincts but their expenditure was often very limited. There were also concerns raised about the need to maintain and encourage local community support for tourism and to enhance cooperation between local businesses and traders. Finally participants thought they needed assistance with more consistent, effective and professional marketing, the provision of information to tourists, the formulation of better property development controls and planning laws and the need to understand tourist markets, motivations and satisfaction.

These two foundation studies conducted by the research team members revealed a number of complex issues related to the nature and impacts of shopping developments. The interviews highlighted the existence of a range of social representations of tourist shopping, which were often in conflict with each other. These diverse social representations were typically based on very different assumptions or beliefs about which tourist markets were attracted to different shopping opportunities and what kinds of experience tourists were seeking. Despite being conducted in very different settings there were consistent concerns over development controls, parking and traffic, the need to support regional producers and enhance income for local residents and the importance of better understanding the tourist perspective. These issues parallel those reported in the available literature which will now be considered as a part of the process of formulating the program of further studies and analysis in this volume.

TSV DEVELOPMENT DYNAMICS

As noted in the previous chapter, there has been a modest amount of academic discussion focussed specifically on tourist shopping. The available literature providing information on TSV development dynamics, impacts or sustainability issues is fragmented and spread across discussions of rural tourism, impacts of tourism on small towns and community development. The available material can be organised in increasing order of specificity under five main themes—explorations of retail and development, TSV development pathways, generic studies of TSV issues and impacts, focussed studies of specific TSVs and creative destruction.

Explorations of Retail and Development

Retailing can be simply defined as the act of conveying a product from the final intermediary in the supply chain to the consumer in an effective and profitable manner (Coles 2004b). Thus, shopping episodes can be examined from the retailer's perspective as well as the consumer's. Beyond the retailer there are also their employees and suppliers and local residents. The issue of economic and social decline is an important one in many peripheral regions around the world (Moscardo 2005a). In the United Kingdom, for example, Powe (2006) argues that many small towns are facing serious challenges as residents are diverted elsewhere for shopping and employment. According to Jackson (1996), small towns in America have also seen their downtown districts decline with local businesses boarded up and abandoned. In this context several authors have argued that tourist/leisure shopping can be an effective economic and infrastructural alternative for declining industries (Coles 2004a; Jansen-Verbeke 2000).

According to Coles (2004b), tourism can be used to the retailer's advantage in a number of different ways. The additional numbers of people in a retail environment can assist in improvements in turnover and the presentation of products to tourists can stimulate long term relationships with brands, or enhance levels of customer satisfaction with the transactional experience (Coles 2004b). Coles (2004a) also lists some other advantages for linking tourism to retail. He argued that the production of goods geared to tourism can support new networks of entrepreneurship in the supply chain. Links here can include new opportunities for selling agricultural and forestry projects to the consumer. For some of these kinds of products—making wood products or chocolates are examples—it is possible to simulate or provide access to the basic production sites thus providing a 'performance' in tourism retailing. These kinds of visual and sensory experiences can be important as attractions and help foster respect for local communities and their ways of life (Coles 2004a; Ritzer 1999).

Pittman and Culp (1995) offer similar conclusions from a more general analysis of retail as a regional development tool. These economists note that traditionally retail has not been considered as a stimulus for regional economic development but that this assumption has been based on analyses of retail within urban centres. In the regional context they conclude that regional shopping, especially outlet centres and tourism-related speciality shopping, can generate jobs, support local production of goods and encourage preservation of local heritage. Robertson and Fennell (2007) provide a more detailed analysis of regional shopping centre developments in the United Kingdom. This research indicated that when such shopping is co-located with entertainment, which attracts leisure shoppers, it can create a significant number of permanent jobs, bring external capital investment into the region, improve transport options and infrastructure for residents, attract new residents and support local businesses.

Robertson and Fennell (2007) acknowledge that retail development can also attract criticism but this is often based upon unsupported assumptions about the value and potential of the economic activities that existed before the new development. In other words there is a tendency to argue that the new development is responsible for the decline of traditional economic activity, but that decline usually results from other forces, often external to the region, and the retail development offers an opportunity to arrest that decline. Powe (2006) concludes that country towns can often provide attractive and distinctive visitor locations for urban residents. Country towns have an important role to play as rural service centres, with those living in the towns themselves and rural hinterlands often making up the majority of the visitors to their town centres (Powe 2006). It appears therefore from these broad considerations of retailing and the roles of country towns that tourist shopping village development represents an important pathway for the future for a subset of these communities. The specific development routes which have been identified in the existing literature pursue this theme.

TSV Development Pathways

Getz (2000) suggests three distinct development pathways for tourist shopping villages: natural evolution, entrepreneur-driven and planned. Natural evolution occurs when tourist-oriented services evolve relatively smoothly in response to gradually increasing demand. In this case, no single business or individual is dominant. Local planning and environmental controls are necessary to manage the growth and to protect heritage and natural amenities. Discussion of this type of evolution often assumes that the growth is driven by tourism, but the interviews in New England and an examination of several TSV case studies suggest that these patterns of development may be driven by amenity migration and/or the spread of sleeper or dormitory communities which are linked to urban centres (Vaughan 2006). Like amenity migration this type of residential development creates both a group of residents seeking business and employment opportunities in the urban fringe areas and a market for various types of leisure shopping.

This process of natural evolution can also occur based on the successful development of an anchor attraction. The TSV of Hahndorf in South Australia developed around visitors seeking access to local German food and wine and the growing popularity of the historic German hotel, the German Arms. Natural evolution can also be stimulated by location. In New Zealand, for example, the development and improvement of the Transalpine highway and scenic railway linking Christchurch to the west coast of the South Island opened up touring routes that brought increased numbers of tourists through the town of Hokitika. This increase in tourist traffic supported the development of restaurants and shops, with a particular emphasis on greenstone carving and jewellery.

The second development trajectory identified by Getz is entrepreneur–driven development. This label applies when an individual or corporation takes initiatives which are followed by others. These first developments are a catalyst, which can generate enough tourist demand to stimulate other initiatives. Johns and Mattson (2005) provide a detailed case study of this kind of TSV entrepreneur led development for Hay-on-Wye, a successful village dominated by book shops. In some cases the entrepreneur is clearly focussed on tourism development, for example, the Conway Scenic Railroad in North Conway, while in others the business may not be especially targeted at tourists in its initial stages. The L.L. Bean store in Freeport is an example of the latter. Getz (2000) notes that there can be challenges associated with this entrepreneurial led pathway as residents opposed to rapid or large scale change might target the dominant entrepreneurs by seeking legal action or political intervention.

Combinations of natural evolution and entrepreneur-driven options in TSV development pathways are also common. Kuranda, a rainforest themed village in north eastern Australia, is an example of such a combination. Initial tourism was stimulated by growing attendance at local alternative markets and increasing numbers of visitors using the Kuranda Scenic Railway. These attractions provided a platform for an entrepreneurial couple to work with the local Indigenous community to create the first version of the Tjapukai Aboriginal Dance Theatre, an attraction that significantly enhanced the profile of the village for tourism. In turn a number of other attractions and shops were built.

According to Getz (2000), it is also conceivable that a TSV can be created where none exists through planned development. For example, a developer could be enticed to invest in the necessary attractions and infrastructure. A village with heritage or natural attractiveness could be targeted by tourism development agencies and provided with assistance to plan for growth. The village of Ngong Ping in Hong Kong represents one example of a fully entrepreneurial vision of building a tourist village where none existed. The point of this development was to augment the appeal of an existing but isolated tourist attraction—Lantau Island's the Big Buddha, which is located on an isolated hill top. The newly constructed shopping precinct was designed as a village linking the exit from the cable car to the base of the Big Buddha. The village was purposefully constructed to generate and profit from visitors walking the one kilometre between these points. This case will be reviewed in subsequent chapters. There exist few other examples of this type of TSV development, although it has been an option pursued in Europe and the United States for the development of factory outlet shopping (Thomas and Bromley 2002). In these cases, the development is not usually based on an existing village.

In his discussion of TSV development pathways Getz (2000) does note a number of issues and impacts. In particular he identifies parking and traffic flow as potentially serious problems in tourist villages which can lead to negative resident attitudes, especially where visitor volume exceeds the physical capacity of small villages. Social capacity issues can also arise as villagers are likely to become sensitised to all forms of development. One concern identified by Getz (2000) as an obstacle to generating local economic benefits is the absence of accommodation in small villages. A further issue of concern and one noted in part in the New England interviews lies in the marketing and theming of the village. Theming adds to the overall marketability of the TSV, but obtaining agreement on, and use of, the theme might be problematic. In particular, concern with preserving authenticity can clash with the desire to develop architectural uniformity, and developers can come into conflict with municipal officials or other businesses in their attempts to develop a design theme (Getz 2000).

Generic Studies of TSV Issues and Impacts

A number of common positive and negative impacts and a range of issues associated with TSVs were reported earlier in this chapter. These generic considerations were established from both the participants in the New England and Australian TSV studies and from the analysis by Getz (2000). Other available evidence on the impacts of and issues associated with overall TSV development can be seen as falling into two main categories—general discussions of tourism and consumption in relation to rural or peripheral areas, and specific analyses of particular villages. This section will consider the first of these categories.

A series of studies of changes in smaller towns has been conducted in the UK by the New Economics Foundation (Conisbee, et al. 2004). This research distinguishes between 'clone' towns and 'home' towns. Based on the extent of independent shops, 'clone' towns are seen as occurring where the individuality of the high street shops has been replaced by a monochrome strip of global and national chains. In contrast, 'home' towns are identified as places that retain their individual character and are individually recognisable and distinctive to both the residents and visitors. Places with higher populations were more likely to be classified as clone towns, and smaller towns, such as country towns, were more likely to be classed as home towns, suggesting that country towns can provide a different type of shopping to most large urban areas (Conisbee, et al. 2004).

Allport (2005) also examined retail aspects of the UK High Street and its ongoing viability as a trading location. This work highlighted the debate about the purported sameness of many retail locations and suggested that a select band of multiple retailers and brands are ever-present on many high streets, leading to a loss of individual town character. Further directions noted included the ongoing convergence between retail and leisure activities and the development of 'retail theatre'. The new integration between retail and leisure has resulted in the intermingling of facilities, such as bars, restaurants and cinemas, alongside the traditional retail offerings. Retail theatre is presented as a response to demand from consumers expecting a shopping experience rather than just a shopping trip. Retail theatre is described as the development of innovative and eye-catching retail interiors (and exteriors) that enhance the environment in which retail products are sold (Allport 2005).

According to Backstrom (2006) since convenience and economic issues are not of primary concern to recreational shoppers, retailers who want to attract them must also attempt to provide value in other ways. Entertainment activities represent one option for highlighting the distinctiveness of recreational shopping. Jansen-Verbeke (1998) argues that the need to combine tourist/leisure activities and retail trade to create retail theatre induces a process of 'touristification' of the retail sector. This process and its outcomes are indicated by not only the shift in the range of goods offered but particularly the way a shopping area is being designed for casual behaviour, and for leisurely browsing. The emphasis is increasingly on fun shopping and whatever could contribute to this leisure experience (Jansen-Verbeke 1998). The shift in retail trade in tourism destinations from a utilitarian function towards a hedonic function, marketing the thrill of the shopping experience rather than the value of the products, fits well into the changing demand pattern of tourists (Jansen-Verbeke 1998).

The threat of standardisation in products and unremarkable environmental design has become a serious issue for these destinations (Getz 2000). In order to effectively compete with other destinations a TSV needs to safeguard the competitive advantages of its 'uniqueness'. Emphasising the cultural links with the host community and its traditions, conservation of the original architecture and understanding the appeal of vernacular architecture are assumed to contribute to the uniqueness and the sense of place perception. Academic authors suggest these features are vital to the quality of the tourist experience. This perception of uniqueness results from a combination of forms and function of the shopping area and depends on both the product mix and on the characteristics of the shopping environment (Jansen-Verbeke 1998).

According to Snepenger, et al. (2003), relationships among the tourists, locals and merchants are by their very nature competitive and may produce tensions within the community. This tension results from the distinctive goals of each set of actors. Tourists visit the area for a leisure experience while locals are going about their daily lives in the community and merchants are seeking to compete in the local economy. The merchants shape the space through the nature of the products, services and store choices they offer, as well as influencing the prices of these goods and services, which in turn influences the mix of consumers found in the retail district. The residents also serve as a critical element in defining the shopping space as they are the key targets in the absence of tourism. Snepenger et al. (2003) also note that the resulting perceived authenticity of a retail space depends greatly upon the shopping behaviour of residents. When they have purchasing power and social class tastes consistent with the tourists, the shopping district functions as a cohesive part of the community. If there is a major separation of these groups economically and psychologically, the shopping space is likely to suit only one group. This will be the tourists if there is enough money to be made from this market but the result for the locals can be a contrived space. Additionally if the entrepreneurial and merchandising forces misread the market needs, possibly by engaging in too much touristification, then the visitors too may not support the setting (Snepenger, et al. 2003). If the income from the visitors is minimal the village will cease to exist or not develop as a shopping village and drift towards simply being a local base for supplying the community.

Focussed Studies of Specific TSVs

This tension between locals and entrepreneurs is described in some detail in a case study of Williams, Arizona in the United States (Davis and Morais 2004). This case study described the conflicts between an external tourism developer, state government policies and local businesses. In this particular TSV the development of an anchor attraction—Williams provides the base for a prominent railway to the Grand Canyon—did bring employment, increased tourist numbers and support for some local businesses. But these positive economic impacts were overshadowed by increasing property rents, significant social conflict over the development and a decline in retail business for some areas of the town. The analysis suggested that deficiencies in town planning and government tourism policies, especially those related to managing public-private partnerships, may have been a significant factor in the case (Davis and Morais 2004).

These themes of the importance of appropriate planning controls and effective public-private partnerships were also noted in a study of Kinsale, a TSV in Ireland described in Case Study 2.3 (Halme and Fadeeva 2000). In this case, however, a proactive and effective partnership was seen as creating a situation where tourist development based around leisure shopping and dining acted as stimulus for heritage conservation and restoration. The authors of this study provided evidence that the tourism development in this village was managed in such a way that it encouraged civic engagement and regional pride and was able to maintain an appropriate balance between commercial interest and a sense of community (Halme and Fadeeva 2000).

Frost (2006) argues that shopping and cultural heritage are usually considered to be at opposite ends of the tourist interest spectrum. He proposes that visiting heritage places is typically seen as a serious pursuit, often linked with education, respect for the past, even pilgrimage. In contrast, shopping may be viewed as far less serious, even trivial. This can result in conflict where an emphasis on the development of shops and commercial activities may have negative effects on the atmosphere, physical fabric and

Case Study 2.3   Kinsale, Ireland

Kinsale is a coastal village on the southern outskirts of Cork (16miles/25kms). It retains architecture and sites from medieval times and has been the site of a number of historic events including the Battle of Kinsale between the English and an Irish-Spanish coalition in 1601. It has a long history as an important harbour with a significant role in trading wine between Ireland, Spain and France. The area is also close to the location of the sinking of the Lusitania in 1915. In addition to its historic and trade importance, Kinsale also has a strong association with sailing and yachting.

Figure 2.4   The presentation of heritage, art and food themes in Kinsale.

(continued)

Case Study 2.3   (continued)

In 1969 the Kinsale Chamber of Tourism established a network to encourage tourism and community development. That network combines a number of organisations including the District Council, the Harbour Board and the Kinsale Good Food Circle. This network chose to develop Kinsale's tourism around its history and as a place for gourmet food. This initiative has been successful and generated visitation levels that have supported the development of other businesses, including shopping. This network has also been associated with the introduction of a number of sustainability initiatives including the adoption of a town wide Fair Trade policy and energy alternatives.

Case Study Sources:

http://www.cork-guide.ie/kinsale.htm (accessed October 2007)
http://www.kinsale.ie/ (accessed October 2007)
http://en.wikipedia.org/wiki/Kinsale (accessed October 2007)
Fadeeva, Z. (2004) 'Translation of sustainability ideas in tourism networks'. *Journal of Cleaner Production*, 13, 175–189.

perceived authenticity of heritage places and where high visitor flows may encourage developments which have little relationship to the heritage of an area. To explore this potential conflict Frost (2006) examined the economic importance of shopping to cultural heritage tourism with a focus on two small Australian TSVs. The results indicated that for such towns the benefits of tourism promotion may come indirectly through shops and cafés rather than directly through admission fees to attractions. Tourists appear to be attracted to these historic towns by a combination of specific cultural heritage attractions, the ambience of their heritage streetscapes and opportunities for eating and shopping. Heritage attractions on their own, however, earn little revenue from the tourists. Instead it is the privately run cafés, restaurants and shops that reap the economic rewards in these heritage towns.

The economic aspects of tourist shopping have also been explored in Australia with a study of antique shops, peripheral regions and tourism in Australia (Michael 2002). In this case the author notes that often smaller towns on the outskirts of major urban centres develop retail options for antiques and collectibles and these tend to cluster together in TSVs. The paper presents evidence that the economic multiplier resulting from antiques shopping can be significant, although no comparisons are provided to other types of tourism or development. Michael (2002) argues that the role of this particular type of tourism shopping has not been recognised and that currently its effective development is hindered by a lack of understanding of visitors and what they seek.

Another study of the economic impacts of tourism in TSVs is provided by Cegielski et al. (2001). They examined three heritage towns in three different states in Australia, Maldon (an established TSV included in the shopping villages research projects conducted by the authors of this book), Burra (an emerging TSV) and Charters Towers (not a TSV). The results from the two TSVs were very similar with each attracting just over 40,000 visitors annually. Average visitor expenditure was AUD$102 for Maldon and AUD$109 for Burra bringing a total annual income of AUD$4.27 million for Maldon and $4.48 million for Burra with a regional impact of AUD$3.82 for Maldon and $4.81 million for Burra which was estimated to support 310 full-time jobs for Maldon and 333 for Burra. The patterns of visitor expenditure showed the importance of shopping to the economic impacts of tourism. Shopping accounted for just under a third of all tourist expenditure (32.9 per cent), with 28.7 per cent accounted for by food and beverage and a further 20.8 per cent spent on accommodation.

The focussed studies of the specific villages together provide evidence for the value of specific research on tourist shopping villages. Conflicts exist and economic advantages have been documented. The discussion also highlights the existence of a number of different social representations of the development pathways or life cycles associated with TSVs. A fuller understanding of the processes involved in the shaping of TSVs is attempted by one set of authors whose work is reviewed in the next section.

Creative Destruction

One program of research into the development pathways for TSVs can be found in the work of Mitchell and her colleagues on several villages in Ontario, Canada (Mitchell 1998, 2003; Mitchell and Coghill 2000; Mitchell, Atkinson and Clark 2001) and most recently in China (Fan, Wall and Mitchell 2008; Huang, Wall and Mitchell 2007). This work is driven by an adaptation of the concept of creative destruction from economics. The concept was first put forward by Joseph Schumpeter in the 1940s (reported in Schumpeter 1975) who proposed that capitalism was based on a process in which innovations were developed and exploited by entrepreneurs to create wealth. But these innovations inevitably contribute to the destruction of the previous economic activities in a sector. In other words, capitalism is characterised by a continuous cycle of innovation and destruction of existing businesses (Furst and Reeves 2008). The core of the creative destruction approach is that there are five (sometimes expanded to six) phases which define the levels of development and growth of the TSVs. The stages, which will be considered in more detail subsequently, are an early commodification phase, an advanced commodification phase, a pre-destruction phase, an advanced destruction phase and a final period entitled post-destruction.

Mitchell (1998) argues that this model of creative destruction as applied to TSVs is based on the relationship of three variables: entrepreneurial investment, consumption of commodified heritage and destruction of the rural idyll. The premise underlying the model is that the desire to accumulate capital drives investment in the production and sale of tradition and heritage. These investments entice an increasing number of consumers (both tourists and amenity migrants). Their expenditure provides entrepreneurs with the profit for reinvestment. As the landscape unfolds, it results in destruction of the old, in the replacement of the pre-commodified landscape with one that is crowded, congested and far removed from the rural idyll that often attracted residents (Mitchell and Coghill 2000). In this context it is important to note that the rural idyll is more a state of mind than a physical reality. As Sharpley (2004: 377) points out, this rural idyll "is a constructed, negotiated experience, the symbolic importance of which may bear little resemblance to the reality".

In addition to the entrepreneurs that drive this process, Mitchell and Coghill (2000) identify other groups stakeholders associated with these towns. They observe the presence of a group they entitle preservationists who typically wish to protect and care for the heritage landscape. Above all, this group fundamentally wants to prevent destruction. There are also producers or creators of artistic heritage. Visual, performing or literary artists contribute to the stock of both tangible and intangible heritage within a community (Mitchell and Coghill 2000). For those artists who do not sell their craft, their need to produce or preserve a time-honoured artistic tradition may be the primary motivations driving their actions. Their very presence and volunteer activity (e.g. displays of craftsmanship) contribute to the ambience, and thus to the visitor experience within a community. For others the need for profit to fund the creative process may also be a motivator (Mitchell and Coghill 2000).

It is the combined motives of the capital-driven, preservation-minded and production-oriented stakeholders that shape the evolution of a heritage-based tourist shopping village. According to Mitchell and Coghill (2000) the magnitude of destruction of the old landscape will depend on the domination of the profit-motivated discourse. In the absence or unsuccessful intervention of individuals embodying other discourses (production and preservation) the destruction of the original landscape may be total. The transformation of these rural landscapes takes more than a tangible form. The influx of visitors, which inevitably accompanies the creation of these spaces, will be seen by some as a threat to the existing way of life. Mitchell, Atkinson and Clark (2001) do note that animosity towards these changes is not uniform across these communities.

Mitchell and de Waal (2009) argue that in TSVs the process of creative destruction occurs in six stages. In the first stage, the commodification of tradition or heritage is initiated. Investments that are made during this period generate financial benefits and cosmetic improvements. The attitudes of local residents are favourable, and the rural idyll remains intact. The next period, that of advanced commodification, is marked by acceleration in investment levels. New businesses are opened, while others are converted to meet the demands of the visiting population. The community is marketed extensively resulting in an escalation in visitor numbers. Those involved in the tourism industry extol its virtues, while others point to the disadvantages associated with growing popularity. It is at this stage that the community begins to witness a partial destruction of the rural idyll (Mitchell 1998). The period of early destruction is one where surplus value is reinvested into businesses that provide for the needs of the expanding visitor population. As the landscape continues to evolve, the numbers of tourists escalate, generating significant problems, including crowding and congestion. A growing number of residents perceive the erosion of their community and, ultimately, a further destruction of their idyllic rural landscape. Specialty shops (sometimes dominated by souvenirs), as well as catering and entertainment businesses evolve to meet the different demands expressed by the visitor and leisure shopper (cf Getz 2000). The development of these services can either displace traditional, resident-oriented businesses or expand the range of shopping and service opportunities. A displacement of resident owners in favour of in-migrant investors or chain stores can occur.

The period of advanced destruction is also one of continual investment (Mitchell 2003). During this stage, consumption levels continue to rise and an out-migration of local residents may occur as individuals witness the disintegration of the sense of community and cohesion that formerly characterized village life. The end of this phase is reached when residents perceive a complete destruction of the rural idyll, thus moving the community into a state of post-destruction. Several scenarios are possible, but Mitchell (2003) suggests that what emerges is the fully-fledged recreational shopping village that appeals to the mass tourist market, not the heritage-seeking consumer. Residents who remain learn to adjust to life in the new landscape, a landscape that no longer contains any vestiges of the rural idyll.

This set of studies represents the only systematic attempt to examine TSV development over an extended period of time using a coherent conceptual framework. It has effectively delineated the key sets of actors and the forces that create tensions in TSV development life cycles and mapped out some of the complexities in these life cycles. But it is also restricted to a particular type of TSV—those on the fringes of major urban centres in densely populated regions with existing infrastructure and a wide range of economic alternatives. Not all TSVs can be described this way. The program has also focussed much more on the destruction element of 'creative destruction' tending to assume that change in existing activities is inevitably a negative outcome. Other applications of the concept of 'creative destruction' view it as a cycle with separate outcomes for different actors under varied conditions (de Figueiredo and Kyle 2004) or as a force for renewal which can foster positive social change and build opportunities for previously disadvantaged groups (Furst and Reeves 2008; Pe'er and Vertinsky 2008). The creative destruction model will be referred to and discussed elsewhere in this volume but other approaches are also needed to capture the processes and outcomes operating in a wide range of TSVs.

A SUSTAINABILITY CONTEXT FOR TSVS

The creative destruction model represents one systematic framework with which to view TSV development. The following section seeks to introduce another perspective to assess the outcome of the changes in and due to TSVs. Moscardo (2008a) argues that we need better frameworks to identify the full range of tourism impacts. A thorough assessment of the contribution tourism might make to the sustainable development of a destination region can only be made if the full array of effects are available. Once this full range of impacts is known it may then be possible to begin to relate the types of development and or pathways that are associated with better outcomes. Two related concepts that could be useful in developing such a framework are quality of life (QoL) and community well-being (Moscardo 2008a, 2009). These two concepts share the underlying assumption that an individual's perceived quality of life and a community's overall well-being depend on their stock of various forms of capital (Costanza, et al. 2007; Malkina-Pykh and Pykh 2007). The forms of capital to be considered include:

- Natural capital or the stock of resources available in the ecosystem to support life;
- Human capital including health, skills and levels of education;
- Intellectual capital which incorporates knowledge,
- Financial capital, the most traditional use of the term capital which refers to the money an individual can use;
- Built physical capital which constitutes the structures and aesthetics of a community's buildings and infrastructure; and
- Social and cultural capital which refer to the extent and quality of trust, social networks and support that an individual has within a community (see Vermuri and Costanza (2006) for more detail).

For tourism to be sustainable it must contribute to both the quantity and quality of these forms of capital across the entire system in which it operates. Figure 2.5 outlines this system.

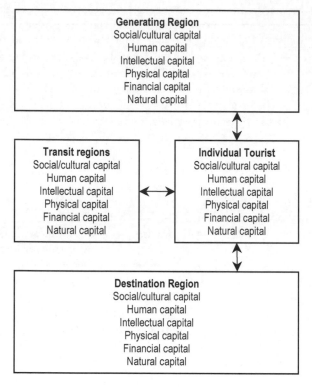

Figure 2.5   Framework for identifying tourism impact areas.

By taking these different forms of capital, using the available evidence in the literature that has been reviewed and focussing on the destination region component of Figure 2.3, we can begin to map out how the development of tourist shopping might impact on a host community. Table 2.2 shows the results of this mapping exercise. The challenge is to link these outcomes to features or dimensions of the tourism development so that more effective pathways can be identified and encouraged.

TSV DEVELOPMENT IN REVIEW

The analyses of TSV development and the consequences of that development for destination communities reviewed thus far can be summarised using five main themes. Firstly, there is a consistent reporting of positive economic outcomes arising from the diversification of the economy associated with tourist shopping development. Secondly, the development is often, but not always, associated with tension and conflict within the local community. These tensions are often seen as a force destroying social capital within the communities.

Table 2.2   Overview of Tourism Shopping Impacts on Destination Community Capital

Type of capital	Positive Impacts	Negative Impacts
Financial	Tourist shopping can provide markets for local producers, local employment and support for local businesses	Rising rents and land prices can displace residents
Physical	Tourist shopping can be an alternative use of heritage buildings and support the restoration and conservation of the physical landscape	Tourist numbers can create crowding, congestion and pollution. The building of facilities and services for tourists can result in negative aesthetic impacts
Natural	Visitor interest can support conservation efforts. Visitor numbers can make certain environmental management systems economically viable and support the construction of greener infrastructure	Infrastructure built to accommodate visitors may have negative environmental impacts. Inappropriate numbers and behaviours of visitors can threaten natural processes and over use resources
Intellectual/ Human	The development of tourist shopping can encourage migration into the region bringing skills and knowledge into the community. Visitors may provide the numbers necessary to support better educational and health services for TSV communities	Changes to the nature of the community may result in some individuals feeling alienated
Social/ cultural	Speciality shops can support local artists and craftsman and encourage conservation of cultural heritage and practices. Positive partnerships and successful developments can create networks that can be used for other economic activities, and encourage local pride.	Conflict over development can break down relationships and undermine trust

The tensions and conflicts hinder more sustainable outcomes from tourism development by eroding trust, slowing decision making and limiting the flow of financial capital. Thirdly, there are many different types of TSV which vary in their political, geographic, demographic and historical contexts. This diversity modifies the ways in which the tourist shopping villages develop and shapes the ensuing outcomes and impacts of growth. Fourthly, while the TSV development pathways and outcomes are influenced by a number of factors, government planning and policies appear to be critical elements.

Finally, much of the conflict is underpinned by divergent views and assumptions about what tourists want, yet very little research has been conducted specifically into the characteristics of tourist markets, or the expectations and experience evaluations of the tourists. There is little research available on the types of tourists who frequent TSVs and whether or not they differ across different types of TSV and at different stages in the development of a TSV. Almost nothing is known about the TSV experience from the visitor perspective—either in terms of what they seek and expect or how they evaluate currently available opportunities. In addition little is known about how TSVs fit into larger travel experiences or how tourists make purchase decisions.

One important framework used to understand TSV development is the creative destruction model, which has considerable value in identifying stakeholders and their discourses. Its applicability to all TSVs remains questionable and some of the assumptions it makes concerning visitor characteristics and community attitudes are untested. A wider sustainability framework based on assessing various forms of capital offers another pathway to improving our limited knowledge of TSV development.

In particular it is clear that the discussion of TSVs' development in the existing literature is often based on statements about assumed tourist characteristics, motivations and behaviours. More specifically, assumptions and claims have been made about issues related to changes to the physical and visual aspects of the villages, the relationship between heritage and tourism, perceived authenticity and village themes, the need to develop the various elements of retail theatre and demand for services and infrastructure. Clearly having a better understanding of the TSV experience from the tourist perspective could be a valuable element in better understanding how TSV development pathways can contribute to more sustainable outcomes for the destination communities that host TSVs. The next chapter will explore these questions and set out a model for understanding the TSV experience from the visitor perspective.

3 A Model of Tourist Shopping Village Experience

INTRODUCTION

A number of social scientists have described leisure shopping itself as a type of tourism (Cox, Cox and Anderson 2005; Falk and Campbell 1997). In his analysis of the shopping mall, Goss (1999: 47) uses the notion of a trip as a metaphor to describe key aspects of a visit to the mall: "The brilliant combined effect of nostalgia, spatial and temporal displacement through transport, and fetishization of commodities, is to contrive the experience of The Mall literally and figuratively as a shopping 'trip', a bodily and imaginary journey to distant places and past times that is undertaken in states of reverie and distraction, and for which the purchase stands as souvenir". Lehtonen and Maenpaa (1997) are more direct, describing key features of modern shopping settings, such as the combination of refreshment, retail and entertainment, the use of themes, the celebration of the senses and the building of a safe enclave, and noting that these are very similar to the features of many tourist destinations.

Given this close link between shopping and tourism and the evidence presented in Chapter 1 on the extent of tourist shopping, we can question why shopping has not been given more attention in the tourism literature and why tourism research has not contributed more to the discussion of shopping? Similar questions have also been raised about shopping more generally (Miller 1998, 2001; Underhill 1999, 2004). Three contributing factors have been suggested. Firstly, the problem could be academic snobbery—shopping is simply not seen as a serious academic activity and may even be considered a socially undesirable activity in the social classes and subcultures to which many academics belong (Miller 1998; Underhill 1999). Similarly tourism has also been seen as a less desirable phenomenon for academic attention (Crick 1989; Nash 2007). Secondly, shopping is such a common activity that we do not reflect on it much and so it often escapes our attention (Miller, et al. 1998). Thirdly, it could be that research into shopping presents academics with an ethical dilemma in that this research could be seen as merely serving to assist businesses to better exploit shoppers. Researchers who venture into this area have to contemplate whether their work seeks to improve benefits for the retailer, property developer, shopper or wider community and at whose cost. Some shopping researchers have avoided this by seeking to understand shopping as a social and cultural ritual with no emphasis placed on analysing the details of what is bought (see the work of Falk and Campbell (1997) and Miller (1998, 2001)). Other researchers are unapologetically on the side of the retailer clearly seeing their research as providing information that can assist retailers to encourage shoppers to buy more (Underhill 1999, 2004). Most, however, do not explicitly address this issue.

The authors of the present book recognise the interconnectivity of these issues, the complex nature of the commercial and social systems in which shopping occurs and the active role that all participants, including shoppers, can play in this system. The aim of the particular analysis described in the present book is to improve our understanding of the overall system to identify points of improvement for multiple actors. We have selected as a starting point the experience of the tourist consumer. This choice reflects three factors:

- It seems to be a critical component in understanding the processes that generate impacts, both negative and positive, on the destination communities;
- Many destination development decisions are made based on untested assumptions about who comes to TSVs, why they come and what they do once there; and
- It is an area where the authors are qualified to make a contribution.

Chapter 2 demonstrated links between different patterns of development and different locations. It also addressed actions of entrepreneurs and tensions between different groups and provided a framework to assess categories of impacts. The actors in these TSV settings often assume that development patterns are linked to different tourist markets and further that changes in experience opportunities are linked to the arrival of new kinds of tourists. Little research has been done to establish these implied links. It was argued in Chapter 2 that if we better understand tourists and TSVs we might better understand the development cycle and its likely consequences for all stakeholders. Therefore, the main aim for this chapter is to build a model of the TSV experience from the perspective of the tourist that incorporates a) research into shopping and shoppers and b) the discussions of TSV development and impacts described in Chapter 2. The present chapter will review key themes and findings in academic approaches to leisure shopping with particular attention paid to rural and tourist shopping research. It will then use recent discussions of the customer experience concept to develop a theoretical context before presenting and explaining the TSV experience model.

ACADEMIC APPROACHES TO LEISURE SHOPPING

Shopping can be defined as "consumption-oriented movement in a space where one has the possibility of making purchases" (Lehtonen and Maenpaa 1997: 143). This definition highlights the core link between shopping and consumption. Miller and colleagues in 1998 offered a history of academic approaches during the twentieth century to consumption as a context for understanding research into shopping. This history divided these academic approaches into five stages. In the first stage consumption was seen as the domain of economics with much emphasis placed on exploring the links between consumption and production. This stage ended as consumption was taken up as a research topic in other disciplines such as anthropology and sociology. The second stage was characterised by a broader range of research topics reflecting a new and wider range of disciplinary attention. In this period research expanded into understanding patterns of consumption, thus incorporating shopping, as well as endeavouring to analyse the growth and nature of consumption places.

Stage three was associated with a further broadening of disciplinary interest and in this stage research began into more specific aspects of consumption such as distribution, the role of service staff and the personal and cultural meanings of the items bought or consumed. An important element in this stage was the growth of studies into consumer behaviour and decision making. This area of research was then, and still is, focussed on understanding the variables that influence how much and how often people shop and what they buy. In this third stage of consumption research, the consumer behaviour work was primarily interested in understanding retail "atmospherics" or "servicescapes" (Baker 1987; Turley and Milliman 2000).

Turley and Milliman (2000) provide a review of this third phase of shopping research. Most of the studies into atmospherics use one of two related models. The first is a basic model from environmental psychology, the stimulus-organism-response or (S-O-R) model (Mehrabian and Russell 1974). This simple proposal argues that physical features of the retail atmosphere act as the stimuli; these create different emotional responses and setting evaluations from the shopper or organism, who then responds by either avoidance, leaving the retail environment, or approach, staying in the retail environment (Turley and Milliman 2000). Shoppers who stay in the retail setting, explore it and have a positive mood are then more likely to purchase products (Babin and Attaway 2000). The second commonly used framework proposed by Baker in the 1980s (see Baker, Grewal and Levy 1992 for more details) builds on this S-O-R model by dividing the stimuli into three main groups—ambient factors, design factors and social factors (d'Astous 2000). Ambient factors are background conditions such as air quality, noise, odour and cleanliness; design factors include architecture, colour, scale, texture, layout, comfort and signage; and social factors which include both the number and type of other shoppers, and the appearance and behaviour of service staff (d'Astous 2000). Table 3.1 provides a summary list of the variables that have been studied and/or proposed as having an influence on shopper behaviour within this tradition. The second column summarises the main findings in each area in terms of the overall shopper evaluations.

Table 3.1   Summary of Variables Studied in Retail Atmospherics

Variables Proposed & Studied	*Contributions to Positive Shopper Evaluations*
Ambient Factors · air quality · temperature & humidity · noise intensity & type · type of background music · odour · cleanliness · lighting	Shoppers prefer clean, well-lit, well-ventilated shops with comfortable temperatures, no unpleasant odours and lower noise levels.
Design Factors · colours · architectural style · scale of buildings & features · type of building materials used · width of aisles · security & safety features · type & features of merchandising signage & displays · access points to & within the store · access to the merchandise · signage & orientation systems · payment procedures · presence of rest areas · organisation or grouping of merchandise · variety & quality of merchandise · price display · presentation of samples & promotions	Shoppers prefer easier access, clear orientation systems, variety of merchandise with clear prices, free samples, rest areas, short queues and easy to understand payment procedures
Social · crowding · interactions with other shoppers · number of service staff · appearance of service staff · characteristics of the shopper including motivations, experience & who they are shopping with	Shoppers don't like crowding but do appreciate opportunities for social interactions with others. They like easy to find & easily identifiable service staff who offer good service (prompt, courteous, knowledgeable, willing to help, reliable).

Sources: d'Astous (2000), Turley & Milliman (2000), Machleit et al. (2005), Ng (2003), Underhill (1999; 2004).

This shopping research stream continues into the present but is limited in a number of critical ways (Aubert-Gamet and Cova 1999). Firstly much of it is too simplistic in its methodological design and lacks external validity. Many of these studies are conducted in laboratories, not real settings, using students to assess written descriptions of retail settings (cf. Babin, Hardesty and Suter 2003) or videos of retail transactions (cf. Morin, Dubé and Chebat 2007). Even when research is conducted in actual retail settings, these field experiments tend to manipulate only a single or small set of variables. Despite limiting the number of variables to allow for greater control, many of these studies report complex findings and evidence of mediating variables (cf. Dubé and Morin 2001). It is very difficult from this work to move beyond very broad generalities such as those presented in the second column of Table 3.1. A second problem is the focus on the single retail store which results in a lack of attention to other important variables. More recently some studies have moved beyond a single store to explore shopping centres or malls and this work has suggested additional variables that might influence shopper cognition and behaviour. These include the variety of stores in shopping centres or malls; the presence of entertainment or leisure facilities, celebrations and/or special events programs; the use of themes; and the existence of an anchor attraction (Ibrahim and Ng 2002; Kang and Kim 1999; Wakefield and Baker 1998).

The third main criticism of retail atmospherics research is that it pays insufficient attention to shoppers and their motivations, constraints and characteristics, their broader shopping experiences and to the rapidly changing nature of these variables (Underhill 1999, 2004). In the shopping centre studies the importance of the characteristics of the shopper was also noted. Wakefield and Baker (1998) argued that features of the centre such as variety, combined with other retail atmospherics and influenced by the shopper's motivation and experience, create a level of 'excitement' which in turn affects the desire to stay in the centre. Together, excitement and desire to stay had direct links to the amount of shopping undertaken within the mall and intentions to return (Wakefield and Baker 1998). Ibrahim and Ng (2002) found that positive evaluations of shopping places were significantly influenced by the social interactions that shoppers had, whether or not they found what they were seeking, their available free time and opportunities to learn about trends and products.

Returning to Miller and colleagues' (1998) history of academic approaches to consumption brings us to their fourth stage which begins with a focus across several disciplines on shopping as a cultural practice or ritual. Research is now conducted in geography on the locations and movement patterns associated with shopping. In this research stage a number of sociologists have begun to examine dramaturgical approaches to shopping. Analysis of shopping reveals its importance in lifestyle and the development of self-identity. For some shoppers this means seeking nostalgia and through that a link is made between heritage and shopping (Miller, et al. 1998).

Work in consumer behaviour continues with retail atmospherics but consumer behaviour research also expands in this fourth stage into understanding shopper motivations and developing shopper typologies (Ng 2003). This work places particular emphasis on what is referred to as leisure, recreational or hedonic shopping which Backstrom (2006) describes as characterised by intrinsic satisfaction, perceived freedom, a focus on entertainment and escape and having social worth. It is this type of shopping that becomes linked to travel.

At the end of the twentieth century Miller et al. (1998) describe a fifth stage where shopping is recognised as a common but complex social activity linked to culture, social interactions and self-identity. In consumer behaviour this work is seen as falling under the banner of consumer culture theory (Backstrom 2006). Several types of research can be identified in current approaches to shopping—issues related to public spaces connected to shopping, discussions of themes in shopping places, research into brands and products as identity markers and research focussed on the meaning and value of shopping for participants (Miller 1998).

Many shopping spaces are also public spaces. Town centres and TSVs are settings where privately owned shops are located within larger precincts that include public spaces managed often by local governments. The distinction is not so clear in shopping centres or malls, which are usually privately owned. Underhill (2004) notes that there continues to be considerable confusion in different US states over the extent to which shopping malls can be considered public spaces. He discusses this in the context of a number of court disputes over mall management actions with regard to different leisure uses of the setting by local residents. He concludes that, while in some states courts have ruled that shopping malls are not public spaces, generally local residents and community groups consider that they are. Certainly shoppers see them as more than places to shop.

This convergence of private retail business and public space creates a number of tensions (Falk and Campbell 1997). Underhill (2004) sets out in detail the problems of managing competing and conflicting uses of the space around shops and the pressure from retailers to control that use in order to attract people more likely to spend money in the shops. He notes a number of tactics that are used to discourage use of the overall shopping spaces by people less likely to spend money in stores. In other shopping settings such as town centres and TSVs there are also issues related to who pays for and manages the provision of public facilities and entertainment programs (Murphy, et al. 2008) and who is responsible for the marketing of the entire centre (Warnaby, Bennison and Davies 2005). One major area of concern here is the development of themes and changes in the presentation of the spaces to match these themes. In the previous chapter we have already described how this tension over the development and marketing of village contributes both to conflicts about how a village should be developed and presented to visitors and resident concerns about the image of their community.

The importance and role of themes in shopping settings is the second area of current approaches to shopping research. Miller and colleagues (1998) argued that the connection between leisure shopping, nostalgia and heritage was established as an area for analysis in their fourth stage. Essentially heritage can be seen as theme for a shopping setting and this theme can be seen as reflecting a motivation for leisure shopping—in this case to return to a perceived simpler past as a way to escape the tensions of current life. According to Goss (1999) this seeking of heritage is one of four common themes used in shopping spaces, the others are a return to childhood, a desire to experience nature and an interest in the primitive or exotic other. In each case Goss (1999) provides examples of how shops and shopping precincts have translated these themes into precinct and store design and presentation. Goss (1999) goes on to argue that these themes reflect a desire on the part of the shoppers to experience something more than simple consumption—they provide a reason for shopping in these particular places thus locating shopping in the larger leisure context.

This work on themes and shopping as part of larger leisure experience is linked to research into brands and products as identity markers. Branding has become a central concept in marketing, starting with consumer goods, especially discretionary items such as cars, clothing, jewellery and cosmetics, and expanding to include a range of services (Hoeffler and Keller 2003). A brand can be defined very simply as "a name, term, sign, symbol or design, or a combination of these, intended to identify the goods or services of one seller or group of sellers and to differentiate them from those of competitors" (Kotler, et al. 2006: 575). The important feature of a brand for the present discussion is that it enhances a product's competitive advantage because it links consumption of the brand to a set of characteristics that are desirable to the buyer (Kotler, et al. 2006). In particular it has been argued that the purchase of a well-known, branded product links the buyer with particular lifestyles and is a marker of personality characteristics to which they aspire (Aaker 1997). So shopping becomes a way of establishing one's identity and associating oneself with a particular lifestyle and presenting that identity and lifestyle choice to others (Aubert-Gamet and Cova 1999).

The final kind of shopping research concentrates on the shopper perspective. Within this area are studies using techniques such as the Critical Incident Technique (CIT) (Jones 1999) and ethnography (Miller 1998). These approaches attempt to understand overall shopping experiences from the perspective of the shopper. This work identifies additional variables that are important to shopping activities and shopper evaluations. Miller's (1998) ethnographic work stresses the importance of shopping as a way to strengthen and celebrate important social relationships through both the shared activity itself, but also through shopping to buy things for others. Miller (1998) argues that shopping is about love and sacrifice. Machleit et al.'s (2005) examination of factors associated with 'uplifting' retail incidents notes that in addition to atmospherics and positive encounters with service staff, other key variables included good prices, finding bargains and getting good value for money. The importance of price and a bargain were also noted in a CIT study conducted by Jones (1999). This study found that positive memorable shopping incidents included opportunities to socialise with others, time to browse and explore, finding unique products, encounters with fun and entertaining sales people and opportunities to get involved with products and engage in activities. These are recurring findings and Cox et al. (2005) conclude that shopping pleasure is associated with mingling with others, bargain hunting, browsing, exploring, novelty-seeking, sensory stimulation and enjoyment of being in a comfortable environment. It is in these discussions of emic approaches that ideas of engagement (Backstrom 2006), delight (Arnold, et al. 2003), entertainment (Jones 1999) and experiences emerge (Arnold and Reynolds 2003). According to Webb (2000) the convergence of entertainment, leisure and shopping and the growth of non-traditional retail settings, such as brand flagship stores and stores in art galleries and museums, has contributed to a growing interest in retail experiences and themed shopping settings.

SHOPPING IN RURAL AREAS

Research into, and discussions about, rural shopping can be characterised as driven by three main issues and grouped into three key themes. The discussion of urban shopping experiences remains relevant but some further issues of importance can be identified. The three main issues are the need to find effective strategies for economic and social regeneration in rural areas, the wide range of different contexts that exist within the broad category of rural and a lack of understanding of consumer or market behaviour in relation to many rural products and services (Findlay and Sparks 2008; McEachern and Warnaby 2006; Paddison and Calderwood 2007; Thomas and Bromley 2003). The three key themes of rural shopping research are food availability and choice, the impact of new retail centres on existing shops and urban and local shopper attitudes and behaviours (Findlay and Sparks 2008).

The most common driver of research into rural shopping is the recognition that many rural areas face a number of economic and social challenges as traditional sources of income change and decline (Thomas and Bromley 2003). There are numerous government strategies designed to address these challenges and the development of large retail centres, factory outlets and warehouse shops is one of these strategies (Thomas and Bromley 2003). Paddison and Calderwood (2007) list a number of benefits of retail as a development strategy. These advantages include some benefits listed in the previous chapters such as income and employment, stimulus for business network development and innovation, greater choice and lower cost for local residents and the maintenance of an active community and social hub. But the universal effectiveness of retail regeneration strategies is constrained and complicated by the wide variety of situations that can exist in rural areas. McEachern and Warnaby (2005) argue that there is no clear rural-urban dichotomy but rather we can see areas as existing along a continuum between the two points. Thus some rural areas may have access to larger regional centres while others may be so remote as to have almost no clusters of residences or services at all. Some may have dispersed settlement with a network of small villages and others may have a single centre. Many rural areas vary significantly in terms of transport access and links (Findlay and Sparks 2008). These different patterns of location, settlement and linkages all influence the impact of retail development (Thomas and Bromley 2003).

According to Paddison and Calderwood (2007), the effectiveness of retail as a regeneration strategy is also limited by a lack of understanding of consumers, a conclusion that is the consistent with the aim of this chapter. This dearth of specific knowledge about consumers has resulted in recent years in a growing number of studies exploring both the behaviours and attitudes of local and urban residents towards shopping in rural areas. McEachern and Warnaby (2006) found an ongoing tension within the attitudes of local residents in rural areas who simultaneously saw their rural communities as providing the positive features of scenery, sense of community, privacy, quietness and a slow pace of life, while at the same time describing the same place as lacking shops, being more expensive and having poor leisure facilities. Snepenger and colleagues (2003) looked at the views and behaviours of both local and tourists in the downtown area of a regional centre, dividing each group into heavy and light shoppers. Overall they found that the profiles of heavy shoppers were similar for tourists and locals but tourists as a whole had higher incomes and less concern about prices. Light local users were the most sensitive to the presence of tourists and possible problems associated with tourist use.

Paddison and Calderwood (2007) concentrated on potential shoppers from urban areas and reported that these shoppers were seeking 'localness' and place distinctiveness in their rural shopping. They especially wanted to buy local food and products and encounter unique expressions of local culture. Powe's (2006) study presents similar results, reporting that urban residents seek more local and specialised shops, distinctive buildings, safety and comfort, a range of different shops, activities for the whole travel party, authenticity, unique local products, quality products and local produce. We can begin to see where conflict may emerge with local residents seeking shops that offer cheaper prices and more opportunities for utilitarian shopping and visitors looking for regionally distinctive quality products.

TOURIST SHOPPING

In Chapter 1 we provided a review of the extent of tourist shopping and developed a typology of the main forms of tourist shopping (utilitarian, social obligation, value for money, self-indulgence/self-development, destination experience and extended leisure (see Table 3.2 for more details)). It was noted that TSVs were most likely to be associated with destination experience, extended leisure and self-indulgence/self-development. This classification was based on location, stage of the holiday, motives and segmentation studies. Shopping motivation, work on souvenir purchase and tourist shopper typologies are three major areas of tourist shopping research. This section will review the other two major areas—factors related to the type and amount of expenditure and evaluations of, and preferences for, tourist shopping places and opportunities. Studies of expenditure have found that how much tourist shoppers spend and what they spend it on is influenced by a range of characteristics including age, gender, travel motivation, income, travel party, cultural background and attitudes such as interest in other cultures (Carmichael and Smith 2004; Choi, et al. 2008; Lehto, et al. 2004; Oh, et al. 2004). At this stage much of the research is descriptive and few consistent patterns have emerged. Further, most studies have focussed only on tourist shoppers with only one study identified by the researchers directly comparing tourist and local resident expenditure across a range of shopping locations. LeHew and Wesley (2007) found from this comparison that overall at any one location tourists spend less than locals as they mix shopping with a range of other activities. The pattern of the expenditure was not examined.

Within the area of evaluations of and preferences for tourist shopping there are both broad survey studies incorporating a range of variables and smaller specialised studies, often using more qualitative techniques, focussing on a limited set of variables or specific locations. In the case of the broad survey studies there is considerable consistency in the conclusions both within the studies of tourist shopping and across studies of tourist shopping and leisure shopping in general. Table 3.2 provides a summary.

The more focussed studies can be grouped into three categories. The first are those analysing the importance of cross-cultural interactions between tourist shoppers and sales staff (Chang, Yang and Yu 2006; Smith and Olson 2001) or differences in shopping behaviour between different cultural groups of tourists (Choi, et al. 2008; Kikuchi and Ryan 2007; Lehto, et al. 2004; Yüksel 2004). As with the studies on tourist expenditure, this research has established that cross-cultural interactions and differences are important influences on tourist shopper behaviour and evaluations but from the limited work undertaken it is premature to establish clear patterns from the findings. The second category of specific tourist shopping studies is about perceived risk. Yüksel and Yüksel (2007) argue that tourist shoppers face additional ... ause they may be unfamiliar and/or uncomfortable with cultural ... related to bargaining and selling. Often, tourists can be aware of the ... y of returning and exchanging purchases as well as being concerned

Table 3.2 Features Tourists Seek and Enjoy in Shopping Opportunities

Features

- Variety of stores and products
- Novel, unique, authentic and distinctive products, especially those not available at home
- Attractive prices/value for money
- Clean, well-lit, attractive stores with interesting window and product displays
- Easily accessible shopping areas in terms of location, having a pedestrian focus and extended opening hours
- Positive interactions with friendly, helpful and knowledgeable staff
- Safe and secure environments and transactions
- Opportunities to experience local culture
- Shops combined with leisure and entertainment activities
- Cheerful, colourful and lively settings
- Streetscapes with a variety of attractive facades

Sources: Yüksel (2004), Wong and Law (2003), Yeung et al. (2004), Tosun et al. (2007), Turner and Reisinger (2001), Reisinger and Turner (2002), Hsieh and Chang (2006)

about product quality and brand imitations. Westwood (2006) notes that these concerns can be a deterrent for some tourists, who will seek sanitised or familiar purpose-built shopping places such as malls, and an attraction for others who will seek out less sanitised informal places such as markets and street stalls. Westwood (2006) further proposes that for this latter group, shopping in these basic transaction spaces provides both more intense encounters with local culture and greater authenticity.

The third category is that of studies concentrating on product characteristics including authenticity. While tourists purchase a wide of range of goods there is a clear emphasis on buying quality products and/or local, unique and distinctive products. A number of studies have explored these types of purchases, focussing particularly on perceptions of authenticity. This research suggests that perceived authenticity varies according to a number of variables including the age and experience of the shopper, characteristics of the product including its link to cultural symbols, being locally and handmade, the quality of the workmanship, the product use, cultural and historical integrity and features of the purchase experience such as the ability to interact with the producers (Asplet and Cooper 2000; Hu and Yu 2007; Littrell, Anderson and Brown 1993; Yu and Littrell 2003). We are dealing here with vestiges of objective authenticity, the notion that the product or experience can be reliably assessed by key characteristics. Many academic researchers now suggest that authenticity is essentially subjective and is determined principally by the judgements observers make which in turn are dependent on issues of experience, status and cultural capital. In this widespread view, perceptions of authenticity tell us more about the observer than what they are observing (Cohen 2002; Pearce 2007).

Finally there are a few studies examining tourist behaviour and evaluations specifically in TSVs. Most of these are, however, simple descriptive profiles of tourists provided by regional or national tourist organisations. For example, in Australia, Tourism Victoria (2006) provides market profiles for regional areas where TSVs are dominant and in Canada the Ontario Ministry of Tourism (2007a) provides similar profiles for visitors to areas where TSVs are core destinations. These types of reports do not provide much insight into what visitors seek and appreciate from their tourist shopping experiences. Four exceptions can be briefly reviewed as the findings in each case are consistent with those previously reported. Firstly a study of visitors to Maldon (Australia) found that they combined shopping with visits to heritage sites and they sought well-preserved heritage buildings, opportunities to experience and learn about Australian history, an authentic experience, good visitor amenities, good information, peaceful surroundings, nice cafés and craft shopping (Cegielski, et al. 2001). Visitors to Hahndorf (Australia) were seeking opportunities to explore, spend time with family, experience good food and wine, learn and experience German heritage and discover something new. There was also an appreciation of the local atmosphere, the variety of activities, friendly locals and key attractions (Tourism Research Australia 2008). Repeat visitors to two Texan TSVs, Wimberley and Fredericksburg, tended to be older, gave greater importance to leisure shopping and saw the TSVs as being within an easy drive from home and as having good quality restaurants (Tiefenbacher, Day and Walton 2000). Finally the authors' own study, which analysed expert ratings of the visitor experiences offered in 29 TSVs in Australia, New Zealand and Canada, concluded that successful tourist experiences in these settings were related to a well-developed heritage theme, good food and wine, facilities and presentations for tourists, accessibility and regionally distinctive merchandise available for purchase (Murphy, Moscardo, et al. 2008).

SUMMARY OF RESEARCH INTO LEISURE, RURAL AND TOURIST SHOPPING

Ng (2003) attempted to summarise research into leisure shoppers and how they respond to shopping situations with a framework that split the variables into those related to the shopping environment and those related to the shopper. The environment was further subdivided into variables related to the environment in general (the realm of much atmospherics research) and variables related to the type of shopping setting such as mall or downtown area. The shopper variables were partitioned into individual characteristics of the shopper, situational factors such as time and access, overall shopping orientation and specific shopping motivations. Ng's (2003) argument was that these person-environment variables combined to create the particular characteristics of any shopping event.

Figure 3.1 is a development of Ng's (2003) framework that summarises and organises the main findings of the literature review thus far including

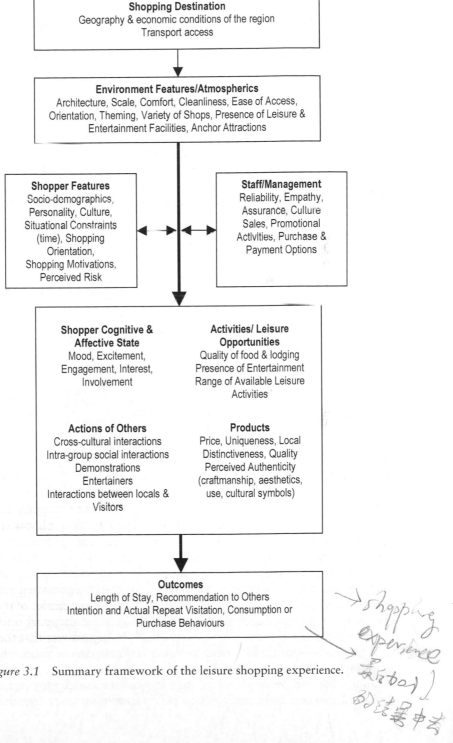

Figure 3.1 Summary framework of the leisure shopping experience.

the additional findings from research into rural and tourist shopping. The framework in Figure 3.1 extends Ng's (2003) work to integrate the additional findings from the literature review in this chapter by suggesting that environment, management and shopper features combine to create a set of activities available for shoppers to engage in, a set of social interactions with others, a set of products to purchase and a particular cognitive and/or affective state on the part of the shopper. These four additional groups of variables then combine to create the overall shopping experience.

THE RISE OF EXPERIENCE IN CONSUMER AND TOURIST BEHAVIOUR

The idea of experiences as the central element of production and consumption has been made popular in recent years by Pine and Gilmore's (1999) book on the experience economy. But it has a much longer history in studies of consumption (Holbrook and Hirschman 1982) and in tourism, which den Breejen (2007) argues can be identified by its focus on the production of experiences. Numerous definitions of the customer experience concept exist, ranging from very broad inclusive approaches such as that of Boswijk and colleagues (2005: 2) in which experience is defined as "a continuous interactive process of doing and undergoing that provides meaning to the individual", to more focussed options such as that provided by Shaw and Ivens (2005: 6) in which a customer experience is defined as "an interaction between an organization and a customer. It's a blend of an organisation's physical performance, the senses stimulated and emotions evoked, each intuitively measured against customer expectations across all moments of contact". It is this latter definition that seems best suited to a discussion of TSVs. Moscardo (2008c) has reviewed the available research into factors associated with both positive tourist experiences and positive customer experiences in general and identified a set of factors consistently associated with both. These are listed in Table 3.3 and as would be expected, the list is similar to that provided for positive leisure shopping experiences. The literature review thus far has identified considerable repetition in the lists of features found to be associated with positive shopping and tourist experiences across different populations, settings and methodological styles. What is not clear is why these features should matter and how they interact? The more recent work on customer experience suggests some answers to these questions. Within this work several related concepts and theories have been used and proposed including dramaturgical approaches, stories, involvement and mindfulness.

Pine and Gilmore (1999) used a dramaturgical approach to both define and describe customer experiences in that they argued that businesses provided a stage and props for a customer experience with staff playing some roles and customers being either other players or the audience. The theatrical

Table 3.3 Key Features of Positive Customer and Tourist Experiences

Feature	Details
Multisensory	Use of all senses in settings and products
Unique or novel	Surprising and/or unexpected features, products or activities
Easy to access	Includes physical access and good orientation and intellectual access through information provisions
Themes	Consistent use of clear and strong themes
Emotive	Encourages and supports affective responses
Interaction or participation	Opportunities for customers to be active participants and experience co-creators
Social	Positive interactions with staff and other customers and opportunities to be social with companions
Personal relevance	Opportunities to personalise the experience and pursue aspects of personal significance
Authentic	Perceived authenticity in relation to features of the setting, interactions with others, the products or services to be consumed and freedom of personal expression
Learning	Changes in understanding and opportunities to develop skills and knowledge
Stories/narratives	Built around narratives, contains roles for customers to play, provides events that can be built into personal stories to tell others

Sources: adapted from Moscardo 2008c.

metaphor is useful for the design of customer experiences in that it divides the customer experience into easily described groups of factors that businesses can manage—setting, props, roles for staff and roles for customers. But the approach is not without its critics. Caru and Cova (2003) point out that customer experiences vary along a number of dimensions and the type of approach taken to understand a customer experience will need to match the type of experience being examined. In particular they are concerned that existing analyses, including those of Pine and Gilmore (1999), often assume that all experiences are clearly bounded and all are aimed at being extraordinary. Baron, Harris and Harris (2001) offer a different perspective, arguing that a dramaturgical approach is a valuable one for analysing and understanding consumption but that mostly academics in this area have used it as a simple descriptive tool, failing to appreciate the many different ways in which a drama can be enacted. Thus many different experiences are inadvertently treated as the same.

Two key features of a dramaturgical approach, as it has been applied to customer experience by Pine and Gilmore (1999) and others (Gentile,

Spiller and Noci 2007; Kozinets, et al. 2002; McGoun, et al. 2003), are worth noting. The first is the importance of themes/narratives/stories in providing coherence, structure and opportunities for immersion on the part of the participants and in providing a way for customers to justify and explain their participation in the consumption experience (Moscardo in press). The second is the importance placed on customer engagement and involvement. This need to involve the customer more actively in the experience is a common theme in both the leisure shopping literature and in more recent discussions of customer experiences (Gentile, et al. 2007). The term involvement has been used in different ways in discussion of shopping experiences. Sometimes it is used as a general term to refer to action in terms of participation or engagement in activities associated with a shopping experience (Backstrom 2006). Additionally it is used to refer to an emotional or affective response to a shopping experience and is associated with excitement and arousal (Arnold, et al. 2003; Jones 1999). Yet again it is used as a more formal conceptual construct with standard definitions and measures (Ng 2003; Wakefield and Baker 1998). The involvement construct was originally defined and a measure created in 1985 by Zaichkowsky. This definition saw involvement defined as the degree of relevance associated with an object or activity based on the level of interest, need and motivation of the individual. In this sense involvement is a set of attitudes based on individual motivation and interest and it is related to higher arousal, greater cognitive attention and stronger affective responses (Wakefield and Baker 1998; Zaichkowsky 1985).

Moscardo (2008c) has argued that given the importance of engagement and involvement in customer experience, the concept of mindfulness may be important in developing a theoretical framework for experiences. Mindfulness theory was developed by Ellen Langer, a Harvard social psychologist (Langer 1997) and it combines the concept of dual processing which is a core assumption in many cognitive and social psychological theories (Evans and Curtis-Holmes 2005) with long standing theories of curiosity, attention and arousal (Berlyne 1960). In mindfulness theory various environmental and/or situational features interact with individual characteristics to firstly capture a person's attention and secondly to encourage them to be either mindful or mindless. Mindfulness is a state characterised by deeper and more extensive cognitive processing of information, higher levels of arousal, greater attention paid to the immediate situation and environmental context and the creation of new behavioural routines (Carson and Langer 2006). The alternative to mindfulness is mindlessness which is characterised by lower levels of arousal, shallow and limited cognitive processing of the immediate situation and the use of pre-existing routines to guide behaviour (Carson and Langer 2006). Mindfulness has been shown to be associated with greater learning from, and better recall of, situations, better decision making and feelings of involvement, interest and satisfaction (Carson and Langer 2006). Moscardo (2008c) provides a review demonstrating that the factors that encourage mindfulness are the same as those that have been associated with positive tourist and customer experiences. Moscardo (2008c) has also extended mindfulness theory in two significant ways. Firstly, she argues for a two stage process in which the first stage involves capturing attention and stimulating interest and curiosity to invite further participation in an experience, and the second stage then encourages mindfulness and more extensive engagement in the experience. Secondly, Moscardo (2008c) proposes that in the leisure/tourism context it is important that customers feel comfortable, safe and oriented so that the focus of the mindful state is on the experience, not features such as safety and wayfinding.

SUMMARY: BUILDING A MODEL OF THE TOURIST SHOPPING VILLAGE EXPERIENCE

Using mindfulness theory it is possible to develop the summary descriptive framework presented in Figure 3.1 into a conceptual model of the TSV experience for visitors. Figure 3.2 presents such a model. This model combines Hall's (2005) proposal, presented in Chapter 1, that tourist experiences can be seen as having distinct phases, with Moscardo's (2008c) work on the stages of mindfulness and the need to manage tourist settings for comfort and orientation. Importantly the model incorporates the research into purchase behaviour of tourist and leisure shoppers reviewed earlier in this chapter to suggest four key stages in the TSV visitor experience. The first is a pre-visit stage where promotion and advertising, interacting with accessibility and location and visitor characteristics, create awareness and encourage visitation. The second stage is arrival in the TSV where it is important to create a positive mood and establish minimum levels of safety, comfort and orientation and to simulate interest and curiosity to encourage visitors to further explore the setting. The third stage is then during the visit where it is important to maintain and support positive mood and comfort and to encourage mindfulness. The final stage is to encourage shopping and purchase behaviour and it recognises that a positive experience for a visitor may not necessarily involve shopping and even if shopping is involved it may not always involve purchase. But if we place this visitor experience within the larger context of the sustainability of the TSV in terms of benefits for other TSV stakeholders then purchase is important. The model also separates the factors into those that contribute to a positive mood and comfort and those that are related to initiating and encouraging mindfulness. Finally, the model indicates the connections between the characteristics of the visitors and each of the stages of the experience.

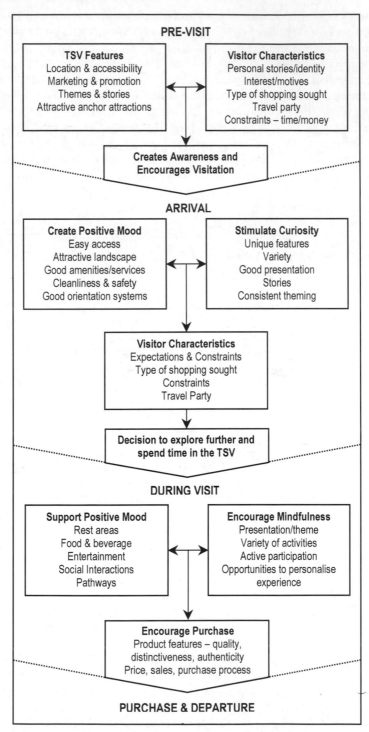

Figure 3.2   A model of the TSV visitor experience.

The model in Figure 3.2 is focussed on the TSV experience for visitors. Figure 3.3 places this component within the larger context of the destination community and other stakeholders, thus combining what has been covered in this chapter on shopping experiences with the previous chapter on the development of TSVs and the perspectives of business owners and residents of these communities. This framework recognises that the type of experience offered to the visitor is partly dependent on the development context, which includes features of the village such as its location and history, development decisions and processes and the actions of entrepreneurs. These features establish the types of opportunities that can be or are offered for the visitor experience and determines the range of tourist types that are likely to visit. The nature of the TSV experience offered for visitors then results in a set of outcomes that include both outcomes for the visitors but also various impacts on the destination place and community.

These two figures highlight five major sets of variables that influence both the nature of the TSV experience and the processes and consequences of TSV development and these will be explored in more detail in the following chapters. The first is the TSV context with a particular emphasis on location, anchor attractions and entrepreneurs. These three features of a TSV directly influence the types of development and tourists attracted and the range of experience opportunities that are offered. These topics are considered in Chapter 4. The second set of variables and factors is the physical setting at the location, which encompasses the streetscapes, landscapes and servicescapes. These elements contribute to the attractiveness of

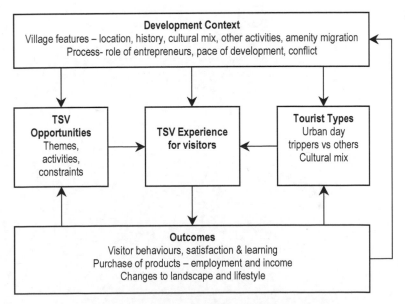

Figure 3.3 Framework for understanding TSV development and impacts.

the destination, the effectiveness of any theme associated with the village and to encouraging curiosity and mindfulness. This kind of background material is considered in Chapter 5. A third set of forces is concerned with how the village is presented to visitors through theming and includes the stories that are associated with a village. Chapter 6 considers this material. The fourth concern is focused on the nature of the activities offered within the TSV experience and the nature and design of such experiences are considered in Chapter 7. The fifth and final set of considerations is the services and amenities that support visitor comfort and influence their behaviour. This material is reviewed in Chapter 8. Each chapter in this volume now pursues one of these sets of key themes.

4 The Importance of Location, Anchor Attractions and Entrepreneurs

INTRODUCTION

This chapter begins the process of providing detailed analyses of the defining features of TSVs and the TSV shopping experience. It considers some of the key organising features, specifically location, types of attractions and the role of entrepreneurs, all of which shape the character of tourist shopping villages. Figure 4.1 locates these features within the TSV Visitor Experience Model. Each factor will be considered in turn but the interaction and integration of these organising forces will also be noted throughout the chapter. As Diamond (2006) has pointed out, many studies of social activities and human settlements proceed on the basis of social scientists benefitting from the natural variability of settings and cases. The use of a large number of villages, which have been studied in some detail in this book, represents exactly this approach of being able to compare and analyse the existing variability of cases. Sometimes however it is valuable to go beyond the typical cases and benefit from the lessons of an outlying or very different example. Such a special case of a recently constructed village will be considered in the final stages of the chapter as it provides some further applications of many of the points raised in the key sections.

LOCATION

The concerns of this section follow the first of the orienting issues to tourist shopping reported by Ng (2003) and included in Chapter 3 in Figures 3.1 and 3.2. There are two important senses to the term location for tourist shopping villages. The first meaning of importance is the position of the village in relation to major source markets. This consideration includes matters of access and transport routes. A second meaning can also be distinguished. This interpretation refers to the setting and site of the village, particularly the scenic value conferred by the perception of locational features such as hillside and mountain elevations, river frontages, seaside or lakeside views or other impressive landscapes

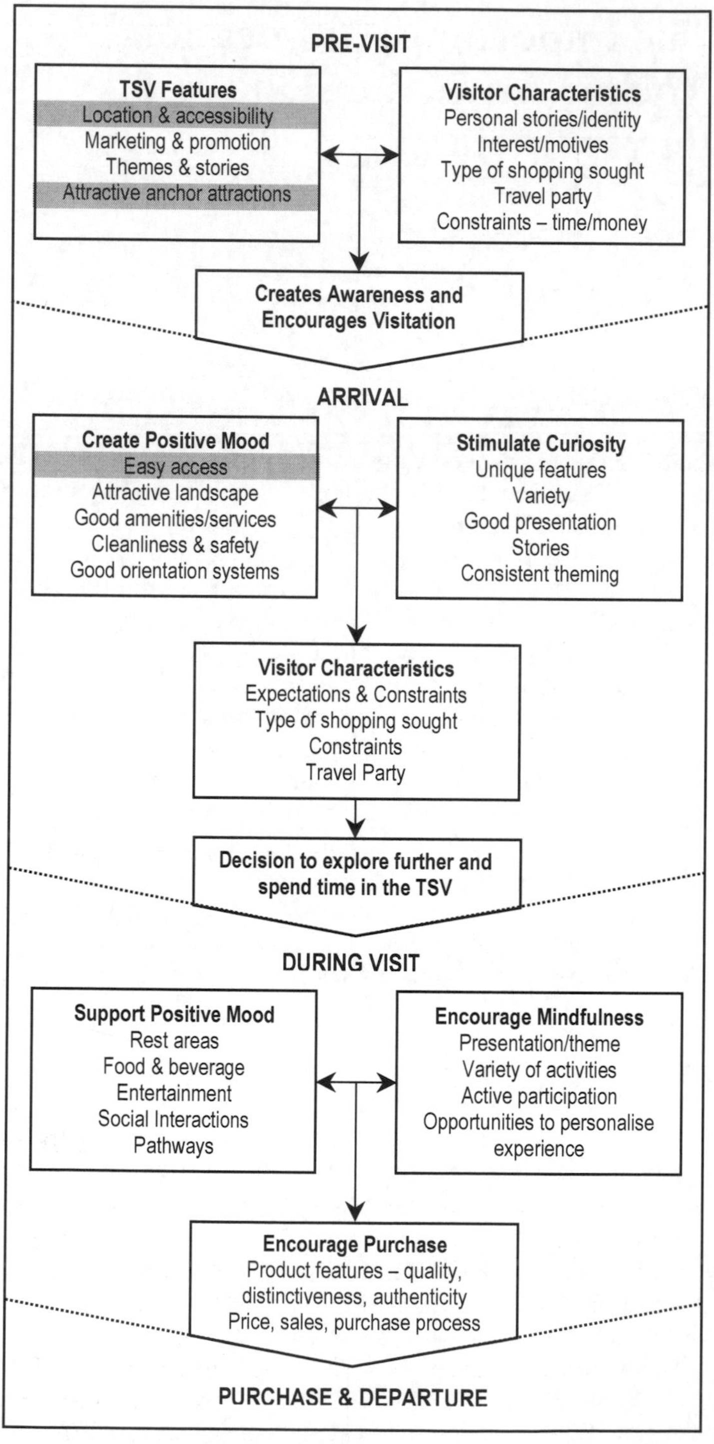

PRE-VISIT

TSV Features
Location & accessibility
Marketing & promotion
Themes & stories
Attractive anchor attractions

Visitor Characteristics
Personal stories/identity
Interest/motives
Type of shopping sought
Travel party
Constraints – time/money

Creates Awareness and Encourages Visitation

ARRIVAL

Create Positive Mood
Easy access
Attractive landscape
Good amenities/services
Cleanliness & safety
Good orientation systems

Stimulate Curiosity
Unique features
Variety
Good presentation
Stories
Consistent theming

Visitor Characteristics
Expectations & Constraints
Type of shopping sought
Constraints
Travel Party

Decision to explore further and spend time in the TSV

DURING VISIT

Support Positive Mood
Rest areas
Food & beverage
Entertainment
Social Interactions
Pathways

Encourage Mindfulness
Presentation/theme
Variety of activities
Active participation
Opportunities to personalise experience

Encourage Purchase
Product features – quality, distinctiveness, authenticity
Price, sales, purchase process

PURCHASE & DEPARTURE

Figure 4.1 A model of the TSV visitor experience.

surrounding the village. It is this latter sense of location which helps form the perception of the rural idyll which is integral to the creative destruction model reported in Chapter 2.

MARKET ACCESS AND TRANSPORT PATTERNS

A prime determinant of tourist shopping village location is its accessibility to a large base market. This base market may be a major city such as Melbourne for Daylesford, Sydney for Leura, Christchurch for Akaroa and Dallas-Fort Worth for Salado. Proximity to major cities may not be entirely necessary for the village to function as a shopping destination if there is a substantial mobile tourism market based in a regional tourism city or travelling through a region. For example, the regional tourism destinations of Queenstown, New Zealand and Cairns, Australia have adjacent shopping villages in Arrowtown and Kuranda respectively. A few villages appear able to survive because of their presence on a touring route. Hokitika in New Zealand and Sneem in Ireland are both examples of being on such routes as well as being conveniently spaced to suit the driving times and patterns of visitors touring the countryside.

The nature of these patterns may be considered in more detail through linking to foundation studies on touring and transport by Lue, Crompton and Fesenmaier (1993), Parolin (2001) and Lumsdon and Page (2004). Additional studies confirming or re-interpreting these basic patterns include work by Tideswell and Faulkner (1999), McKercher (2001), Lew and McKercher (2006) and McKercher and Lau (2008). The contribution to understanding tourist village location here lies in sorting through the travel patterns and spatial arrangements which can comprise a day trip or touring route. Lue et al. (1993) propose five patterns for pleasure vacation trips. Parolin (2001) proposes three patterns for day trip touring in Australia based on his study of a region south of Sydney. These two foundation patterns and an adaptation of these ideas for tourist shopping village touring are presented in Figure 4.2.

The material presented in Figure 4.2 highlights some special features of the trip patterns associated with tourist shopping villages. The bypass single destination pattern is allied to both the single destination pattern identified by Lue et al. (1993) and the linear model noted by Parolin (2001) but adds in the feature that many villages are within easy reach of main interstate or motorways or highways. There is an advantage to the village if it is on a side road adjacent to a highway in terms of easy access and there is the further point that other traffic flows through the village are scaled down.

The en route pattern of Lue et al. and the non linear pattern of Parolin have affinities with the through-route pattern. All stress that touring can be broken into segments or multiple parts of a journey with the through-route notion emphasising that tourists visiting shopping villages, unlike local

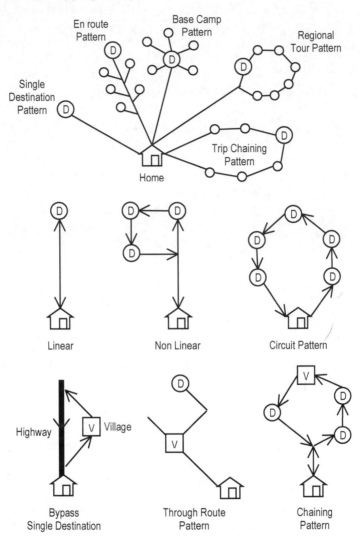

Figure 4.2   Spatial patterns for touring trips and visiting shopping villages.

residents, may not be returning to a home base. In this instance the location of the village may gain a strategic advantage if it is reached by travellers around morning tea, lunch time or afternoon tea time. This may apply to coach tours as well as independent travellers since the opportunity for coach passengers to use the eating and rest room facilities of intermediary towns in a day's itinerary can add a set and predictable volume of visitors to the town's businesses. Sneem, at the bottom end of the Ring of Kerry (Ireland), is a prime example.

McKercher's (2001) work, which identifies differences between through travellers and main destination visitors in Albury, New South Wales, provides some parallels to the present distinction. McKercher noted that through travellers were often overlooked in terms of their importance to tourism. The distinctions McKercher made were for visitors who had at least stayed overnight in the location of interest, whereas the present use of the term through travellers addresses those who are spending shorter parts of a day in a village. The third shopping village pattern presented in Figure 4.2, the chaining pattern, is analogous to both the regional tour pattern and trip chaining pattern of Lue et al. and the circuitous pattern of Parolin. The essence of this kind of touring lies in travellers maximising the diversity of their day's route and while there may be some overlap between the initial and the final stages of the journey there is an effort to not repeat the journey.

It is useful to connect these trip patterns to the interpretations of the role of transport in the tourist experience (Lumsdon and Page 2004; Moscardo and Pearce 2004). In the views of these authors the transport involved in accessing tourist experiences can vary from an experience that has to be endured to one that is thoroughly enjoyed and is indeed a part of the attraction. Lumsdon and Page (2004) cite scenic car trails as high on their continuum of transport types which are intrinsic to the tourist experience while Moscardo and Pearce (2004) suggest that self-drive touring and the time in the car can, in a positive way, dominate the day's activities. In this context a village will be poorly located if it requires that the visitors endure rather than enjoy the drive. Plentiful traffic and crowded roads or indeed dangerous, winding and poor roads are likely to make the drive unappealing and limit the prospects to create or grow a shopping village. Differences in travellers' responses to the prospects of driving to a village appear to be quite marked and present a considerable measurement challenge for that body of transport work which tries to model trip behaviour using basic demographic and distance-time-cost variables (cf. Taplin and McGinley 2000). It would seem to be important in future studies which attempt to predict the acceptable distance and travel times which might apply to the development of shopping villages to pay close attention to the dominant attitudes of potential visitors to the driving routes as well as to the appeal of the village.

There are other concepts and findings which arise in the context of studying driving routes. Thomas (1998) constructed visitors' personal town maps by integrating information collected from sketch maps and survey questions. The approach taken to building all of the information collected was to conceive of the tourists' memory and image for the towns as consisting of layers. In this account of the drive travellers' experience of places, the physical factors accessed by the town maps form a fundamental layer. It was further suggested by Thomas that these physical factors typically include the main street, the town centre, the town park, the body of the town and the town surrounds. Using these divisions as the basis for summarising the questions put to the drive tourists in a structured survey, Thomas was able to add layers of town imagery to the basic physical descriptions and layout. The additional material directs attention to the feel of the town (or parts of the town) and to the needs for improvement from the driving tourists' perspective. In summary, this approach depicts a layered view of the cognitive map of towns with the physical core obtained in the town maps overlaid by a commentary on the emotive properties of parts of the town. The final output of Thomas' efforts are a little like describing villages with a hand drawn map across which are scribbled items of social advice for personal recollection or directives to others. Further developments of how tourist shopping village visitors mentally map the villages and their characteristics offers a promising additional line of work within this study of locational effects.

It would be a mistake to assume that tourist shopping villages are always the province of self-drive travellers. In Europe and the United Kingdom in particular, the access to villages through coach travel is important. If a village is included on standard tourism coach packages, particularly from large urban centres, then its presence as an economically sustainable year round tourist shopping village is more assured. Two outstanding examples of the powerful presence of the coach tourism market among the villages studied are Adare in Ireland and Volendam in the Netherlands. Indeed the popularity and reputation of these shopping villages is so powerful that in explaining this volume and research program to interested parties in Europe, citing the examples of Volendam and Adare was often very effective in communicating the kinds of locations being considered.

The notable feature of Volendam is its standard role in being included in all half day and full day tours from Amsterdam. It lies within a convenient one hour travel time from both the centre of Amsterdam and Schipol airport and its flourishing as a tourist shopping village is in part due to the combination of easy access and its extensive presentation of diverse and traditional Dutch themes and stereotyped products. The centrality of the coach market to Adare is equally impressive and is visibly manifested in the arrangements which the local council have constructed in terms of a very large but discrete parking area, ample restaurant space, plenty of toilet facilities and a service centre for the coaches. Undoubtedly there are many other Irish villages which feature the same charms of thatched houses, attractive gardens and craft shops but Adare's success is its provision for the coach market as well as its centrality to those visitors arriving at the increasingly well-used Shannon airport and staying in the accompanying tourist centres in central and western Ireland.

VILLAGE SITES

Convenience site

The convenience and scenic value of the routes to the village represent basic features of the villages' locational status. The site of the village itself is another important influence on visitors' appraisals. Many villages actively promote their immediate environment and site. In the language of much tourism research, village promoters are socially constructing a meaning for their place and inviting a tourist gaze which is focussed on specified attributes (cf. Urry 1995). Often the well-promoted attributes are physical, such as attractively vegetated valleys (e.g. Arrowtown in New Zealand), rivers and river banks (e.g. Bourton-on-the-Water in the UK), impressive gorges (e.g. Cheddar in the UK and Elora in Canada), rolling hills (e.g. Hahndorf and Yarra Glen in Australia) and mountains (e.g. Mount Tamborine in Australia and Stowe in the US). A few villages have a seaside location; Kinsale and Dingle in Ireland, Akaroa and Hokitika in New Zealand and Volendam in the Netherlands and others are lakeside, such as Niagara-on-the-Lake and Bayfield in Canada. Many have emerged from their original role in serving farming communities. Case Study 4.1 describes the village of Montville and fits this pattern.

As the cultural geographers have noted for many years the appreciation of these rural landscapes is learned and has much to do with our needs to understand how the world we view has been produced. Lowenthal (1975) observed: "As we erode and alter the inherited past, we more and more contrive our own. Creatures of historical processes beyond our control, we shape landscapes and artifacts to conform with illusory histories, public and private that gratify our tastes" (1975: 36)

Understanding the origins of our reactions does not alter the emotional appeal of many landscapes for the visitor and de Botton (2002) suggests that the dominant aesthetic traditions of the nineteenth century—an appreciation of the wild and grand landscapes known as the sublime and the more ordered landscapes referred to as the picturesque still penetrate the viewing consciousness of most western travellers. In particular the appreciation of the picturesque, which is essentially the enjoyment of a balanced, ordered and well-organised aesthetic, is applicable to the scale and indeed the enjoyment of many village locations (cf. Urry 1990). The following examples illustrate the promotion of the sites in either sublime or picturesque terms. Cheddar in England is described as nestled within the most magnificent gorge, Akaroa in New Zealand is a jewel set in a stunning harbour, Sedona benefits from its presence set amidst barren and craggy hills (see Case Study 4.2), Kuranda in northern Australia is presented as a unique tropical village in a magnificent (World Heritage) rainforest and Adare in Ireland is portrayed as the prototypical neat and picturesque small Irish community. The images shown in Figure 4.4 and the village sites often have such appeal that they are standard inclusion on calendars.

Case Study 4.1   Montville, Queensland, Australia

Montville is a linear shaped tourist shopping village on the coastal rim of the Blackall ranges in southern Queensland. The village sits along the edge of the escarpment and offers views overlooking the nearby settlements of the Sunshine coast. Montville is 1.5 hours driving time from the centre of the city of Brisbane (population 2.1 million) and 30 minutes from the beachside settlements and resort environments of the Sunshine coast. It has a small resident population (less than 900) but the main road along the mountain range connects Montville to other small communities, notably between Maleny and Mapleton, which also serve as accommodation bases for local citizens and visitors alike.

Figure 4.3   Montville contains a mix of architectural styles.

The area was first settled in 1887 and became a key centre for dairying and timber production. In more recent times the decline of both these former industries in the area has seen a greater focus on small alternative farming enterprises and tourism. Montville has a distinctive central area in the style

(continued)

Case Study 4.1   (continued)

of a village green and the streetscape consists of largely wooden buildings with a subtropical architectural style painted in traditional nineteenth century colours. Originally developed as an arts and crafts centre with key shops specialising in clocks, antiques and art, the recent developments in the village strip have been diverse and include clothing stores, home wares and a variety of restaurants. In addition to the day trip visitor market there are a number of specialist accommodation properties including bed and breakfast operations and rainforest cottages in and near the village.

The contemporary appeal of the village lies partly in its many shopping opportunities and its setting in a lush vegetated environment. Large trees are a feature of the village green and form a backdrop to the village. The civic efforts to provide facilities for visitors have been extensive and streetscaping is well-developed and harmonious throughout the shopping strip.

Case Study Sources:

Reader's Digest (1993) *Illustrated Guide to Australian Places*. Surry Hills, NSW: Reader's Digest.
http://www.brbta.com/history_montville.php The Blackall range The Calm behind the Coast. (accessed May 2010).
http://www.montvilleguide.com.au/ Montville Town Guide (accessed May 2010).
http://www.queenslandholidays.com.au/destinations/sunshine-coast/places-to-visit/montville/index.cfm Sunshine Coast (accessed May 2010).
http://www.oesr.qld.gov.au/queensland-by-theme/demography/population/tables/erp/erp-components-change-no/index.shtml Population of Queensland regions (accessed May 2010).

ATTRACTIONS

Another level of analysis of the features of a village lies with a consideration of the attractions within the village. The special emphasis on attractions in this section of our appraisal of tourist shopping villages has links with several other topics. The attractions of a village as discussed here are separate from the themes of the village and the activities available in the village. The promotion of the village may integrate the main attraction into its village labelling such as when Hokitika in New Zealand is presented as the jade capital of New Zealand. The largest and dominant stores and production buildings are the key attractions while the activities available for visitors may include watching gemstone and jewellery making as well as strolling between stores comparing products and possibly purchasing some of the items.

Framke (2002) outlines some related multifaceted perspectives on the meaning of the term attractions. In essence he considers the range or the drawing power of the attraction. He notes the long history of tourism scholars using the words attractions and destinations, with most business-oriented researchers seeing attractions as embedded in the larger term destinations. He also observes that there is a social-cultural approach to the study of attractions (Leiper 2000; MacCannell 1976; Urry 1990). This

Figure 4.4   Sedona, Arizona (top) and Cheddar, England provide examples of TSVs in spectacular landscape settings.

approach offers the insight that while marketing personnel and tourism professionals conceive of the world as comprised of sets of well-defined destinations, visitors in their multi-location visiting trips may be combining attraction elements from several regions. Adopting this approach, a visitor

Case Study 4.2   Sedona, Arizona, U.S.

Sedona is located in the Upper Senoran desert in Arizona. It is this location amongst a series of red sandstone formations that is the basis of one its common descriptions 'red rock country'. It is within easy driving distance from Flagstaff (29 miles/47 kilometres) and just over two hours drive from Phoenix (116 miles/187 kilometres). It has a resident population of just over 11,000 and is described in its community plan as a gateway community offering access to the surrounding protected natural areas.

Figure 4.5   Images of Sedona.

Case Study 4.2   (continued)

The first white settlers arrived in the 1870s, forcibly displacing the Native American tribes who lived in the region. The settlement remained rural and undeveloped until the 1950s when a combination of retirement resort development and growth in second homes and tourism resulted in rapid change. Sedona's location was a prime factor in this development through its scenery, warm, dry climate, lower land prices and perceived positive quality of life. Sedona was also a drawcard for film makers being a location often used for western films, further adding to its tourist appeal. Finally, the location was also a source of another Sedona characteristic - its appeal to new age spiritualists who believe that the red rock formations in the region contain a number of energy "vortexes" that are sacred. Today tourism is a major activity in the town with multiple resorts, spas, and a large number and variety of shops.

Case Study Sources:

http://en.wikipedia.org/wiki/Sedona_Arizona (accessed May 2010).
http://www.visitsedona.com/ (accessed May 2010).
Allen, F. (1999). The new old west. American Heritage, September, p. 30.City of Sedona (2010) Community Plan Update. http://www.sedonaaz.gov/Sedonacms/index.aspx?page=613 (accessed May 2010)
Gober, P., McHugh, K.E. and Leclerc, D. (1993). Job-rich but housing-poor: the dilemma of a western amenity town. *Professional Geographer*, 45(1), 12–20.
Ivakhiv, A. (1997). Red rocks, "vortexes" and the selling of Sedona. *Social Compass*, 44, 367–384.

interested in antiques may visit antique shops in a set of villages and small towns rather than one key antique shop in one shopping village destination (Michael 2002). In summary, an attraction may function as source of interest within but also beyond the village destination in which it is embedded.

A related set of points about attractions stems from work on the hierarchy of attractions and patterns of visiting attractions within that hierarchy (Cooper, et al. 1993). In this model attractions are seen as not only having varying degrees of drawing power, but the most important attraction is the first to be visited. In this model visitors then allocate the remainder of their time to the remaining attractions according to their decreasing or diminishing degrees of importance. This is consistent with the advice of Baedekar, the prominent and formative German tourist guide book writer, whose definitive statements of what to see and in what order influenced much nineteenth century travel (Holloway 2002). While some early evidence for this approach was provided in studies of visitors to the Channel Islands, other studies indicate a more chaotic pattern of visiting for many markets and travellers (McKercher 2004; Mings and McHugh 1995; West 2005). For tourist shopping villages the applicability of a hierarchy of attraction visits according to the prominence of the attraction needs further investigation. McKercher and Lau (2008), working at the level of the special administrative region of Hong Kong, identified 78 discrete movement patterns in their study of visitor itineraries. These could be reduced to 11 movement styles. While these patterns include all of the tourists' travel (e.g. to restaurants, for local shopping and to natural areas as well as attractions) there is no evidence presented in the study, at least at this scale, which would imply a hierarchy of attraction importance approach. This study reinforces findings from earlier work where McKercher (2004: 19) concluded that: "tourist movements are highly individualistic. Each visitor picks and chooses from the many activities [sic attractions] available to create a personalized itinerary that suits their interests".

Another line of work using the cognitive mapping methodology also identified a good deal of individual variation in the mapping of towns and communities (Pearce and Thomas 2010). This cognitive mapping approach was founded by Lynch (1960) whose work provided a method, a coding scheme and a purpose for the use of sketch maps in studies of residents' and visitors' views of their towns (Banerjee and Southworth 1990). The method used is to ask people to draw a freehand sketch of an area—it could be a neighbourhood or a village or a whole city. A coding scheme to score the maps was also devised—essentially a five part system, specifically: landmarks, districts nodes, edges and pathways. The purpose of using sketch maps which Lynch promoted was to use the sketching process to access the visual images people have of places, effectively tapping into another kind of language they use to store their experiences. Lynch termed the most commonly recognised or anchor attractions the nodes of the city or town. Despite the individual variability in the maps already noted it is possible to aggregate the individual responses of visitors and provide summary or aggregate maps of visitor recall of towns. The resulting data indicated that for many locations there are key anchor attractions which nearly all people recall and use to centre their image of the place (Young 1999). These considerations suggest that some of the villages in the study are likely to also have anchor attractions which can be better defined here as the very visible and well-publicised main reference points of the village. Anchor attractions should arguably appear on all village maps and be a dominant part of the listings of places to go and things to see even if the order in which visitors go to the attractions remains unknown.

There is though some debate in the tourist attraction literature about the use of metaphors and the way in which these terms constrain and shape analytical thinking. The term attraction for example, while very commonly used, has been seen as naively representing a form of environmental determinism, even magnetism, and neglects context and the highly social and active process of visitors' making sense of the places they visit (Framke 2002; Leiper 2000; Pearce, Benckendorff and Johnstone 2001). Adding the noun anchor to this term attraction might be thought of as confounding the problem. Importantly, the term anchor is meant to apply to the tourist and the experience of the visitor as well as to indicate a stable foundation point or building block (or blocks) around which the village entrepreneurs can add ancillary shops, facilities and services.

A survey of the tourist shopping villages studied in detail in this research program indicates that single dominant anchors are not very common. There are some. Blarney Castle and the lure of kissing the Blarney Stone to acquire the legendary talkativeness of the Irish is undoubtedly the anchor around which the village of Blarney has been able to construct its shopping. Until its movement closer to Cairns, the Tjapukai dance theatre, a performance of international acclaim staged by local indigenous dancers, was certainly the key anchor for the village of Kuranda. In Stratford, Ontario (see Case Study 7.1), the major theatre staging Shakespearean plays is a key anchor for that setting. The Blue Bell ice cream factory is the prime reason why the Texan village of Brenham attracts visitors. More commonly it appears that the tourist shopping villages have several smaller anchors rather than a single dominant node. These smaller anchors may be prominent hotels, art galleries, antique stores and the larger themed merchandising stores such as quilting shops, jewellery stores or local produce outlets. There is a marked advantage in having several anchors rather than the one. If the existing dominant anchor moves then the village may struggle to re-establish a public identity without its key component. An interesting analogy may be drawn here with the small towns which base their tourism appeal on iconic figures, the heroes and heroines of public life. As these figures age or their popularity declines the appeal of the town as a destination may have to struggle to reinvent itself as more than the home of a once famous politician, writer, artist, musician or sportsman (Pearce, Morrison and Moscardo 2003; Tang, et al. 2009).

As a final consideration in the analysis of attractions in tourist shopping villages the concept of emergent authenticity can be usefully applied. As previewed in Chapter 3, in the long history of the application of the authenticity concept to tourism settings it has become apparent that subjective authenticity, that is the values the visitor brings to the setting, dominates the assessment of the setting (Cohen 2002; Wang 1999). While visitors may inspect the properties of the setting to determine their view of its authenticity the variability in their cultural capital, effectively their knowledge and background, influences how they determine the staged or authentic qualities of what they are viewing and experiencing. An important contribution to this discussion in the academic literature is that the appraisal of authenticity is a dynamic and changing process and some attractions and setting features, while initially copies or facades of others, may in time acquire their own perceived authenticity. This process has been termed emergent authenticity and there are attractions and even services in tourist shopping villages which are candidates for such perceptions. As an example the main hotel in Hahndorf (see Case Study 6.1), a settlement with a history of German influence, is arguably not very much like a German hotel but in the Australian context its long established tradition of serving German food and its internal décor and atmosphere mark it out as likely to be perceived as authentic. It is, of course, a case of emergent authenticity.

The discussion of authenticity which has developed in tourism studies has arguably become highly specialised. Undoubtedly many business personnel in TSVs, as well as community members and visitors continue to use the term authentic as an evaluative label which they firmly believe has an objective basis in the qualities of their village and its shops and products. While careful scrutiny of the basis for their assertions and judgements does reveal the kinds of logical flaws exposed by the work of Wang, Cohen and others, it is also apparent that popular use of the term 'inauthentic' is almost synonymous with the pejorative term 'touristy'. The meaning of this label parallels the concept of "touristification" as outlined by Jansen-Verbeke (1998) and discussed in Chapter 2. Both academics and TSV stakeholders using the term inauthentic in this fairly broad ranging fashion are implying that there is a highly commercial orientation to the village and its shopping experiences and the interests of local residents are subordinate to the presentation and sales of goods to its visitors. The judgements using the label authentic or the lack of authenticity in this same way were also present in the responses of the Australian residents reported in the authors' second study in Chapter 2.

ENTREPRENEURS

Tourist shopping villages, with a few exceptions, are the territory of small or even micro-businesses. The modest scale of tourism investment in tourist shopping villages, at least when compared to the financial scale of airlines, theme parks and mega resorts, makes the popular image of an entrepreneur in tourism—a Sir Richard Branson or a Conrad Hilton—inappropriate. Instead, the scale of the operations usually means that the kind of entrepreneurs active in tourist shopping villages are more likely to be prominent leaders who act as their own managers rather than being charismatic characters engaged in taking calculated risks with large amounts of capital and employing executives to run the company (Murphy and Murphy 2004). It also means that villages tend to be the products of multiple individual efforts to gain access to the shopping markets rather than the vision of one person or one corporation. Cooperative and competitive entrepreneurial tensions tend to exist side by side, often literally. There can be, for example, positive synergies between attractions and eating establishments but two similar shops may struggle to survive and compete for customers to the detriment of both. Further, beyond each shop door there are issues of maintaining the appearance of the street and public areas and the roles of commercial and government enterprises in undertaking this maintenance and development is often a contested and much debated issue requiring both leadership and cooperation.

It is useful here to distinguish leaders from entrepreneurs. While there are many definitions of leadership in the business literature, several approaches to the topic share an emphasis that leaders harness people's energy towards common goals (cf. Clegg, Hardy and Nord 1997; Van der Wagen and Davies 1998). There have been fashions and periods of change in the style of leadership thought to be effective. Some original conceptualisations emphasised a command and control approach, others delegation, yet others social influence. More recently approaches built on creating a shared vision or adopting a coaching role have been prominent (Blackman 2008). Examples of people playing a leadership role in the development of shopping villages include Tom Patterson, who pioneered the Stratford Festival Theatres, and Brian Doherty, who developed the George Bernard Shaw Festival Theatre (see Case Studies 7.1 and 7.3).

Murphy and Murphy (2004) review the case of one Australian entrepreneur and leader whose achievements are relevant to the scale of a tourist shopping village. Arguably, the small town in the study is very similar to many of the Australian villages studied by the researchers and described in Chapter 1. The case in question is the town of Beechworth in North East Victoria which has a community of 3,000 people and a predominantly rural service function. The bakery in Beechworth was purchased by a baker Tom O'Toole, and through creative marketing, teamwork and an emphasis on the attitude of staff he has created a substantial regional business worth several million dollars annually. In a lively book about his experiences as a small town leader and entrepreneur he reports that a secret to his success, beyond the great enthusiasm for his staff and plain hard work, was the blending of the bakery into the community through sponsorships and community support. In particular the effort to attract people to the town and create a shared vision of what Beechworth could be became a cornerstone of his marketing and ultimately expanded his operation to include outlets in other Victorian villages (O'Toole and Tarling 2000).

While the Beechworth story is an example of an active, even dominant entrepreneur in a small town, a review of the histories of shopping village development collected through the websites and ephemeral literature reveals that the trajectories of development and the creation of the towns is usually much less spectacular and could be described as slow organic growth. This kind of description can be linked to the stage or step models of growth. The most dominant of these in tourism stem from the work of Butler (1980) and the many treatments of his Tourism Area Life Cycle model (Butler 2006a; 2006b). While previous consideration about the development of tourist shopping villages has been undertaken in Chapter 2 and future prospects are considered in both Chapters 9 and 10, it can be noted here that entrepreneurs external to a location are often conceived as pivotal to the rapid expansion and development of tourism in that setting. As Johnston (2001) and Haywood (2006) have pointed out in just two of the many studies tinkering with or re-interpreting the Butler model, there may be other ways of thinking about development other than a life cycle curve. It may be that the constraints of a tourist shopping village are such that villages show an oscillation around a mean size rather than being an expanding entity which ultimately collapses and then needs re-invigorating. Further discussion of these issues will also take place in Chapter 9 dealing with challenges and problems of tourist shopping village management. For the purposes of the present remarks about entrepreneurs it can be noted that in some circumstances, and here Hokitika is a good example, government investment in regional development may be a parallel to entrepreneurial activity and provides the boost the village needs to be a credible destination.

An additional perspective on the kinds of entrepreneurs operating in the tourist shopping villages comes from studies of what have been termed lifestyle businesses (Andrews, Baum and Andrew 2001; Morrison 2006). The concentration of this work has tended to be on small accommodation owners in rural areas but many of the issues raised arguably apply quite well to small retail businesses in the shopping village context. At the very least these parallel studies provide a source of analogous cases for researchers to build hypotheses and better explore the supply side of TSVs. A number of studies of these lifestyle businesses have suggested that their operators are very concerned about containing the growth of their operation so that the owners would not have to get trapped into bureaucratic approval processes and the management of diverse employees (Di Domenico 2005; Stone and Stubbs 2007; Wilson 2007). These findings were particularly applicable to those business owners who had joined the same kinds of rural communities as being investigated in the TSV research.

Popcorn and Hanft (2001) among others have identified shifts in public values in western countries which account for the rise of the rural lifestyle entrepreneurs. In particular the processes of 'cashing out' and 'downsizing', which refer to transferring assets usually from one kind of urban situation to a more rural location with a less stressful employment role, appear to be common in a number of countries. The descriptions 'sea changers' and 'tree changers' are applied to these relocating residents who are also termed amenity migrants (Murphy 2002). Typically this involves guest house, bed and breakfast accommodation or some forms of farm tourism and natural resource use. Undoubtedly some of the retailers in TSVs share this background. For other retailers who have always lived in the region of the TSV the appeal of staying in their own communities with modest income levels may be a preferred lifestyle option compared to making more money but being forced to work in less congenial contexts (Ateljevic and Doorne 2000; Getz and Petersen 2005).

There are visible outcomes of these lifestyle entrepreneurial motivations in some of the TSVs. The opening times of some shops are often limited, even unpredictable, which may reflect the owner's interest in times which suit them rather than all of the public. In the United Kingdom in particular there has been a long tradition of half day closing. In some rural areas it is still possible to arrive in a tourist shopping village and, with the combination of local holidays, half day closing and idiosyncratic decisions by the retailers, to find few shopping options available. For the northern hemisphere shopping villages in particular, seasonality effects can compound the relaxed opening times. Baum and Lundtrop (2001) note the harsh effects of seasonality in locations such as Scotland, Norway, Finland, Sweden and Canada. Natural seasonality in the form of very cold weather as well as snow and rain can be driving forces affecting retailing and many small tourism businesses. In January and February in particular the effects can be pronounced in terms of customers' accessibility to the more remote locations, a lowered enthusiasm for travel generally and the availability of staff. By way of contrast in Australia and at some locations in the United States such as Arizona and Texas, extremely hot weather may produce its own seasonality effects in terms of an unwillingness to travel and walk along village streets. The way in which individual businesses and entrepreneurial activity respond to these seasonality pressures will determine if the villages effectively shrink in certain seasons or remain fully functioning attraction centres for the whole year.

Ateljevic and Doorne (2000) provide a model which features four quadrants describing the way lifestyle businesses deal with the world (see Figure 4.6). Its applicability to the retailers of tourist shopping villages has not been directly assessed but it holds potential to explain the individual entrepreneurial choices such retailers face. In each of the four quadrants of the model there is a tension between holding to the values which promote a lifestyle orientation to business and being drawn away from those values towards more commercial and larger business concerns. The first quadrant is concerned with the way businesses deal with their customers. A distinction exists here between cultivating a rather homely and richly interpersonal style versus transactions which are characterised by a simple commercial relationship. A second source of differentiation between lifestyle businesses and more commercial concerns is the machinery of the business organisation. Here there can be simple administrative arrangements, sometimes restricted to one to two family members which can be contrasted with complex governance arrangements and obligations characterising the more formally structured, larger operations. The ways in which the businesses are integrated into the local community is another quadrant Ateljevic and Doorne use to differentiate the operations. The contrast here can vary from significant involvement in community activities and decision making to relative independence. The final sector shaping the nature of the operation is the style of the management arrangements varying from an individualistic approach embracing cooperation and the generation of ideas and change through a bottom up approach to a top down decision making system. It can be suggested that some of the value orientations implicit in these business arrangements and orientations within TSVs underlie many of the development conflicts and contrasts discussed in Chapter 3. The further development of business-based research using these dimensions could add to the literature on both TSV and lifestyle entrepreneurs (see Chapter 9).

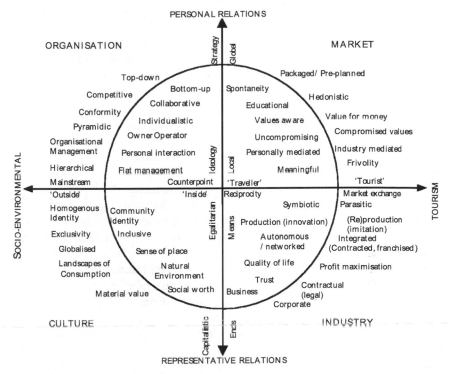

Figure 4.6 Perceived value positions (Source: Ajetlevic, I. and Doorne, S. (2001) "'Staying within the fence': Lifestyle Entrepreneurship in Tourism." *Journal of Sustainable Tourism*, 8:5, p. 387.)

AN EXAMPLE INTEGRATING THE THEMES OF THE CHAPTER

The integration of the effects of location, anchor attractions and entrepreneurs is well-illustrated by a case outside of the frame of the closely analysed villages. The village is Ngong Ping on Lantau Island, Hong Kong. This village has several quite distinctive, even remarkable, features. As a first and obvious point it is in Asia, thus distinguishing it geographically from most villages discussed (although Wall and Mitchell have studied a number of villages in China). The second feature of Ngong Ping is that it is virtually a brand new village, entirely designed and created by the visions of entrepreneurs exploiting their knowledge of the location and anchor attractions. The story of Ngong Ping needs some explanation. The village was built in 2005. It is a tourist shopping village in the specialist sense that it is constructed entirely to serve tourists. No local community lives in the village, although there are modest residences for local people with a much longer tradition of settlement just a kilometre away. The stimulus to build the village arose to connect and profit from the terminus of the new Ngong Ping Cable Car and the traditional anchor attraction in this part of Lantau Island, the 60 year old Giant

Buddha (Tian Tian) statue. This cableway was originally built and managed by the same company responsible for the Skyrail Cableway to the Australian village of Kuranda. The cable car is a 5.7 kilometre two track gondola and commences adjacent to Tung Chung station, an important connection point in the rail and transport system of Hong Kong. The cable car provides a new transport system to the giant Buddha statue which previously could only be reached by a lengthy (over one hour) and tortuous bus journey. The distance between the cable car and the giant Buddha statue is approximately one kilometre which is not a daunting walk but was certainly discouraging to some. The entrepreneurial challenge was how to provide a more attractive product to Hong Kong residents and other visitors.

The entrepreneurial solution was to add a tourist retail shopping precinct designed along a linear path. Importantly, this shopping strip was supported by a set of additional attractions. It is noteworthy that in the newly constructed village these attractions are connected to the cultural and spiritual traditions of the area. These additional attractions include the Walking with Buddha interpretive display (an easily digested rendition of the life of Buddha), the monkey's tale theatre (a cartoon-based film providing children's entertainment with a minor moral message) and the Ngong Ping tea house (an elegant presentation of the art of tea drinking). Interested readers are referred to http://www.np360.com.hk/html/eng/np360_exp/village-index. html. The challenges and potential contradictions involved in providing a spiritually-based entertainment theme in an overtly commercial setting have been noted in studies of this type of entertainment (Bryman 2004; Pearce 2008). In particular, while the attractions de-emphasise material acquisitiveness, the adjacent souvenir shops, restaurants and mixed retail offerings actively promote consumption. In the village strip there are set pieces of street performance including kung fu demonstrations, jugglers and acrobats. Since the cable car is the main point of access at the eastern end of the village and the bus terminal accesses only the back of the north western part of the village, the one and only main street is entirely free of cars and vehicles.

These arrangements and facilities at Ngong Ping provide a virtual test of academic issues in tourist shopping village organisation. While a notable concern of the arguments about tourist shopping villages revolves around the creative destruction model, Ngong Ping is the exemplar of commercial creative construction.

In summary the themes illustrated by this special instance of a constructed shopping village broadly validate the attention being paid in this chapter to location, anchors and entrepreneurial leadership. The future success of Ngong Ping lies in maintaining some of the spiritual and peaceful feel of the mountain top location, a set of qualities quite precious and hard to find in the crowded environment of Hong Kong. While Ngong Ping is dependent for its fame on the giant Buddha statue its ancillary attractions are not unimportant as they distinguish the setting from the array of retailing and eating experiences found in shopping malls everywhere. Further, the way in which the entrepreneurs have constructed the village is of particular interest. Arguably, Ngong Ping is a Chinese themed reinterpretation of Kuranda, a well-established Australian tourist shopping village. It represents a new example of hybridisation, a term coined by Bryman (2004) to characterise the growing interconnections and lack of differentiation among entertainment forms. In this case the hybridisation is arguably between a traditional shopping village and a theme park's retail section. The case emphasises the future commercial and community value of synthesising the best elements and key components of tourist shopping villages from a multi-country framework.

Village needs differentiation

5 Shopping Village Streetscapes and Servicescapes

INTRODUCTION

This chapter traces further steps in the journey exploring TSV characteristics. The focus narrows from the material considered in Chapter 4 where the regional contexts in which TSVs exist and the local landscapes in which TSVs are embedded were considered. Additionally in the previous chapter the role of anchor attractions in contributing to the appeal of these TSVs was noted and the entrepreneurial efforts to create the villages were considered. The information presented in this chapter focuses directly on the resultant environmental and social forms of the villages. The discussion corresponds to the second section of Figure 3.1 in Chapter 3 under the heading Environmental Features and Atmospherics. Like the forces identified in Chapter 4, the physical and social features considered here act as significant influences on the quality and richness of the visitors' TSV experience. These attributes are highlighted in the TSV Visitor Experience Model presented in Figure 5.1. The environmental features reviewed in this chapter have an important role in encouraging mindfulness which is our consistent approach to understanding the TSV experience.

A specific model to focus on and integrate these influences is provided in the following figure (Figure 5.2.). The key elements featured in this figure can be outlined as follows. The framework presents the environment as three interacting spatial settings: the landscape, streetscape and servicescape. These three interacting settings provide a sense of 'place' in which the postmodern consumption of tourist shopping villages takes place. The landscape includes broader destination variables that provide the setting for the tourist shopping village. Environmental cues such as vegetation and signage may spill over into the streetscape. The streetscape is the exterior presentation of the TSV, or more accurately, the area of the town that is the object of the tourist gaze. Streetscaping includes the use of paving, trees, gardens, water features, street art, signage and street furniture, which may add (or detract) from the village atmosphere. The streetscape also includes social factors, physical and design factors and ambient factors. These elements in turn cascade into the servicescape. The servicescape is perhaps the most well-researched of the three settings as social factors, physical and

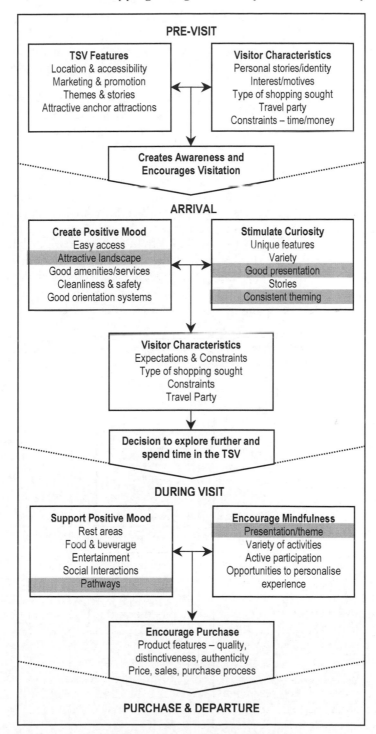

Figure 5.1   A model of the TSV visitor experience

design factors and ambient factors combine to create the interior environments of individual shops.

The way in which visitors respond to these environmental cues may be mediated by a variety of personal characteristics. Cultural origins have been shown to have a strong influence on the importance individuals place on contextual factors such as the environment (Hall 1969; Yu 1995). The appeal of environmental cues such as colour, music and product variety may be mediated by demographic characteristics such as age, life cycle stage, income and gender or psychographic and behavioural characteristics such values, attitudes and motives.

Bitner (1992) indicates that the servicescape not only impacts on customers, but also on employees. In adapting this to TSVs, it could be argued that environmental cues mediate the way in which hosts (employees, entrepreneurs and residents) respond to the environment. Residents who perceive that changes to the village environment have impacted on their quality of life might respond negatively. Entrepreneurs might view the environment, as this chapter does, as a collection of factors which can be manipulated to encourage desirable visitor responses such as repeat visitation, increased length of stay and increased expenditure. Employees who

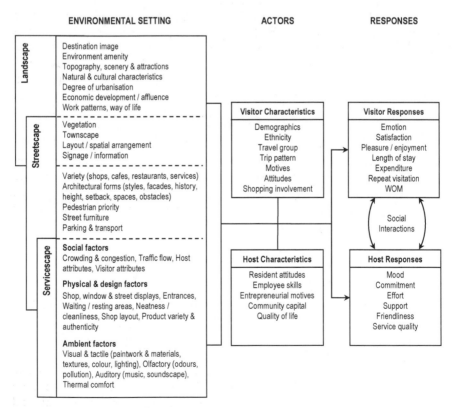

Figure 5.2   The elements of the tourist shopping village structure.

find the environment stimulating and rewarding to work in might respond more positively.

Social interactions between visitors and hosts in the environment are influenced by the responses of individuals. Residents who are proud of their village and perceive a lifestyle congruent with their aspirations may be more involved with tourist activities and may be friendlier to visitors. Likewise, employees who are appropriately skilled and are stimulated by the environment might respond more enthusiastically to visitors. The quality of these interactions in turn reinforces visitor responses such as length of stay, satisfaction and expenditure.

The remainder of this chapter is concerned with the three core elements of the TSV environment: the landscape, streetscape and servicescape. The discussion explores research findings from a range of settings, including shopping malls, tourist precincts, markets and rural towns. The chapter also draws on a number of detailed case studies of shopping village environments in North America, the United Kingdom and Australia.

THE VILLAGE LANDSCAPE

The term landscape has a range of connotations and interpretations rooted in various disciplinary traditions. Daugstad (2008) observes that as a field of research, landscape studies are complex and somewhat chaotic. In particular, she argues that in the discipline of geography, there has been an overemphasis on the visual dimensions of the landscape. In this chapter the landscape is presented as a broader concept, encompassing multisensory aspects of the broader environment in which TSVs are commonly found. The discussion of landscape first considers the concepts of rural destination image and environment amenity as a way of understanding what attracts visitors to the setting. Discussion then shifts to the particular multisensory landscape elements that make rural locales attractive. Finally, this section recognises that the TSV experience is often embedded in a larger townscape and that the presentation of TSV precincts can take many forms.

Environmental Amenity and Images of the Countryside

It has been argued that for many visitors the appeal of rural landscapes is the result of the need to escape their urbanised home environments (Cloke 2003). Continuing with this theme, Bunce (1994) suggests that the desirability of rural landscapes is due to their contrast to modern industrial and suburban landscapes and lifestyles. He argues that this desirability has led to a romanticised construction of rural landscapes representing values such as a sense of belonging and community, harmony between nature and humankind and a simple way of life. This idealised view of the rural landscape and community is frequently referred to as the 'rural idyll' (Cloke and Milbourne 1992; Mingay 1989; Newby 1979). Images of picturesque working farms and rural service towns help to attract visitors who view the countryside not merely as a space of *production*, but also as a space where they are the *consumers* of landscape and lifestyle amenity (Cloke 2006; Halfacree 1997). Tonts and Greive (2002) argue that those regions that possess some combination of amenity landscape, heritage architecture and good access to metropolitan centres have been the focus of attention of people seeking out the countryside ideal.

Hopkins' work on the destination images of rural areas also provides some useful insights for understanding the landscapes in which TSVs are commonly situated. In his semiotic analysis of the slogans of rural towns in Southern Ontario, Canada, Hopkins reported a strong focus on the environment, locality advantage, heritage and ideal community. An analysis of logos also revealed two further themes of agriculture and recreation. It is interesting to note that these themes have previously emerged in the TSV analyses reported in Chapter 3. Hopkins (1998: 78) concludes that the images used to market rural destinations create the expectation of "a spatial and temporal retreat from the urban environs, a place close to nature, rich in community ties, where life is lived at a slower pace in settlements situated amidst idyllic, nostalgic settings".

This quote illustrates the ethereal nature of the characteristics that attract people to country landscapes. Visual qualities of the landscape are not mentioned explicitly but the importance of the setting is implied. A number of researchers have explored the visual elements that make rural and natural landscapes attractive. This research highlights the importance of vegetation, human elements and scenic landmarks.

Vegetation in the Landscape

Vegetation is a major visual cue, with trees, shrubbery, grass, pasture and open spaces being very important landscape amenities (Kaplan 1985; Ulrich 1986). The density of vegetation in a landscape also appears to have a significant impact on visual quality (Arriaza, et al. 2004; Sayadi, Roa and Requena 2005). Trees, in particular, have been found to have a positive effect on landscape preferences (Lynch and Rivkin 1959; Thayer and Atwood 1978). The presence of wildflowers and pasture are also likely to attract visitors. Rural landscapes which contain pasture, trees and livestock appear to be more appealing than those containing cultivated crops but the research in this area is far from conclusive (Pérez 2002; Vanslembrouck, Huylenbroeck and Meensel 2005).

Human Elements in the Landscape

The preference for natural elements should not be interpreted as an indication that people prefer rural landscapes without human elements. The work of Pérez (2002) has indicated that man-made features such as stonewalls add to the attraction of the rural landscape. In addition, Sayadi, et al. (2005) have found that irrigated rural landscapes are more appealing than virgin landscapes or abandoned farmland. Arriaza, Cañas-Ortega, Cañas-Madueño and Ruiz-Aviles (2004) found that the perceived visual quality of rural landscapes increased with the degree of wilderness of the landscape, the presence of well-preserved, man-made elements, the percentage of plant cover, the amount of water, the presence of mountains and colour contrast. Positive human elements included farm houses and buildings, however, visual quality decreased with the growing presence of human elements such as roads, power lines and industry.

Scenic Landmarks

The fact that a landscape may contain landmarks also impacts on the visual quality of the landscape. Some landscapes contain iconic features which serve to attract visitors to the broader rural environment. These may include mountains, lakes, volcanic features, national parks, endemic fauna and flora or other attractions. For example, the landscape surrounding Sedona in Arizona offers a spectacular setting which not only serves as a backdrop for tourist shopping but also supports a range of other activities. Likewise, the tourist precinct of Cheddar is located within a gorge which supports a range of recreational activities such as rock climbing and caving (see Case Study 5.1). Some landscapes include human features such as castles, which serve to attract visitors. In some cases these landscape features serve as anchor attractions as discussed in the previous chapter.

Case Study 5.1   Cheddar, United Kingdom

Cheddar is a large village in Somerset and is best known for being located immediately adjacent to Cheddar Gorge, the largest gorge in the United Kingdom. The Gorge attracts about 500,000 visitors per year and it is estimated that over 1,000 people are employed by the tourism industry in Cheddar (Nagle 1999) Cheddar Gorge acts as a major anchor attraction which in turn creates demand for a number of tourist shops in the village. It lies within an Area of Outstanding Natural Beauty and is a candidate for Special Area for Conservation status. The Gorge is historically significant because it contains a number of caves that have been the centre of human settlement since Neolithic times.

Britain's oldest complete human skeleton, the Cheddar Gorge Man, was found in one of the caves in 1903 and is estimated to be 9,000 years old. Older remains from the Upper Late Palaeolithic era (12,000–13,000 years ago) have also been found. As a result the caves at Cheddar are the focus of significant visitor attention, with a number of tours based around these archaeological attractions. The cave entrances have been extensively developed and the experience, based around a number of tours, has been heavily commercialised. Visitors can also learn about the historic significance of the site through a visitor centre and the Cheddar Man Museum of Prehistory. Exhibits include orig flint tools and human remains excavated from the caves.

(cont

Case Study 5.1   (continued)

Figure 5.3   Entrance to Gough's Cave (top); cheese and cider
are major tourist products (bottom).

The village also gives its name to Cheddar cheese and has also been a major centre for cider and strawberry growing. Many of the shops, restaurants and cafes in
the village are focussed around the production and sale of these local foods and
produce. Cheddar's popularity as a tourist destination began with the opening of
Cheddar Valley Railway in 1870. The railway became known as the Strawberry
Line, because it passed a number of strawberry-growing fields. Cheddar straw-
berries are still grown in the area and when in season can be purchased by visitors
from roadside stalls. The railway line is no longer operating but part of the line
has become the focus of visitor attention as a long distance countryside walk.
Local community groups and politicians have orchestrated a campaign to convert
the remainder of the old railway line into a network of safe paths for walkers and
cyclists, further adding to the drawing power of the village.

(continued)

Case Study 5.1   (continued)

The village is also a major destination for adventure sports such as caving, rock climbing and abseiling. The Cheddar Yeo in Gough's Cave is Britain's biggest underground river while the Gorge Cliffs are Britain's highest inland limestone cliffs. There are about 350 officially graded climbing routes on the 27 cliffs that make up Cheddar Gorge. These cliffs also provide a spectacular setting for the village and the many tourist shops, cafés and restaurants.

Case Study Sources:

Nagle, G. (1999) Focus on Geography: Tourism, leisure and recreation, Cheltenham, Nelson Thornes, pp. 54–56.
http://www.cheddarvillage.co.uk/ (accessed 31 May, 2010)
http://www.cheddarcaves.co.uk/ (accessed 31 May, 2010)
http://www.enjoyengland.com/destinations/find/south-west/somerset/cheddar-gorge.aspx (accessed 31 May, 2010)
http://www.thestrawberryline.co.uk/ (accessed 31 May, 2010)
http://en.wikipedia.org/wiki/Cheddar_Gorge (accessed 31 May, 2010)

Multisensory Cues in the Landscape

In addition to the visual consumption of the landscape, it has been argued that tourists want the personal experience of tasting, feeling and hearing stories about the landscape (Daugstad 2008). Auditory cues of the rural landscape include an absence of stressful sounds associated with urban environments, such as traffic, telephones, sirens and alarms. These sounds are replaced with birdsong, sounds of livestock and the movement of water through the landscape. At the same time, visitors to rural areas are assaulted by a variety of smells. Concomitant with the visual cues of the seasons are smells such as spring flowers, or dry leaves in autumn. Some shopping villages are to be found in areas where herbs such as lavender are cultivated, and combined with the visual stimulus of these fields, they help to establish a sense of place. A sense of taste and smell may be triggered by the local food and produce associated with the region. Daugstad (2008) found that food is a major ingredient of the landscape experience, and that tastes and smells associated with cooking can provide strong environmental cues. It would seem that the presence of roadside stalls selling local produce provide further opportunities to 'taste' the landscape.

FROM THE LANDSCAPE TO THE VILLAGE STREETSCAPE

Visitors' first impressions of any TSV include the spatial relationship between different elements of the *townscape*. The 'tourist shopping' precinct or area which forms the focus of the tourist gaze may be an integrated part of the broader townscape, or alternatively, it can be separated from the more functional and utilitarian services used by local residents.

The village of Cheddar provides an example of a segregated village form, with the tourist precinct clearly delineated from the commercial, residential and accommodation component of the village by a stream. Natural features such as waterways or man-made features such as rail lines often serve as a convenient divider. In other villages the tourist shopping area may be a single street (often a 'high street') which is densely occupied by tourist shops but is linked with a broader network of streets offering amenities for locals. In all of these variations, the tourist precinct is separated, whether by design or evolution, from residential services which can reduce conflicts between visitors and hosts.

Undoubtedly the most common pattern is the one where tourist and resident services are mixed together, creating greater potential for some of the impacts explored in Chapter 2. The spatial relationships between different parts of the village have an impact on visitor orientation, visitor flows, perceptions of congestion and crowding and visitor satisfaction. While research in this context is limited, studies in urban settings have found that tourists prefer layouts that offer clear lines of sight (Kemperman, Borgers and Timmersman 2009). However, in small villages, the sense of discovery associated with exploring small laneways and arcades may add positively to the experience. A number of forms are evident in the shopping villages investigated in this book (see Figure 5.4).

The most common form is a linear 'high street' arrangement with visitor amenities on either side of the street. The street often follows a natural feature, such as a river or an engineering feature such as a rail line or major road. The tourist precinct of Cheddar provides an example where the main road winds its way through a gorge. Bourton-on-the-Water provides another example, where the main street and a modified waterway are fringed with visitor facilities. A variant on the single linear model is

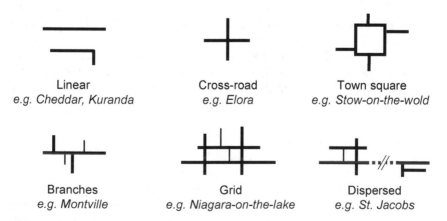

Linear	Cross-road	Town square
e.g. Cheddar, Kuranda	*e.g. Elora*	*e.g. Stow-on-the-wold*

Branches	Grid	Dispersed
e.g. Montville	*e.g. Niagara-on-the-lake*	*e.g. St. Jacobs*

Figure 5.4 Spatial forms of TSV visitor precincts.

an 'L' arrangement where two streets dominate the precinct. Kuranda is an example of the L pattern. A more developed spatial arrangement involves laneways, side streets and arcades branching off from the main tourist strip. The pedestrian arcades of Montville, which take visitors away from the main street, provide an example of this arrangement. A further form occurs when tourist shopping is focussed around a core feature such as a village square. This arrangement is common in English villages, such as Stow-on-the-Wold. Larger shopping villages may exhibit a grid pattern of several streets and this creates a fourth form. Niagara-on-the-Lake is a good example of a grid pattern. The village of Hay-on-Wye also exhibits a grid pattern, although the pathways are more organic. A final form can be identified, one which involves some distance between two shopping village areas in the one community. The Mennonite village of St. Jacobs, Canada has two distinct precincts, the 'village' and the 'market district' separated by a three kilometre drive through the countryside. The village precinct has a more traditional heritage village focus, while the market district contains farmers markets, furniture outlets and factory outlet shopping. The two areas are marketed collectively as 'St. Jacobs Country' (see Figure 5.5).

THE VILLAGE STREETSCAPE

In addition to the spatial arrangement of the streets and shops within TSVs, a number of other features create the exterior shopping environment for the villages. The streetscape is both a social arena and a traffic artery (Lillebye 1996). Yüksel (2007) argues that it is particularly important for managers to pay attention to the exterior shopping environment because it must be considered acceptable and pleasing before visitors will choose to explore store interiors. These views are consistent with the elements of the TSV Visitor Experience Model outlined in Chapter 3 which structures the discussion in this section. Table 5.1 provides an overview of the environmental and some social cues that can be found in the TSV streetscape. As with the consideration of the location and landscape surrounding the village reviewed in Chapter 4, visual elements are important but at this closer scale of experience multisensory features of the environment grow in importance.

Physical and Design Factors in the Streetscape

Vegetation has been identified as a major factor in determining the visual amenity of a streetscape (Fukahori and Kubota 2003). Vegetation can be used in a variety of ways to improve the TSV streetscape. Techniques that have been observed in villages around the world have included the use of trees, flowers, shrubbery and native vegetation. Trees break up continuous

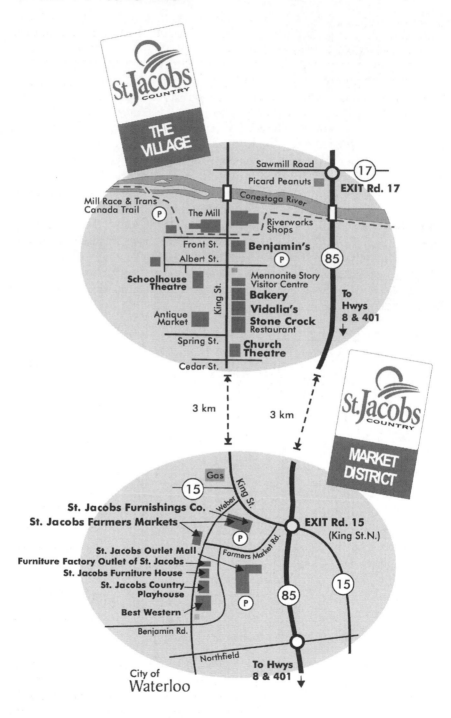

Figure 5.5 Visitor Map of St. Jacobs, Canada. Courtesy of St. Jacobs Country.

Table 5.1   Environmental and Social Cues Found in TSV Streetscapes

Environmental Cues	Typical Features
Physical/design factors	
Vegetation	Well-maintained small to medium street trees with wide canopies, woody flowering perennials, bright perfumed annuals, climbers on buildings, hardy drought tolerant species, fragrant herbs
Architectural styles	Heritage facades, distinct rural or ethnic styles, use of natural materials (stone and timber), use of colour
Use of space	Low built forms, set back from road, separation between buildings
Store variety	Restaurants, pubs, cafes, bakeries, local produce, arts and crafts, galleries, antiques & collectables, toy shops, boutique clothing, Christmas shops, fudge & lolly shops
Signage	Small, quaint, country-style, old-style lettering, use of rustic materials. Themed entrance signage, directional signs and interpretation
Street decoration	Consistent presentation of amenities such as lamp posts, bins and seating, street art, pavement art, water features, picket fences, café-style umbrellas
Pedestrian areas	Separation from road, wide walkways, arcades, frequent crossings, consistent use of paving in natural tones to add interest and texture
Displays	Prominent street and window displays of products
Water	Running water, fountains, streams
Social factors	
People	Street theatre, music, costumed/uniformed 'actors'
Transport	Nostalgic modes of transport, steam trains, horse & cart, vintage cars, removal of modern transport and parking from main streetscape
Ambient factors	
Soundscape	Birdsong, livestock, running water, breeze through vegetation, street music, absence of urban noises
Olfactory	Village smells, cafés, bakeries, coffee shops, fragrant flowers & herbs, smoke from log fires, absence of urban pollution

building facades and provide delineation of space, shrubs provide a sense of scale to settings and grass and ground cover help to define pavement edges (Smardon 1988). Flowers add colour and texture and can draw the tourist gaze away from less attractive elements of the streetscape. A study conducted by Antupit, Gray and Woods (1996) found that vegetation is the most important element in creating 'great streets'. The research provides some evidence that people feel more positive, calmer and more relaxed when viewing or being around plants (Kaplan 2001; Ulrich 1984). Customer patronage has been found to increase with the presence of trees and customers are also willing to pay more for products in retail settings that are accompanied by quality landscaping (Wolf 2005a; 2005b).

Of all vegetation types, trees can have the most dramatic effect on the streetscape (Todorova, Asakawa and Aikoh 2004; Wolf 2005a). Villages such as Hahndorf, Montville and Kuranda in Australia; Niagara-on-the-Lake and Bayfield in Canada; and Bourton-on-the-Water in England have many mature trees in the streetscape. The presence of trees and other vegetation also provides a habitat for wildlife. The presence of birds in particular adds to the soundscape of the exterior environment. While trees might be liked by visitors (Lohr, et al. 2004; Ulrich 1986), their presence in the streetscape can create some challenges. Poor landscape design, lack of maintenance or bad selection of tree species can create problems such as allergies from excessive pollen production, interference with signage or powerlines, chemical emissions and pollutants from trees and maintenance activities, waste disposal, infrastructure damage and water consumption (Lohr, et al. 2004; Nowak and Dwyer 2000).

Flowers, shrubbery, grass and climbers can also add to the presentation of the streetscape. When examining the preferences of Japanese pedestrians Todorova et al. (2004) found that low and ordered arrangements of brightly coloured flowers were the most favoured among a set of choices that also included soil, grass and hedging. Flowers and shrubbery have been used to great effect in a number of TSVs with extensively landscaped streetscapes. Niagara-on-the-Lake offers perhaps the most stunning example of the use of flowers in the streetscape, with extensive plantings of annuals on median strips and sidewalks in spring and summer. The use of flowering woody perennials such as roses and camellias are also evident in many village streetscapes and their presence adds not only to the visual presentation but also provides pleasant scents. Likewise, the use of herbs such as lavender and rosemary provides pleasant olfactory cues as pedestrians move past these plantings. Not much has been written about vines and creepers, but their use on historic buildings can add to the sense of nostalgia and authenticity. Creeping ivy, wisteria and other climbers are particularly evident in heritage village settings (see Figure 5.6).

The use of lush vegetation and mature trees does pose some challenges for villages located in dry regions. The village of Sedona, in Arizona has an average annual rainfall of 440 mm (17.3 inches). The village has overcome this challenge by using drought tolerant species such as grasses and small leafed plantings of hardy herbaceous shrubbery, succulents and cacti. Flowering annuals such as petunias are used sparingly to add colour. The Tlaquepaque shopping precinct, which is removed from the main shopping strip, overcomes the low rainfall by creating a microclimate amongst buildings and the shelter provided allows vegetation to flourish. The result is an

Figure 5.6   Use of flowers at Niagara-on-the-Lake (top), shrubbery and vegetation at Montville.

environment that is relatively lush and contrasts with the harsh surrounding countryside.

In addition to vegetation, architectural styles and building facades play a major role in the physical presentation of the streetscape. Research on historic tourism shopping precincts appears to be fairly limited and narrow in scope, with a particular emphasis on geographic or planning perspectives, rather than architectural factors (Griffin and Hayllar 2006). Many TSV streetscapes contain heritage buildings which provide cues about the history, ethnicity and prosperity of the region.

It would appear that there is no simple architectural recipe for 'building' a successful shopping village. Consistency can be achieved either by using distinctive regional architectural styles or by the careful selection of building materials and colours (see Figure 5.7 for examples). Getz (1993) notes that deliberate architectural and historic theming appears to be actively used by entrepreneurs as a tool for developing the attractiveness of TSVs. Extensive use of modern materials such as glass, steel and concrete do not appear to be common. It can be suggested that it is the contrast between the village architecture in whatever forms and materials and that of more anonymous shopping centres which appeals to many visitors.

Architectural style is also influenced by building setback, height and space. Some successful shopping village streetscapes contain buildings that are well set back from the road, to allow visitors to admire the facades. The buildings are rarely higher than two levels, creating a sense of scale that results in villages being described as 'quaint' or 'charming'. As discussed in Chapter 4 this aesthetic is an appeal to the picturesque. The space around each building is often vegetated, setting buildings apart from each other and allowing visitors to appreciate not just the facades but also the three-dimensional beauty of the buildings. Some of the spaces between buildings contain historic monuments, cemeteries, parks and gardens, which create a sense of place by adding to the heritage and authenticity of the village experience (cf. Hayllar and Griffin 2005).

The variety of stores in the streetscape adds to the appeal of the shopping environment (Jansen-Verbeke 1991). Shopping villages sometimes contain three or four very similar shops which are often trying to sell the same or very similar products. This repetition may reduce the village's appeal for visitors. There are exceptions though as some products gain an advantage if there is a collection of product types such as the reputation of Hay-on-Wye for bookstores or Strathalbyn's specialised stores selling Australian antiques. It would seem that collectors and specialist (self-development) shoppers might relish the repetition but general shoppers, as described in the typology in Chapter 1, are likely to be less favourably disposed to these villages.

A broad range of dining options, from café-style to fine dining would appear to be important. Restaurants, pubs, cafés, bakeries and purveyors of local produce all add to the culinary delights of the village. Fast food chain outlets are not commonly found in shopping villages and

Figure 5.7 Use of atypical architectural elements, Williams and Eumundi.

this niche appears to be filled by businesses such as bakeries and coffee or tea shops. In terms of shopping products, most villages contain various local arts and crafts shops, including many that provide traditional handicrafts such as timber carvings, glassware, jewellery, haberdashery, textiles, quilts, toys and other home wares. Antiques and collectables are also common but are not found in all villages and their viability is being seriously undermined by online collectables trading. Some villages have a clear focus on the arts and subsequently feature a number of galleries showcasing painting, sculpture and photography. Other speciality stores are readily found in TSVs; for example, surprisingly few villages can be found without Christmas shops or fudge and confectionary shops.

Related to the variety and presentation of buildings in the streetscape is the display of signage and merchandise. Coordinated and themed signage has been recognised as an important element in the presentation of TSV streetscapes (Getz 1993). Consistency of presentation is an important consideration across all of these various markers. Some villages present very clear welcome signs which act as entry statements to the tourist shopping precinct. These signs are further reinforced by consistently themed directional and interpretive signs. The rainforest village of Kuranda not only makes extensive use of themed street furniture, but also carries this theme into its directional signage and street signs. The signage used by vendors is also an important component of the streetscape. Local government agencies often play an important role in TSVs by using ordinances and by laws to set parameters regarding the size, style, lettering and use of colour of signage. As a result, signage is often quaint, with a distinct country-style lettering and images (Getz, Joncas and Kelly 1994). Buildings are adorned with eccentric or unusually shaped signage made from rustic materials such as timber (see Figure 5.8). Signs are often much smaller than would be found in metropolitan environments.

The display of products complements the use of signage by adding meaning to the role of individual stores. Window displays are common in retailing, but many TSV vendors extend these displays onto verandas and into exterior pedestrian areas. These displays can add considerably to the streetscape but essentially are designed to draw visitors into individual shops (Edwards and Shackley 1992; Sen, Block and Chandran 2002). Street displays provide visitors with important information to help them make decisions about whether to enter the store. An eclectic mix of paraphernalia is not an uncommon sight on TSV sidewalks but care needs to be taken not to clutter the streetscape. Examples are provided in Figure 5.9.

The physical design and presentation of the street itself can provide important visual cues which may affect visitor enjoyment. Two dimensions of the physical design are noteworthy for TSVs: street decoration and pedestrian comfort. A variety of decorative approaches are used to improve the visual amenity of streetscapes. Functional features of the streetscape such as street furniture (bins, street lamps, seating) can be

Figure 5.8   Themed directional signage in Niagara-on-the-Lake and Kuranda.

Figure 5.9   Street displays of products at Montville (top) and Bayfield.

Figure 5.10 Decorative bins and lamp posts at Montville.

designed to enhance or fit in with the architectural strengths or theme of a village. The consistent use of attractive and quality street furnishings for the entire length of the shopping street provides yet another visual cue which impacts on visitors' perceptions of tidiness and cleanliness. The decorative lamp posts and bins provided in Montville present a particularly good example of how these mundane elements of the streetscape can be designed as attractive and unique features (see Figure 5.10).

Pedestrian walkways are an important consideration, both in terms of aesthetics and functionality. Paved walkways are commonly used in TSVs but paving has higher maintenance requirements than concrete or asphalt because of the tendency to shift and become uneven. While surfaces such as cobblestone are attractive in older villages, the uneven surface can create accessibility problems, particularly for the disabled, elderly or parents with strollers. Most villages appear to avoid plain concrete walkways in favour of paving, with paving often presented in earthy tones (e.g. brown, ochre, bluestone or sandstone hues). This is consistent with the work of Fukahori and Kubota (2003), who found that pedestrians favoured dark brown and stone paving colours. Paving can be enhanced through the use of paving art. Montville and Kuranda provide particularly good examples of villages that have given considerable attention to the walkways (see Figure 5.11). The use of paving decorations is one technique of embedding street art into the streetscape.

Figure 5.11 Paving art at Montville.

Several villages also make extensive use of street sculptures to add to the
appeal of the street. Sedona, Montville and Kuranda feature good examples of streetscape sculptures, monuments and interpretive plaques.

Water has been identified as an important element in the landscape,
but it is also used by some shopping villages to create a calm and relaxing

streetscape. In some villages natural waterways are visible from shopping streets, while in others entrepreneurs or planners have brought water into the streetscape through the use of fountains and water features. The presence of water can affect pedestrians' perceptions of thermal comfort, while moving water impacts on ambient cues by providing visual and auditory stimuli. Water may also have a tactile dimension, as observed in Bourton-on-the-Water, where, at least in summer, visitors wade into the stream which forms a focal point for the village. This setting also provides a habitat for ducks and other birds, further adding to the unique streetscape (see Case Study 5.2). Similarly the Avon River and its black swans are a focal point in Stratford, Canada. In Sedona, a fine mist of water is sprayed from buildings onto pedestrian areas to humidify the air and improve pedestrian comfort.

The width and gradient of pedestrian pathways and their separation from vehicular traffic also has an impact on the visitor experience. Successful TSVs use several techniques in addition to the points already discussed to enhance the comfort of pedestrians. Some villages have used raised pedestrian crossings or paved crossings to slow traffic and improve pedestrian access. Walkways are typically wide to facilitate accessibility and to lower negative perceptions of crowding. It is common to find that walkways are laid out in a meandering pattern, with gentle curves flanked by gardens, vegetation and street art. This arrangement seeks to induce a calmer strolling behaviour but there is also a subtle manipulation in

---

Case Study 5.2   Bourton-on-the-Water, United Kingdom

Bourton-on-the-Water is one of a number of historic English villages located in Gloucestershire, England in the Cotswolds area. The village is located along the ancient Roman Fosse Way about 140km (85 miles) from London. The village is close to a cluster of shopping villages that include Stow-on-the-Wold, Broadway, Chipping Campden and Burford. It is often described as the 'Venice of the Cotswolds' because the river that runs through the village is spanned by several attractive small eighteenth century road and foot bridges framed by neat tree-shaded greens and tidy stone banks.

Bourton has a rich heritage stretching back to at least the Stone Age, when it was the site of an encampment. Stone Age and Bronze Age burial mounds are common throughout the area while Iron Age currency bars from about 300 BC have been found on the site. The village was a strategically important settlement for both the Romans and the Saxons. At some point in its history, the river around which visitor activity is focussed was channelled through the centre of the village in order to provide a sufficient flow of water to power three mills. The river is flanked by a number of historic Cotswolds buildings which host tourist shops, restaurants and cafés. Many of the buildings and cottages are over 300 years old and are typically built with honey-hued Cotswold stone. Many of the grand buildings, manors and abbeys in the areas were financed in the Middle Ages by the wealth created from wool.

(continued)

Case Study 5.2   (continued)

Figure 5.12   The river and tourist shops at Bourton-on-the-Water.

In more modern times, tourism has replaced wool as a major economic activity. Aside from the attractive historic settings offered by many Cotswold villages, the region has played an important role in the arts and crafts movement instigated by the artist and writer William Morris in Britain in the 1880s. Morris liked the area and persuaded other artists and crafts people to base themselves in surrounding villages such as Chipping Campden. This provided a strong foundation for the traditional handicrafts, home wares and art that attract many day-trippers.

Case Study 5.2   (continued)

Aside from the attractive historic setting, Bourton has a number of tourist attractions including its well-known model village, which is a 1:9 replica of the village and includes a model of the model village itself (a model within a model). The village is also home to a model railway, the Cotswold Motoring Museum, an ornithological theme park, a maze and a farmers' market. A number of long distance countryside walks can be accessed from Bourton-on-the-Water.

Despite its untouched historic appearance the village receives heavy visitation, particularly in spring and summer, and is well-supported by modern infrastructure. Two large car parks on the outskirts of the village provide parking for hundreds of cars and large coaches.

Case Study Sources:

http://www.cotswolds.info/places/bourton-on-the-water.shtml (accessed 31 May, 2010)
http://www.bourton-on-the-water.net/ (accessed 31 May, 2010)
http://www.cotswoldswebsite.com/ (accessed 31 May, 2010)
http://www.bourtoninfo.com/ (accessed 31 May, 2010)
http://www.digital-brilliance.com/hyperg/history/ (accessed 31 May, 2010)

directing the gaze of pedestrians to particular points of interest. Pathways are often separated from the roadway by gardens, creating a perception of increased pedestrian safety and providing a buffer to the unpleasant externalities associated with roads and vehicles (e.g. radiant heat, noise, air pollution). Some villages make use of laneways and arcades that extend perpendicular to the streetscape, and offers visitors refuge from the hustle and bustle of the main thoroughfare.

It is clear from the discussion thus far that many elements of the streetscape can influence visitor satisfaction, length of stay, expenditure and repeat visitation. Nevertheless, the streetscape must be managed in an integrated manner involving all stakeholders. A failure to undertake cooperative planning can result in street clutter. Davis (2002) observes that street clutter erodes the special character, value and distinctiveness of an area. He goes on to argue that clutter works against the concept of distinctiveness because "it forms a visual mist in every foreground, which obscures the buildings and forms that create the unique distinctiveness of a place" (231). It is clear that in successful TSVs there has been considerable coordination between landowners, tenants, local government planners and residents. The importance of coordination, cooperation and funding is discussed further in Chapter 9.

Social Factors in the Streetscape

Social factors, including employees and other visitors, impact on the way that visitors perceive the streetscape. Jansen-Verbeke (1991) argues that the social and emotional appeal of the shopping environment is a fundamental consideration. She identifies the liveliness of the open space, animation, entertainment, amusement and surprise as key features of leisure shopping environments. Perceptions of crowding and the characteristics of other visitors have been shown to have a major impact on visitor satisfaction in leisure settings. Large crowds, congestion and traffic gridlock are certainly not consistent with most visitors' image of a day away from an urban setting. The popularity of some TSVs, particularly at peak periods of the year, can be a major source of dissatisfaction for both visitors and residents. The issue of seasonality was considered in Chapter 4 and dealing with capacity will be discussed further in Chapter 9.

A number of steps can be taken by shopping village managers to enliven the streetscape. Volunteers may be employed to act as greeters or guides, street vendors can sell light refreshments, and performers can be used in a variety of ways to interact with visitors. Costumed ladies are used to greet visitors and provide information about the shopping village at Windsor Castle (see Figure 5.13). In summer uniformed street vendors can also be observed selling ice-cream from old-style street carts in the Cotswold village of Broadway. These social elements are clearly contrived and can assist interactions with locals. The visible local Mennonite population in St. Jacobs add to the distinctiveness of this Canadian village (see Case Study 6.2).

An important social element which is evident in some villages is the preservation of older forms of transport. For example, a number of villages in the Australian Victorian highlands are enhanced by the 'Puffing Billy' steam train. Likewise scenic railways and railway stations are important anchor attractions for villages such as Kuranda and Williams. The presence of horses and carts is strongly associated with the local population at St. Jacobs, but they are also used as novelty forms of transport in Niagara-on-the-Lake and Williams. Vintage cars can also be found strategically parked in the streets of many villages. Approaches to managing the contemporary transport aspects of shopping villages are discussed further in Chapter 8.

Ambient Factors in the Streetscape

The sonic environment, or soundscape, can be defined as: "the totality of sound phenomena that lead to a perceptual, aesthetic and representational comprehension of the sonic world" (Augoyard, Karlsson & Winkler, 1999 in Hedfors 2003: 25). Anderson, Mulligan, Goodman and Regen (1983) found that appraisals of outdoor spaces depended largely on the sounds present in the environment. While much research has examined the use of sound and music in interior servicescapes (see next section), research in exterior environments is limited. Pleasant elements in the exterior soundscape of shopping villages might include birdsong, running water, the gentle

Figure 5.13   Hosts and performers in the streetscape at Windsor and Broadway.

caress of a breeze through vegetation, the sounds of livestock in nearby fields, cowbells, the clatter of horses and carts, church bells, town criers and music from street performers. Unfortunately these sounds are also easily drowned out by unpleasant noises created by traffic, buildings, construction and maintenance, crowding and congestion. Examples include the sound of a tour bus idling or the hum of air-conditioning. Southworth (1969) suggests that solutions to the problem of traffic noise can include careful location of noisy activities, new types of highway and street design, special vehicle design and masking of existing noise by added sound. The shape of spaces, wall materials and vegetation along the street are also critical in noise control and if badly designed, create a resonating chamber and amplify noise.

Beyond sound, the presence of scents in the streetscape can also serve to create positive experiences by evoking pleasant memories of past experiences. The sense of smell is considered to be the most closely attached to memory and feelings because the olfactory bulb is directly connected to the brain's centre of emotion, the limbic system (Wilkie 1995). Experiencing particular odours can therefore trigger deeply embedded memories of the past (Bowring 2006). The types of scents likely to evoke positive emotions in the TSV streetscape are smells of food and beverages such as coffee and bakery items and the fragrance of flowers and herbs. In autumn, the scent of drying leaves may evoke positive emotions, while in some mountain or cool climate villages the smell of a log fire may induce feelings of relaxation and comfort.

THE VILLAGE SERVICESCAPE

In addition to the external environment, an important influence on the experience of TSV visitors is the stores themselves. The atmosphere created by these shops is therefore influential in shaping satisfying and mindful visitor experiences. The previous discussion has alluded to the fact that a great deal has been written over the last 20 years about interior servicescapes. The literature has been particularly prolific in the retail area, where the terms 'atmospherics' and 'servicescape' introduced in Chapter 3 appear to be used interchangeably. The needs of visitors and their attentiveness to the cues and factors discussed in the following sections are modified by the kinds of shopping in which they are involved. As with the streetscape, the literature has focussed on physical and design factors, ambient factors and social factors in the servicescape, and this framework will again form the basis for the discussion below (see Table 5.2).

Physical & Design Factors in the Servicescape

Numerous studies have examined variables concerned with the interior of retail spaces and their effect on shopper's perceptions. Studies exploring

Table 5.2   Environmental Cues Found in Tourist Shopping Village Servicescapes

Environmental Cues	*Typical Features*
Physical/design factors	
Use of space	Small, narrow walkways, often cluttered with products, limited use of tall shelving
Product variety	Individual stores specialise in particular product categories, breadth of products but often one of a kind or limited number of the same product, local hand-crafted products or produce
Signs & labels	Small, quaint, country-style, old-style lettering, labels often hand written, emphasis on products themselves not elaborate labelling
Displays	Low to eye level displays, emphasis on showcasing products and produce with great care taken in placing products, organic rather than orderly arrangement of displays, products often not grouped
Colour & texture	Earthy tones (e.g. timber, stone) or heritage schemes, walls sometimes textured (e.g. stone, timber)
Floor coverings	Hard surfaces, tiles, timber, stone, slate
Furnishings & shelving	Usually timber, sometimes glass, rarely metallic
Social factors	
Hosts	Traditional outfits, ethnic clothing styles or costume
Visitors	Expectations are for an uncrowded experience
Ambient factors	
Lighting	Natural light, supplemented by warm, soft lighting schemes
Sound	Quiet music, slow tempo, relaxation, classic or jazz styles, rarely pop or rock.
Olfactory	Coffee, baked items, confectionery, incense, handmade soaps, timber, candles

several simultaneous variables in the general interior have found that overall perceptions do influence outcomes such as approach/avoidance, length of stay and sales (Akhter, Andrews and Durvasula 1994; Baker, et al. 2002; Donovan, et al. 1994). Since the focus of TSV shopping is on recreational rather than utilitarian shopping, especially destination experience and self-development shopping, the need to get in and out of the store quickly or to easily find merchandise is unimportant. The browsing behaviour of shoppers suggests that contrary to the research on store layout, a more cluttered, less organised environment is more suitable for TSV stores. Such an environment encourages visitors to linger and creates a sense of pleasure and 'discovery' when 'finding' unique or locally distinctive products. The chaotic layout of some shopping village stores appears to be deliberately designed to encourage visitors to spend as much time as possible in the store.

Vrechopoulos, O'Keefe, Doukidis and Siomkos (2004) identify three major types of store layout:

1. *Grid:* a rectangular arrangement of displays and long aisles that generally run parallel and/or perpendicular to one another.
2. *Freeform:* a free-flowing and asymmetric arrangement of displays and aisles, employing a variety of different sizes, shapes and styles of display.
3. *Racetrack/boutique:* a store layout which leads the customer along specific paths to visit as many store sections or departments as possible, because a main pathway facilitates customer movement through the store (e.g. IKEA).

The grid layout that dominates utilitarian shopping environments, with its ordered linear presentation of pathways, walkways and aisles, is rarely evident in TSV stores. Freeform layouts are frequently employed, particularly in larger TSV stores. This layout provides visitors with considerable freedom to move in any direction and may reduce perceptions of crowding. The racetrack layout is also common in TSVs and in some cases ensures that visitors must pass all of the merchandise before being able to exit. While this layout might create an interesting and entertaining shopping experience it may not be well-suited to crowded environments.

The presentation of handicrafts and produce in TSV stores is often almost chaotic, with a focus on striking displays rather than fastidious categorisation and ordering of products. Labels and interior signage are often small and handwritten. In many instances the products are locally produced and may be one of a kind. When this is not the case, many displays still tend to create the illusion of exclusivity by only displaying a small number of items from the same product line. Often these items are interspersed with associated themed items to create a pleasing display (see Figure 5.14). The use of shelving that extends beyond eye level is a rarity, with products being displayed at eye level or below. Walls are often cluttered with artwork or wall hangings displaying more products.

In successful shopping villages the interior design often flows from the exterior cues discussed earlier. Therefore, heritage colours and use of natural materials such as timber is commonplace. Some interiors provide opulent, refined and ornately decorated settings dominated by high quality timber finishes. The apothecary at Niagara-on-the-Lake, with its extensive use of dark timber panels, exemplifies this approach. Other interiors tend more towards rustic internal finishes which include artefacts from the rural environment, such as wine barrels, milk pails and other relics in the display of merchandise. Figure 5.15 provides a good example of this approach. Floor coverings tend to be hard rather than soft, with timber, slate, stone and tiles used rather than carpeting. The sound of people traversing these surfaces

Figure 5.14 Display of goods in TSV servicescapes.

adds to the interior ambience. Often the interior design of stores is driven by the heritage values of the buildings themselves and this in itself contributes to the unique and nostalgic ambience. There are of course exceptions to these positive and broadly appealing design considerations. There are

Figure 5.15   Traditional interiors at St. Jacobs (top) and Mount Tamborine Gallery Walk.

shops featuring mass produced products and conventional souvenirs. Shops in towns like Cheddar and Gatlinburg spring to mind. However, even this approach to retail contrasts with the uniformity of glass and steel shopping environments in urban areas although a proliferation of such shops can become the target for negative community sentiment as described in the New England study reported in Chapter 2.

Social Factors in the Servicescape

Social factors impacting on the servicescape can include the number and type of people in the setting as well as their behaviours. Aubert-Gamet and Cova (1999) argue that while the environment provides a range of stimuli, it should also be conceptualised as a personal construct. The setting is not only a spatial construct but also a social construct in which the customer is an active part of the environment. This view highlights the desire of postmodern consumers to be part of the production process and to experience immersion in thematic settings with others rather than merely viewing finished products. In addition to offering physical support and tangible evidence of the service, the environment should also present social artefacts as well as serving as an evocative background for social interactions and activities.

The presence of other visitors in TSV servicescapes affects the quality of the experience. While recognising that crowding can have a significant positive impact in certain hedonic settings (e.g. sports events, night clubs, bars), visitors to TSVs are likely to be seeking some escape from crowds. Crowding and congestion can be a common social problem particularly in villages that are in an advanced stage of the development life cycle. The small, quaint, cluttered shops described earlier are not amenable to large numbers of visitors. The management of people in the servicescape therefore becomes very important, as do efforts to reduce *perceived* crowding. Perceived crowding has been defined as "a feeling of being confined, cramped, or restricted because of one's physical surroundings" (Wakefield and Blodgett 1994: 69). Customers who perceive stores to be crowded restrict themselves to superficial forms of interaction with store personnel and fellow shoppers, engage less in exploratory shopping, delay unnecessary purchases and reduce shopping time (Harrell, Hutt and Anderson 1980). Perceived crowding can be tempered by other environmental cues such as music, lighting, smell and the physical layout of the store. For example a store that plays soothing relaxation or classical music, burns incense and has a freeform layout so that patrons do not become trapped by fellow shoppers is likely to modify the visitors' negative reactions to others.

Ambient Factors in the Servicescape

Music is an ambient cue that is easily controlled and more readily changed, and for that reason it has been the most commonly studied interior ambient cue. It is clear that music can have a significant impact on sales, customer arousal, length of stay, perceptions of time and perceptions about products and other aspects of the service setting (Dubé and Morin 2001; Morin, Dubé and Chebat 2007). The impact of music has been found to be mediated by the age of the customer (Yalch and Spangenberg 1990), music tempo (Milliman 1982, 1986), volume (Sullivan 2002) and music preference (Caldwell and Hibbert 2002; Herrington 1996). Music in general and classical music in particular has been shown to enhance the experience of customers in service settings (Areni and Kim 1993). Milliman (1982, 1986) found that slower tempos and lower volumes resulted in retail and restaurant patrons shopping and eating at a more leisurely pace, which in some instances resulted in increased sales. The presence of music has been associated with more positive moods and shorter perceived waiting times when experiencing service delays (Cameron, et al. 2003).

The musical properties of TSV stores appear to be largely consistent with the literature. Music is often played at a low background level and live music inside stores is uncommon. In terms of style, the tempo tends to be slower, with genres such as classical music, jazz, soul, relaxation and world music being common. These music characteristics would appear to be a good 'fit' with other exterior and interior environmental cues which project a heritage and rural image rather than a modern urban image. In addition to music, the soundscape of individual shops may at times be filled by the sound of video demonstrations related to the manufacture of specific products.

While olfactory cues are important at the streetscape level, as already discussed, they play a significant role in the interior servicescape of TSVs. The role of smell in TSV stores is perhaps more important than in many utilitarian retail settings. Many of the unique handcrafted products available in TSV stores carry strong scent cues. Products such as soap, candles, timber crafts, leather and furniture have distinctive aromas which can evoke powerful memories in consumers. Moreover, the oils and cleaning products used to maintain merchandise may add to the sensory qualities of a store. Some TSV entrepreneurs deliberately attempt to enhance the aroma of their stores through the burning of scented candles or incense, or through careful placement of potpourri or scent diffusers.

A distinction must be made between product-specific scents and ambient scents. Ambient scents, that is scent that is not emanating from a particular object but is present in the environment, may be of greater interest than product-specific scents, because they could affect perceptions of the store and all its products, including those products that do not have distinctive odours (Spangenberg, Crowley and Henderson 1996). Research has found that smell has a greater impact on consumer decision making when there is some congruence between the ambient scent and the type of product being sold (Mitchell, Kahn and Knasko 1995; Ward, Davies and Kooijman 2007). Chebat and Michon (2003) found that the presence of pleasant ambient odours did not result in a more positive affective state, but they did influence perceptions of the shopping environment and product quality. Scents have also been shown to influence customers' intentions to visit and return to a store (Bone and Scholder 1999). This suggests that the use of ambient odours, such as potpourri and incense, may have an impact on how visitors perceive TSV stores, although the impact of these specific odours has not yet been explored in the literature. The opportunity exists for individual stores to use signature scents that customers will identify with that particular store (Davies, Kooijmanb and Warda 2003).

The third ambient variable which has been discussed in the retail literature is the use of lighting. Since many TSV stores are not tucked away in concrete shopping malls, the presence of natural light tends to be a feature. In some stores entrepreneurs have capitalised on the views of the surrounding landscape by installing large display windows that allow visitors to appreciate the landscape while at the same time letting in a great deal of natural light. Some of the stores in Montville and Leura provide particularly good examples of this approach. More generally in the retail literature, authors have written about the use of artificial lighting to establish the basic ambiance and mood of stores. The research suggests that lighting can influence the store image as well as the examination and handling of merchandise (Areni and Kim 1994; Baker, Grewal and Parasuraman 1994). In particular, bright light was found to result in higher rates of product examination and handling but lighting levels did not influence sales (Areni and Kim 1994). The artificial lighting observed in most TSV stores is dim, rather than bright. Research exploring the colour of lighting is less well-developed but recent findings have suggested that while cooler lighting results in higher levels of arousal, customers generally prefer warmer lighting and perceive it to be more pleasurable (Park and Farr 2007). The use of warmer lights in most shopping village stores appears to be consistent with these findings.

CONCLUSION

This chapter has provided a detailed analysis of many specific environmental and social cues evident in many successful TSVs. While these environmental cues have been presented and discussed individually, they are part of a system with many complex interactions. It is the combination of these environmental and social cues that helps to create a postmodern setting which visitors perceive as unique and different and which gives each village its character. In the case of villages that have been redesigned and planned, the manipulation and management of the cues discussed in this chapter deliberately create the imagery and predisposing conditions for shoppers to relax, engage with the merchandise and possibly open their wallets.

6 Themes and Presentation

INTRODUCTION

Shopping is the central theme of this book and in previous chapters we have established that shopping is a major activity for tourists in rural villages and small towns, a common motivation for visiting these places and a central part of their development. But shopping is very rarely used in the promotion and presentation of these destinations, few of these destinations openly label or refer to themselves as shopping villages (see Table 6.1) and shopping is seldom included in the tourist narratives about their experiences. There are several reasons why people do not mention shopping when discussing TSVs. Firstly, there could be a general view that shopping alone is not considered a worthwhile leisure activity and must be connected to something else to be socially acceptable. Secondly, it may reflect variation in the motives of different members of travel parties, in which some may be explicitly interested in shopping and others either interested in other activities or simply willing to participate to make the shoppers in the group happy. Finally, it may reflect the existence of different types of tourist activities and attractions in villages. Shopping in TSVs takes place within a larger tourist experience often built around a particular theme and it is this larger context that distinguishes shopping in TSVs from shopping malls or urban precincts.

The slogans and phrases given in Table 6.1 are examples of the kinds of themes associated with TSVs. In Murphy, Moscardo, Benckendorff and Pearce's (2008) analysis of the success as a tourist experience of 29 TSVs in Australia, New Zealand and Canada, themes emerged as a critical element. This study concluded that a strong theme, especially one based on heritage and local food and wine, made a significant contribution to a positive tourist experience. The importance of themes also emerged in the review of research into leisure shopping in general and customer experiences reported in Chapter 3. Thus the use of themes and their presentation was included in the TSV visitor experience model. Figure 6.1 presents the TSV Visitor Experience Model introduced in Chapter 3 highlighting

Table 6.1   Promotional Slogans for a Selection of Shopping Villages

Village	Marketing Slogan or First Phrase Used in Marketing Material
Blackheath	Getaway to the Greater Blue Mountains
Castlemaine	Arts, atmosphere – the rest is history
Hahndorf	Australia's oldest surviving German settlement
Kuranda	Village in the rainforest
Montville	True village charm – the calm behind the coast
Bayfield	Heritage village on a Great Lake
Stratford	Canada's premier arts town
St. Jacobs	Acquaint yourself with a gentler time
Adare	Picture postcard village
Kinsale	Take one spectacular location, season liberally with Norman, Spanish, English influence, add one major battle and let it simmer for 400 years – the result, Ireland's fine food capital
Arrowtown	Where history is very much alive
Hokitika	Hub of the west coast gold rush
Hay-on-Wye	Town of books
Bethel	Maine's most beautiful mountain village
Salado	The best art town in Texas
Sedona	Red rock country

the different points where themes and their presentation are involved. In the pre-visit stage the use of themes, often presented through stories, in promotional materials provides a way for visitors to make connections to their interests, identity and motives. During the arrival phase good presentation, including stories and the use of consistent themes, can contribute to stimulating visitor curiosity and encouraging them to explore more. Finally, during the visit, presentation and themes are important factors in encouraging mindfulness.

This chapter will analyse in more detail the roles, presentation and development of themes in TSVs. It will begin by defining themes and describing in more detail the roles of themes in visitor experiences. It will examine the presentation and evolution of themes in TSVs before analysing themes and stories in some detail for four TSVs. These discussions of the role, presentation and evolution of themes in TSVs will particularly emphasise the importance of stories, perceived authenticity and regional distinctiveness.

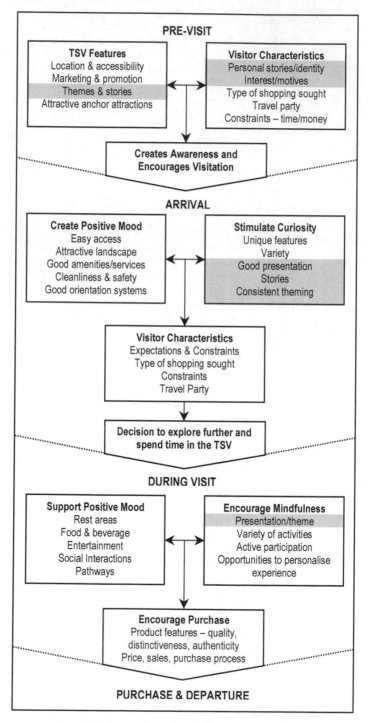

Figure 6.1 Highlighting the role of themes and presentation in the TSV visitor experience model.

THE ROLE OF THEMES IN TSVS

Themes have been discussed at some length in the both the literature on customer experiences and research into the effectiveness of interpretation, which is the presentation of information about a place or topic through the use of media such as guided tours, museums, brochures and information signs (Moscardo and Ballantyne 2008). In this interpretation literature a theme can be defined as "a singular statement that captures the meaning that we hope will be retained in a visitor's psyche" (Ham 2003). It is the central idea associated with place or topic that connects that place or topic to the audience, brings together other pieces of information, provides a point of interest and enhances memory for a place (Moscardo, Ballantyne and Hughes 2007). Interpretation studies have shown that themes can encourage visitors to be mindful by capturing their attention and by providing a way for them to link the place or topic to their personal interest or history (Moscardo, et al. 2007). Themes can enhance memory of an experience because they provide a coherent structure to information, making it easier for visitors to comprehend the information that is presented (Moscardo, et al. 2007). Interpretation studies have also found that themes are particularly effective in enhancing visitor experience when they are expressed through stories (Pierssene 1999).

Stories are explicitly linked to themes in the customer experience field (Boswijk, et al. 2005). Davis (1999), for example, defines themes as "pre-existing and well-understood narratives". McGoun et al. (2003) describe the use of themes as important in creating "a place for the entertainment of its visitors in which everything is designed to tell a story in which the visitor is encouraged to play a part" (649). As in the interpretation literature, themes also provide coherence through combining elements and information (Davis 1999). Themes as expressed through stories can encourage an emotional response from customers (Knutson and Beck 2003; Pullman and Gross 2004). Themes also serve as symbolic markers succinctly describing the nature of the experience on offer so that customers can select experiences that are consistent with and confirm their own identities (Davis 1999). For tourists, Hennig (2002) proposes that there are six types of theme or story that can be used to organise experiences:

- Opportunities for individual freedom;
- Seeking paradise;
- Experiencing the noble savage living in harmony with nature;
- Self-improvement through exposure to art and culture;
- The pursuit of social equality; and
- The redeeming power of nature.

The argument is that visitors seek experiences built around themes that best match their self-identity. In a similar argument, Goss (1999) proposes that four themes are associated with authenticity and these are often used to present shopping experiences and give visitors the opportunity to experience an idealized world. The four themes proposed are nature, primitive or ethnic culture, nostalgia for childhood and heritage. These four themes fit very well with the promotional material for TSVs presented in Table 6.1. An alternative way to look at stories and themes is to see them as providing a justification for the shopping or consumption experience. Hollenbeck, Peters and Zinkhan (2008) argue that shopping becomes more socially acceptable when it is framed within the context of activities such as:

- Opportunities for self-development;
- Learning, especially about heritage and/or environments;
- Building social connections to others;
- Being creative; or
- Experiencing culture.

In summary, themes can play a number of roles in the TSV visitor experience. They can attract visitor attention and allow them to make connections to their interests and identity, thus enhancing destination competitiveness and encouraging visitors to select a particular TSV. Themes can provide coherence to an experience, linking together information and activities, making it easier for visitors to organise and remember their experiences. Themes encourage an emotional response to an experience and assist in creating a perception of authenticity. Finally, themes provide a justification for visitors when explaining their behaviour to others. Themes are expressed most clearly through stories.

STORIES IN TOURIST EXPERIENCES

Stories are a specific type of narrative that present a series of events in a particular sequence which includes a beginning, ending and plot linking the events (Adaval and Wyer 1998). Stories are also distinguished by their purpose, which is to entertain (Brewer and Lichtenstein 1982). Woodside and colleagues (Hsu, Dehuang and Woodside 2009; Woodside, Cruickshank and Dehuang 2007; Woodside, Sood and Miller 2008) have adapted and applied a number of concepts from consumer researcher about stories to tourist reports on travel experiences, developing a story telling theory. This theory assumes that because people think in narratives and store information in their memory in stories, that they find it enjoyable to listen, relive and repeat stories. The theory then proposes that tourists seek to organise and make sense of their experience by creating and telling stories about that experience. Woodside and colleagues go on to present evidence from a number of different destinations that tourists do organise their memories and presentation of travel experience through stories. Thus it can be argued that experiences organised around stories are likely to be more attractive to visitors. The final component of the story telling theory is that stories that allow visitors to enact archetypes in classic myths are the most attractive (Woodside, et al. 2008).

The research into the use of themes and stories in both interpretation and consumer experience studies provides some consistent findings. In the case of themes there are two consistent conclusions across both areas of research. The first is that themes should be integrated into all aspects of the experience contributing to a sense of immersion (Benckendorff, Moscardo and Murphy 2006; Pullman and Gross 2004). The second is that some themes are stronger in their appeal and impact than others. More specifically, themes related to physical danger and survival under threat, families and family interactions, maintenance and enhancement of social relations, heroism, altruism and unique physical environments have been shown to be more effective than others (Davis and McLeod 2003; Sugiyama 2001). In the case of stories the research suggests that to be effective stories must present some sort of challenge and must allow the visitors to get involved in the story and personalise it in some way (Woodside, et al. 2008).

THE PRESENTATION OF THEMES AND STORY TELLING IN TSVS

Table 6.2 gives a summary of the various ways in which themes can be presented in a TSV. The key is for consistency through all the elements. In addition to expression through the elements listed in Table

Table 6.2   Methods of Presentation of Themes in TSVs

TSV Aspect	Presentation Options	Example Hahndorf
Promotion (websites, brochures)	Use the theme in slogans and descriptions of the offered experience, use images consistent with the theme	"Oldest surviving German settlement" With a sub-theme around German food and wine
Servicescape (landscaping, architecture)	Select architectural, streetscaping and land-scaping consistent with the theme	Retention of original archi-tecture and attempts to integrate new buildings into the existing heritage style
Events & festivals	The selection of events and festivals consistent with the theme	Arts festival based around a local German artist, Oktoberfest
Merchandise	Goods for sale consistent with the theme	Specialist food, German bread, butcher and hotel, and wine cellars
Activities & attractions (museums, galleries, etc)	Site visits, displays and activities that match the theme	Tours of a farm which is home to a German Jam company that sells in the TSV
Interpretation (guided tours, information centres, signs)	Information about the theme provided through these options	Tours of the artist's house

6.2, themes can be presented through the stories associated with a TSV. Stories about a TSV can be presented in the marketing of the TSV, in the interpretation onsite at a TSV, by the people who live and work in a TSV and by other visitors.

Exploring Themes and Stories in Hahndorf, Sedona, Kinsale and Bourton-on-the-Water

In order to better understand the role of themes and stories, a series of more detailed analyses of the data from the Tourist Shopping Village Project were conducted. This analysis of themes and stories in the TSV experience was conducted in two main stages. The first stage involved an evaluation of key features of 57 shopping villages in Australia, New Zealand, Canada, the United States, England, Ireland and Wales. The second stage consisted of in-depth analyses of four case study villages—Hahndorf in Australia, Sedona in the United States, Kinsale in Ireland and Bourton-on-the-Water in England.

The first stage updated the analysis reported in Murphy, Moscardo, Benckendorff and Pearce's (2008) study with an extended sample of villages. Table 6.3 lists the measures derived from a review of literature on factors that contribute to positive tourist experiences in built tourist attractions. The overall aim of this first stage was to explore the role of themes in the TSV visitor experience. The Murphy Moscardo, Benckendorff and Pearce (2008) study focussed on understanding the factors

---

Case Study 6.1   Hahndorf, South Australia

This village is located in the Adelaide Hills which are located on the outskirts of the South Australian State capital of Adelaide. It is one of several villages in the region that seek to attract visitors through their presentation as examples of the "rural idyll" with many of the original European buildings still in use and locations in scenic rural landscapes. The region is also home to many wineries and specialist food producers. Hahndorf has all these characteristics but in addition presents itself primarily through its German settlement heritage.

The first European settlement in the late 1840s was established by a group of German settlers who survived a challenging voyage under the care of Captain Dirk Hahn. The name Hahndorf was a gesture of gratitude for the Captain's leadership. These settlers were mostly farmers and established a wine-making tradition that continues to the present time as well as fruit orchards. One of these, Beerenberg Farm, is now a major tourist attraction and famous within Australia for its jams and fruit sauces. During the first World War the town changed its name to Ambleside as part of a response to widespread anti-German sentiment. But this was later reversed and in the 1970s the village began to celebrate its German heritage. In addition to the German food, wine and history, Hahndorf is also the home of the German Australian artist Hans Heysen and his house is open for tours.

(continued)

Case Study 6.1 (continued)

Figure 6.2   Images of German food and wine themes in Hahndorf.

The village is a State Heritage Area with 22 heritage listed buildings with strict design guidelines and planning regulations for new buildings. The village is now a popular destination for German food and wine, arts and German themed festivals and events and it shopping. The shops cover German themes, childhood nostalgia, art, food and general Australian rural crafts.

Case Study Sources:

http://en.wikipedia.org/wiki/Hahndorf,_South_Australia (accessed November 2007)
http://www.adhills.com.au.tourism/towns/hahndorf/body.html (accessed November 2007)
Dept. Environment and Heritage (2009) Hahndorf State Heritage Area. http://www.environment.sa.gov.au/heritage/shas/sha_hahndorf.html (accessed May 2010)

that contributed to perceived overall success as a tourist experience. But the discussions in Chapter 2 of issues related to the impact of TSV development on destination residents suggests that on its own this may be an inadequate measure of the overall success of a TSV. Further the results presented in the 2008 study suggest that the expert panel may have determined overall success based on perceptions of the overall scale of development, the extent to which the area was developed exclusively for tourist use and the evidence of planning for tourism through streetscaping and provision of visitor facilities. This approach to success places an exclusive emphasis on the needs of visitors and does not include the needs of destination residents. The review of TSV development pathways in Chapter 3 suggest that TSVs are more likely to bring positive benefits for destination residents if they offer regionally sourced and distinctive products as these are the most likely to bring benefits to local producers. So in this case the analysis was particularly interested in the role of themes in both the regional uniqueness of the shops and merchandise and the perceived overall success as a tourist experience.

Table 6.3   Features of Tourist Shopping Villages Included in the Inventory

Rating Scales *1= Low...7=High*	*Themes: presence & strength of theme* *1=weak...7=strong*
Perceived overall success as tourist experience	Distinctive Food/Local Produce
Shopping diversity	Heritage/History
Architectural cohesiveness	Creative & Performing Arts
Regional uniqueness of shops/ merchandise	Crafts
Food & wine	Environmental
Accommodation	Antiques
Frequency and extent of markets	Ethnic/Cultural
Frequency and extent of festivals	Health/Sports/Outdoor Recreation
Level of integration with village	
Density	
Accessibility (time, effort, money, transport networks)	
Streetscaping	
Gradient	
Marketing professionalism	
Perceived scale of development	
Tourist exclusivity	
Visitor logistics (toilets, car parks, seats, info centres)	
Effect of seasonality	
Extent of heritage conservation	
Aesthetic surrounds (i.e. landscape)	
Familiarity with village	

The first step in this stage was to factor analyse the features to reduce the number of variables. Table 6.4 provides a summary of this analysis. The factor analysis confirmed that regional distinctiveness was a key outcome variable as it emerged as a single item factor independent of other factors. The results also confirmed that overall success was associated strongly with the provision of tourist facilities such as car parks, the extent to which the village provided shopping opportunities exclusively for tourists, the level of development and the extent of streetscaping.

The second analysis conducted was a linear multiple regression analysis that used regional uniqueness as the dependent variable. Independent variables entered into the regression were the factors reported in Table 6.4 and the ratings of theme strength for all the themes identified. The final model was statistically significant (F=4.3, p<.0001, R square = .23) and the independent variables that demonstrated a significant relationship to the dependent variable in order of the strength of the relationship were

Table 6.4   Results of Principal Components Analysis of Shopping Village Features

Rating Scales	Factors				
	1	*2*	*3*	*4*	*5*
	Success	Service	Physical Design	Surrounds	Other
Extent of visitor logistics	.78				
Scale of development	.78				
Tourist exclusivity	.78				
Perceived overall success	.76				
Streetscaping	.64				
Extent of accommodation		.79			
Provision of food & wine		.71			
Provision of events/festivals		.70			
Marketing professionalism		.64			
Shopping diversity		.41			
Extent of heritage conservation			.85		
Architectural cohesiveness			.73		
Level of integration with the rest of village			.56		
Dispersed versus concentrate			.53		
Accessibility				-.76	
Aesthetic quality of surrounds				.67	
Flat versus steep				.55	
Seasonality					-.76
Markets					.59
% of variance explained	19%	14%	11%	8%	7%

theme strength for unique food and wine, crafts, heritage and ethnic culture. Further analysis found that having a heritage theme alone was rarely associated with either regional uniqueness or perceived overall success. The most effective combinations of themes appeared to be ethnic cultural heritage and unique food and/or wine, heritage and arts or crafts, environment and health/recreation and access to a particular environment. In order to explore these themes further a set of four shopping villages were chosen as case studies for more in-depth analysis. These four villages rated highly on both regional uniqueness of shops and merchandise and perceived success as a tourist experience. Each is also an example of a different theme or theme combination. Sedona (United States) combines art, crafts and access to a particular environment; Kinsale (Ireland) combines heritage with arts, crafts and fine dining; Hahndorf (Australia) combines ethnic heritage with regional food and wine; and Bourton-on-the-Water (England) which is primarily an example of a heritage/arts and crafts themed TSV. For each of the cases the following information was analysed in detail:

- Advertising information provided on official websites and in brochures made available in the village for visitors; and
- Ten travel stories provided on the Web by tourists to each case study village.

The weblogs were gathered from searches of sites such as Lonely Planet's Thorn Tree website (http://thorntree.lonelyplanet.com/), travel booking and information sites such as Trip Advisor (http://www.tripadvisor.com), sites devoted to travel diaries and images (http://www.travelpod.com/ and http://blogs.bootsnall.com/) and from general searches using Google to locate individual sites detailing travel experiences at one of the four target villages. For each village every second story located was chosen until a total of 10 stories were gathered. Both the advertising material and travel stories were content analysed with a particular emphasis on the themes associated with each village and the repeating of any stories about the village. Firstly they were examined for evidence of the recognition of the core marketing phrase identified in the advertising material. Secondly, the main phrases or words used to describe the village were identified and listed. In addition the importance of the village theme was examined in terms of whether or not the story included details describing the village theme or explanations of the significance or meaning of the village.

Table 6.5 summarises the content analyses of the four TSVs. Bourton-on-the-Water is presented as an authentic village remaining as it was, offering a nostalgic heritage experience that is also a way to experience the larger Cotswold region. Hahndorf has a very clear image—it is a German cultural experience supported by good food and wine. This TSV is strongly, clearly and repeatedly linked to the story of its first European settlers and their triumph over adversity. It offers a cultural and self-development opportunity for

Table 6.5 Results of the Content Analyses of the Promotional Material

Village	Content Analysis Results
Bourton-on-the-Water, England	Slogan/common phrase – Venice of the Cotswold/perfect English village Most commonly used words – river, scenic, unique, charming, quaint, original, pretty, most visited No stories presented Shopping for antiques and crafts listed as an activity Summary – exemplar of the Cotswolds region in architecture and food
Hahndorf, Australia	Slogan/common phrase – Australia's oldest surviving German settlement/a piece of Europe Most commonly used words – German, original, traditional, historic, scenic, wineries, food Story of the original German voyage and settlement, story of Hans Heysen the artist, story of the village name changes through the world wars Shopping for food and wine listed as an activity Summary – unique German historic settlement with great food and wine
Kinsale, Ireland	Slogan/common phrase – Take one spectacular location, season liberally with Norman, Spanish, English influence, add one major battle and let it simmer for 400 years – the result, Ireland's fine food capital/ quaint area of antiquity Most commonly used words – historic, picturesque, sailing, popular, art, fine food Stories of the Battle of Kinsale, the sinking of the Lusitania, history of the wine cellars and wine trade with Spain and France Shopping for art and fine food promoted Summary – convergence of culture, history and fine dining
Sedona, USA	Slogan/common phrase – red rock country Most commonly used words – red sandstone, spiritual, new age, classic westerns, beauty, colours, unique geology, eclectic, interesting Story of the first European settlers Shopping discussed extensively Summary – gateway to unique natural environments.

visitors with exposure to history, architecture, art and fine wine and food. A combination of wine, fine dining and history are also at the core of the promotion of Kinsale. Kinsale is presented as a meeting place for cultures (Spanish, French and Irish) through trade in wine. The focus on gourmet food is particularly strong and reflects deliberate action by local groups to develop this feature of the village. Sedona has a very different presentation as a gateway to unique natural environments. Like Bourton-on-the-Water, regional distinctiveness is important in the promotional material for Sedona. Sedona is the only village that actively promotes shopping as both a core activity and reason for visiting. But it is presented as a special and different kind of shopping: "When you shop in Sedona, you are likely to be delighted and surprised. There is so much to discover ... Shopping in Sedona is more of a sightseeing adventure than a stop in a mall. Sedona's shopping districts are nestled among the town's world-famous red rocks" (Sedona Chamber of Commerce 2010).

The analysis of the weblogs suggests that the use of stories in the Hahndorf promotional material is effective in encouraging visitor interest. All but one of the 10 weblogs repeated the German theme and four repeated the story of German settlement in detail. In addition four included some discussion about feeling like they were in Europe. Shopping was mentioned by only three visitors and it was about the opportunity to purchase regionally produced food. These weblogs were also the most positive of the four villages examined with seven recommending a visit to the village to others. Only two mentioned other villages in the area.

The next most often recommended TSV was Sedona. In this case it appeared that the highlight was its unique physical location. The following are a selection of the phrases used to describe the surrounding environment:

- "The colors still amaze me";
- "Spectacular canyons and distinctive stunning scenery";
- "It's all red rocks, green trees and blue skies";
- "Magnificent rock formations, mostly red in colour";
- "Spectacular with giant mountains of colourful rock";
- "Truly beautiful with amazing red rock formations";
- "Simply stunning";
- "SO beautiful";
- "Sculptured red rocks are magnificent shapes"; and
- "You just can't get over how amazing this place is".

The colour, rock formations and the blending of the architecture into the environment were all notable features reported in the weblogs. Sedona was also associated with shopping with six weblogs reporting the activity and three of these commenting on the unique nature of the experience. Only one story was included in the weblogs and it was a personal story of the visitor's unsuccessful quest to find a new age vortex in the red rock country.

Shopping was mentioned in only one weblog about Kinsale and only three recommended a visit to Kinsale to others. The weblogs were generally positive and focussed on descriptions of the physical features of Kinsale—architecture, winding streets, harbour and historic attractions. The core element of the Kinsale weblogs was the fine dining experience. The importance of its history and its trade with Spain and France were only included in two weblogs and in both cases the stories presented were linked to the visitors' being told the story by a guide at a historic site. This highlights the importance of interpretation in presenting TSV stories to visitors. The only other story included in the sample of weblogs was about seeing a dolphin the harbour. Most of the Kinsale weblogs also mentioned other nearby villages with Kinsale presented as one stop in a multi-destination trip. Shopping was not presented as a core activity.

Bourton-on-the-Water was also presented in the majority of weblogs as one village amongst a set of Cotswolds villages that offered very similar experiences and only one visitor made a recommendation specific to Bourton-on-the-Water. Several noted that it, like several villages in the region, was an example of a perfect English village. Three weblogs repeated the slogan "Venice of the Cotswolds", but in each case the visitor felt the description was inaccurate. Only one story was reported and it was about the challenge of visiting the areas in heavy rain. Three discussed shopping and particularly noted the attractiveness of unique, original independent stores.

Overall this analysis suggested that regional distinctiveness and strong and consistent presentation of themes through the architecture and activities offered in a TSV are important elements of an attractive visitor experience. For visitors, regional distinctiveness is most readily associated with architecture, food and wine. Visitors also responded very positively to the use of stories in the presentation of TSVs.

THE EVOLUTION OF THEMES AND STORIES IN TSVS

The challenge for those promoting a TSV is to find a story and/or theme that is appealing and can be easily linked to the TSV and its history or location. The previous analysis suggests that the ability to meet this challenge is partly determined by the location and history of a TSV. Thus Sedona and Hahndorf have been able to make the most of their unique location and cultural history respectively. Other TSVs have been able to build themes around events, historic sites and famous characters associated with the location. Without a unique story and a theme that both attracts visitors and connects them to the TSV location, it can be difficult for a TSV to develop a competitive profile.

Another challenge for TSVs is to find stories that are acceptable to the residents. For example, the Mennonite Community surrounding St. Jacobs is an important drawcard for tourists. However, it is difficult to fully develop the theme through active interpretation because Mennonites are traditionally very private people and most limit their contact with the outside world. Tourist exposure is limited to observing the daily lives of Mennonites from afar and to business transactions with those who choose to use the village as a place to sell their produce, small goods and baking. The story telling is limited to static displays and video footage in the Mennonite Museum (see Case Study 6.2). In Chapter 2 we reviewed a number of issues and conflicts related to the development of tourism in TSVs. Many of these conflicts were related to differences in the stories that different groups associated with their village. A more thorough examination of the stories of locals may be a useful exercise both to manage conflict and to generate unique and authentic themes for the experience offered to tourists.

Case Study 6.2   St. Jacobs, Ontario, Canada

St. Jacobs was first known as 'Jakobstettel' which means 'Jacobs Village'. St. Jacobs was officially named in 1852, the 'St.' being added 'for the sake of euphony' and the pluralisation was in honour of the combined efforts of Jacobs C. Snider and his son by the same name – founders of the Village. The first creamery in Ontario (the third in Canada) was begun in St. Jacobs in 1874. During its 98 years of operation, St. Jacobs Creamery won prizes and wide acclaim for the superb quality of its butter.

The Mennonites trekked from Pennsylvania in Conestoga Wagons and settled in and around St. Jacobs in the late 1700s and early 1800s, making St. Jacobs one of the original Mennonite settlements in Ontario. Today, the rural areas around St. Jacobs Country are populated with many Old Order Mennonite farmers who retain the religion, customs and lifestyle of their nineteenth century forefathers. Interest in this unique group of people has increased dramatically over the past 20 years and visitors from all over the world want to learn about the culture of the Old Order Mennonites.

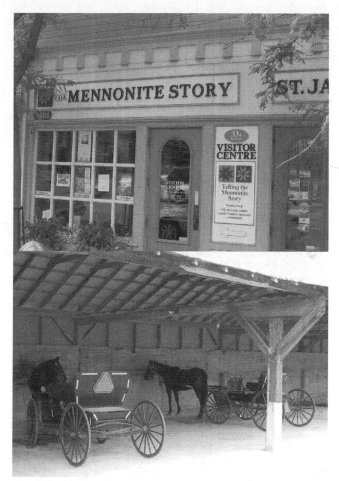

Figure 6.3   The use of the Mennonite story at St. Jacobs.

(continued)

Case Study 6.2   (continued)

The evolution of St. Jacobs as a tourist shopping village began in the 1970s when The Stone Crock restaurant, specialising in Pennsylvania Dutch cuisine, opened in the former grocery store and the flour mill were converted to the Country Mill and Village Silos. The Mill and Silos are home to a range of fashion boutiques, craft shops, galleries and historic exhibits. The Village is a haven for both contemporary and traditional crafts, many being made onsite in Village workshops, such as brooms, weavers, glass and metal studies, and a soapery. The Village is also well-known for the range of handmade Mennonite quilts available for purchase.

The market district is home to the popular St. Jacobs Farmer's and Flea Market, consisting of more than 600 vendors selling meats, cheese, baking, local crafts, home decor, furniture, clothes, tools, house wares, and more. The rich agricultural heritage of the region means that there is a range of fresh produce from local farm gardens as well as from across Ontario.

In the 1990s the traditional drawcards to the region were somewhat controversially added to with the introduction of the St. Jacobs Outlet Mall. Despite being housed in a 'barn-like' structure in order to fit in with the neighbouring Farmer's Market, the introduction of this style of shopping, along with the Best Western Country Inn, is a clear divergence from the original ethnic heritage and arts and crafts retail focus, and from the more traditional bed and breakfast accommodation.

Case Study Sources:

http://www.stjacobs.com/html/history.html (accessed May 2010)

7 The Interactive Shopping Village Experience

INTRODUCTION

This chapter develops an understanding of the shopping experience itself. In contrast to previous chapters which have provided a rich array of information on the contexts in which tourists shop, the material considered in the following sections focuses on the design and planning of the visitor experiences. The core elements of this chapter are highlighted in Figure 7.1. It will be argued throughout this chapter that the shopping experience is a hybrid of visitors' involvement in and evaluations of the available activities, products, services and places engineered by the retailers and local authorities (Tosun, et al. 2007). It is not a passive experience, either physically or cognitively. Shopping is a recreational activity that involves planning, looking, touching, browsing, thinking and buying. The nature of the experience is constructed by visitors in the sense that their motives for attending shopping settings influence their attention, length of stay and behavioural routines. A starting point for the consideration of the visitors' experiences lies with the topic of visitor motivation. There is some direct material assessing and considering this issue and some less direct but interesting information from market segmentation studies. Some of this material on market segmentation studies and visitor motives for shopping was discussed in Chapter 1 of this volume. A select sample of that material and some additional material is presented in the following section with a specific focus on the motivation for types of visitor experiences. These research efforts will be developed and discussed in the first part of this chapter. Subsequent sections of the chapter will review some of the processes and opportunities which can be implemented to engage visitors and fashion their experiences.

VISITORS' NEEDS AND MOTIVES

Shopping may fulfil people's need for enjoyment and relaxation, and is sometimes seen as providing an escape from their daily routines (Timothy 2005). For tourists, the quest for a pleasurable shopping experience may be more significant than the acquisition of products. It has also been suggested

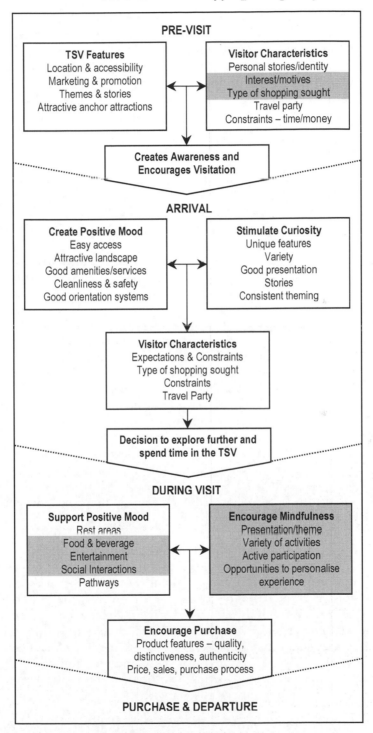

Figure 7.1 A model of the TSV visitor experience.

that the likelihood of returning to a shopping district such as a village is quite likely to result from experiences where the entertainment and novelty value of the setting is high (Yüksel 2007).

Elements of spontaneity, captivation, arousal and excitement are fundamental motivations for hedonic forms of shopping (Tauber 1995) and should be incorporated into retail marketing strategies. Hedonic consumption has been defined as those facets of behaviour that relate to the multisensory, fantasy and emotive aspects of consumption (Holbrook and Hirschman, 1982 as cited by Arnold and Reynolds 2003). Hedonic shopping motives can be separated from the task orientation of utilitarian shopping motives, although both share the power to direct behaviour (Babin and Attaway 2000). In particular hedonic motives encourage a lingering and slow appreciation of the shopping environment while utilitarian motives shape fast transactions where the convenience to the shopper is often paramount.

Tauber (1995) identifies both individual and social motives for shopping. Individual motives include escape, self-gratification, learning about new trends, physical exercise and sensory stimulation. Social motives are equally important and diverse. Throughout history the marketplace has traditionally been a centre of social activity. In the contemporary world social components of shopping settings persist and are powerful. Key social motives include communication with others having similar interests, peer group attraction, opportunities to establish status and authority and the interactive pleasure of bargaining. The multiplicity of hypothesized individual and social hedonic motives suggest that individuals may go shopping when they need attention, want to be with peers, desire to meet people with similar interests, feel a need to exercise or simply want to engage in diversionary leisure (Tauber 1995). In the context of tourist shopping villages, the importance of viewing the visitor experience as a complete leisure experience is evident.

Several studies have identified segments of shoppers with differing activity participation profiles. Carmichael and Smith (2004) identified five rural shopper segments. Respondents in the 'shopping vacation only' segment were mostly female, had lower incomes and tended to be on day trips. The 'short vacation' and 'getaway and visiting friends and relatives' segments also participated in a small number of other activities (e.g. VFR, and visiting a theme park or a museum). However, the 'outdoors and sports' segment was highly active, participating in a wide range of activities during their trip (VFR, sports and outdoor activities, sports events, bars and nightclubs and sightseeing). Finally, the 'long vacationer' segment was on a trip of seven days or more and was highly active. They participated in sightseeing, visiting historic sites and visiting friends and relatives. These findings are consistent with those of Littrell et al. (2004), who found that shopping was an important activity to a group of senior travellers classified as cultural tourists, based on their focus on attending theatre, concerts and festivals, visiting galleries and museums and eating local food. The three identified clusters, Active Outdoor/Cultural Tourists, Cultural Tourists and Moderate Tourists, illustrated linkages between preferred travel activities and a variety of shopping behaviours. Among these senior travellers, shopping was integrated with a range of other activities, including recreational pursuits.

Moscardo (2004) segmented visitors to North Queensland, Australia based on the importance of shopping in destination choice and shopping behaviours. The results revealed that 'serious shoppers' had high levels of participation in most of the activities available in the region and high levels of attendance at many of the commercial tourist attractions in the region. The 'non-shoppers' were quite different to the serious shoppers. The non-shoppers chose the destination for different reasons, had the lowest participation rates for most activities and were markedly less likely to attend tourist attractions. The 'arts and craft shoppers' shopped only for local arts and crafts, stated that opportunities to shop were not important to their destination choice, and were significantly more interested in experiencing indigenous culture and meeting locals. The 'not-so-serious shoppers' engaged in a range of shopping activities, despite not rating shopping opportunities as an important destination choice factor. This group had high levels of participation in general, but especially in active, outdoor, marine-based activities.

A report by the Ontario Ministry of Tourism on U.S. and Ontarian shopping travellers identified and compared six shopper segments based on the main focus of their purchase—clothing, shoes and jewellery, books and music, antiques, gourmet foods, arts and crafts and garden centre (Ontario Ministry of Tourism 2007b). The report revealed that those whose main interest was shopping for clothes, shoes and jewellery participated in the fewest number of different activities while on a trip. They primarily engaged in dining at restaurants that offer local cuisine, visiting local cafés and strolling around the city to observe its buildings and architecture (Ontario Ministry of Tourism 2007b). In addition to these activities, other common pursuits for at least one-third of travellers included visiting a casino, visiting an amusement park, sunbathing or sitting on a beach. The segments other than clothing shoppers were also likely to visit historic sites/buildings or a nature, national or provincial park. The gourmet foods and garden centre segments were the most active shoppers. The gourmet food segment exhibited a desire to eat in local and high end restaurants and cafés, and visit wineries, art galleries, and seaside resorts more so than the garden segment. They were less likely to visit parks, zoos, and botanical gardens, appearing to have less interest in activities that normally appeal to families travelling with children (Ontario Ministry of Tourism 2007b).

The importance of the combination of shopping and dining was further explored by the Ontario Ministry of Tourism in additional research on the

American market. It revealed that during 2004–5, 60.4 per cent of adult Americans went shopping and dining while out of town on a trip of one or more nights (Ontario Ministry of Tourism 2007d). Relative to the average U.S. Pleasure Traveller, shoppers and diners were slightly more likely to participate in culture and entertainment activities. The majority visited historical sites, museums and art galleries, theme parks and exhibits, casinos, theatres, comedy clubs and fairs and festivals. They were also somewhat more likely to have visited cultural exhibits as well as food-related attractions. In terms of outdoor activities, shoppers and diners were most likely to participate in ocean-related activities and wildlife viewing. They were also more likely than the average U.S. Pleasure Traveller to go hiking, climbing and paddling, to exercise and jog and to play games and individual sports. These kinds of studies from the destinations where the researchers have studied tourist shopping villages begin to build a complex pattern of types of shoppers with subtly different patterns of motives and behavioural choices.

In another study in one of the regions where tourist shopping villages are quite common, Frost (2006) examined two heritage centres in the state of Victoria in the southern part of Australia. He considered visitor activity patterns in the small towns of Castlemaine and Maldon, which have developed as venues for tourist shopping and hospitality in the Goldfields region, which lies just over 100 kilometres to the west of the main city of Melbourne. Both towns have large numbers of cafés and food shops, many of which duplicate the ambience of sophisticated metropolitan establishments. Tourism Victoria (2008) visitor statistics for this region indicate that 83 per cent of international visitors to the Goldfields shop for pleasure, 93 per cent dine at a restaurant and/or café, 53 per cent visit history/ heritage buildings, sites or monuments and 49 per cent visited museums or art galleries. Frost's (2006) research indicated that the main heritage activities participated in by visitors were visiting historic buildings, visiting historic mining areas, riding a restored steam train and visiting a museum. The main shopping and hospitality activities were eating at a restaurant or café, visiting antiques shops and visiting a gallery or craft shop. The data confirmed the observations that heritage and shopping are important elements of the tourist experiences in both towns. The results also indicated that those who engaged in shopping were more likely to stay overnight, visit historic buildings, parks, gardens and museums and to ride steam trains (Frost 2006).

THE SHOPPING VILLAGE AS A COMPLETE LEISURE EXPERIENCE

It is clear from the studies reviewed in the previous section that shopping tourists engage in many activities other than shopping. Carmichael and Smith (2004) claim that the variety of activities of rural visitors reflects the fact that tourist trips are often multipurpose and while many of these activities, including shopping, may not be the main reason for the visit, together they form an attractive rural tourism product. Rural areas tend to have an attraction base for nature-based and cultural tourism, and the staging of festivals and events is a strategy often adopted by rural areas to enhance tourist-visitation.

The activity profile of shoppers, particularly those in regional areas, highlights that a successful shopping village will not just focus on its shops and the products they sell, but the overall leisure experience provided to its visitors, both within the shops and in terms of additional recreational activities on offer in and around the village. Complementary leisure activities can also serve to increase length of stay in the village, encouraging overnight stops rather than day visits. Many of the operators who participated in the Australian focus group study identified the fact that their village was in close proximity to national parks, bushwalking and bike trails provided a major strength for their location. Combined with a variety of accommodation and quality dining experiences, tourist shopping villages can offer an appealing weekend or short stay to potential visitors, rather than just a day trip or a couple of hours of leisurely shopping.

The literature on 'experiential marketing' and entertaining experiences can inform this closer examination of enhancing the offerings of tourist shopping villages. Arnold and Reynolds (2003) comment on the fact that many retailers are responding to the threat of Internet-based shopping by leveraging the 'brick and mortar' advantages that virtual retailers cannot match—higher levels of service, highly trained staff, and an entertaining and fun retail environment.

The entertainment aspect of retailing, or 'entertailing' is increasingly being recognised as a key competitive tool that focuses on satisfying hedonic shopping motives (Arnold and Reynolds 2003). The Canadian Tourism Commission reports on the Vaughan Mills shopping centre north of Toronto, Ontario. This centre claims to have coined the term 'shoppertainment' and places an emphasis on a richly-textured high-quality shopping experience. The shopping complex includes a NASCAR Speedpark, featuring indoor and outdoor race and go-kart tracks. There is also an upscale bowling lane and the largest specialty hockey store in Canada. The retail hockey complex is being designed as a themed, interactive environment with an indoor ice pad, providing opportunities to try out the merchandise before committing to purchase. According to the marketing director, Jamie McLean, to refine the experiential journey even further, the shopping centre is broken up into six neighbourhoods and six transition courts, themed to expose visitors to meticulously conceived architectural environments at six entrance ways. MacLean explains that the over-arching theme is 'Discover Ontario' with neighbourhoods themed for lakes, natural, rural, small town and city. As a result Vaughan Mills is not just about shopping; it is about adventure and the emotional connection that appeals to all the senses. The mall has also developed extensive partnerships with the tourism industry through a standing package promotion with seven local hotels and 70,000 coupon books distributed annually to tourists (Canadian Tourism Commission 2007).

In their examination of postmodern ballparks, Ritzer and Stillman (2001) highlight the increasingly blurred line between leisure sites and consumption settings. They claim that in the past a visit to a leisure site was mainly about leisure, and the consumption that occurred there involved mainly the site and the activities that transpired in it. Today, however, the vast majority of leisure sites involve the consumption of a wide array of goods and services. For example, they note the increasing presence of shopping malls, food courts, breweries and museums within the 'boundaries' of ballparks. Conversely, visiting a consumption site in the past mainly involved obtaining goods and services; leisure-time activities were secondary. However, many of today's consumption sites have internalized elements of once fairly distinct leisure sites. Thus people now go to consumption sites to engage in leisure-time activities and consumption itself has become the major leisure-time activity for many people. In theoretical terms, whatever boundaries existed between leisure and consumption have 'imploded,' as have those between the settings that we think of as being devoted to each (Ritzer and Stillman 2001). Among other things, the implosion of leisure and consumption stimulates the imagination of consumers by creating a spectacle that combines the fantasy qualities of the leisure industry with the commodities of the consumption industry. Such settings are designed to be more magical and involving than those that are either purely about leisure or consumption.

Richards and Wilson (2006) argue that one of the major problems that places face in a competitive global environment is how to maintain, develop and utilise their distinctiveness, which increasingly focuses on producing distinctive experiences for consumers. The word 'experience' is widely used in leisure, retail and other service sectors to describe the essence of what consumers are seeking and paying for (Morgan 2006). Pine and Gilmore (1998) contend that it is memorable experiences rather than product or service quality that create sustainable competitive advantage and that an experience occurs when the service is performed in a unique and memorable way in which the consumer is involved as a participant. Unique and memorable experiences are achieved through dramatising the service encounter, appealing to all the senses and telling stories about the brand.

According to Williams (2006), experiential marketing has become a cornerstone of many recent advances in areas such as retailing, branding and events marketing, however, marketing in the tourism and hospitality sectors does not appear to have explicitly engaged the theoretical issues involved. Experiential marketing was first introduced by Pine and Gilmore (1998), who explain the concept by saying that when individuals buy a service, they purchase a set of intangible activities carried out on their behalf. By way of contrast, when individuals buy an experience they pay to spend time enjoying a series of memorable events that a company stages to engage them in a personal way. Experiential marketing is about taking the essence of a product and amplifying it into a set of tangible, physical, interactive experiences which reinforce the offer. It has evolved as a response to a perceived transition from a service economy to one personified by the experiences in which we participate. According to Williams (2006), the fact that their product is almost always experiential puts tourism and hospitality marketers in a unique position to apply the principles of experiential marketing to their activities. The challenge is that simply having an intrinsically, inherently experiential offering is very different from actively and deliberately marketing that offer in an experiential manner. Experiential marketing helps firms to avoid the commodification trap and Williams (2006) claims that those who go beyond service excellence and market experientially will lead the creation of value in the sector. While prior economic offerings—commodities, goods and services—are external to the buyer, experiences are inherently personal, existing only in the mind of an individual who has been engaged on an emotional, physical, intellectual or even spiritual level. Thus, no two people can have the same experience, because each experience derives from the interaction between the staged event (like a theatrical play) and the individual's state of mind (Williams 2006). The kinds of experiential marketing reviewed in the preceding sections depend in part on a core base of well-designed local experiences. Attention will now be directed towards some recent consideration of the elements and components of experience design and commentary on the relevance of these ideas for tourists' experiences in shopping villages will be presented.

EXPERIENCE DESIGN

Pine and Gilmore (1998) suggest that experiences can be considered with a four cell structure defined by two dimensions. The first corresponds to customer participation; at one end of the dimension there is passive participation, in which customers do not affect the performance at all. At the other end of the spectrum lies active participation, in which customers play key roles in creating the performance or event that yields the experience (Pine and Gilmore 1998). The second dimension of experience describes the connection, or environmental relationship, that unites customers with the event or performance. At one end of the connection dimension there is absorption, at the other end, immersion. For example, on the participation construct someone watching a film in a cinema would be passive, whilst someone dining in a restaurant, active. In a similar manner someone watching a tourism spectacle such as a parade from a hotel balcony, can absorb the event taking place beneath them, whilst someone on the street would be immersed in the sights, sounds and smells that surround them.

According to Pine and Gilmore (2002), any company can move to differentiate its offering by creatively orchestrating multiple dimensions of one's hospitality business as distinct theatrical events within an overall experience. Guests obtain a memorable experience when a company intentionally uses services as the stage and goods as props to engage individual customers in an inherently personal way. In the hospitality and lodging industry, almost any service can be leveraged to stage a more compelling experience (Pine and Gilmore 2002). Experiences, like goods and services, have to meet a customer need; they have to work; and they have to be deliverable. Just as goods and services result from an iterative process of research, design and development, experiences derive from an iterative process of exploration, scripting and staging—capabilities that aspiring experience merchants will need to master (Pine and Gilmore 1998).

Harris, Harris and Baron (2003) claim that in retailing the notion of 'theatre' has seen widespread global adoption across most sectors as a means for creating memorable experiences for consumers. Baron, Harris and Harris (2001: 103) note that "retail theatre is generally presented as a 'fun' experience involving spectacle and excitement". However, they also note that there is little evidence that there has been any serious attempt by retailers to go beyond the use of the theatre metaphor as a purely literary device that creates a theatrical vocabulary for generating attractive sounding ideas. The exceptions are where themed retail environments have been created with the purpose of employing retail theatre to encourage consumers to animate the theme. This concept of retail theatre can be incorporated both by individual shops in a TSV and by the village as a whole.

The Family and Company Toy Store in Stratford, Ontario Canada provides a good example of the first application. The 'stage' is set before customers even enter the store with outdoor displays spilling onto the sidewalk, including permanent chess and checker boards set up for the public to use. Once customers make their way into the store they encounter staff dressed in various costumes who not only greet but interact with customers by demonstrating toys and performing magic tricks on a small magic theatre stage. A craft area is also set up at the rear of the store to host workshops and birthday parties. For children this is not just another toy store, it is a magical and memorable experience where they are encouraged to touch and feel the merchandise, not just look.

Despite the fact that Stratford is a theatre town, home to Canada's Shakespearean Festival Theatre (see Case Study 7.1), none of the other stores take advantage of the logical theatrical opportunities to the same extent as Family and Company. The theatre itself has many opportunities for visitors to engage behind the scenes in activities which range from concerts, tours, lectures and discussions to multi-day workshops for budding thespians. There is great potential to bring more 'theatre' to the downtown shopping area. If the scope of retail theatre is broadened to incorporate a TSV as a whole, there are many opportunities for business owners and tourism authorities to work together to provide an integrated and entertaining experience to visitors through the use of, for example, street entertainment and performers, live music, arts and crafts demonstrations, and festivals and events. However, care needs to be taken to ensure that the 'theatre performance' is consistent with the culture and theme of the village and is perceived to be not only unique but to have a degree of authenticity.

Dholakia and Schroeder (2001) comment on the Disney approach to marketing and the concept of consumption spectacles. The spectacles in the Disney environments are not merely static attractions; there is a constant creation of spectacles through 'happenings'. On any single day during tourist season, Disney theme parks across the world create as many as a

---

Case Study 7.1　Stratford on the Avon, Ontario, Canada

Stratford, Ontario, Canada which lies on the Avon River and has a total population of around 30,000 is one of the largest shopping villages. The village is a two hour drive from Toronto, 2.5 hours from Buffalo and three hours from Detroit. While Stratford is surrounded by fertile farming land, it is best known for its Shakespearian history. The area was first settled in 1832 and named after Stratford-upon-Avon, England, of Shakespearean fame. The annual Shakespearean Stratford Festival started in 1953 and has been a major contributor to the local economy since that time. The Festival attracts close to half a million theatre goers and tourists to the area and runs from April to November. Financial information for the Stratford Festival for 2007 indicates that 61 per cent of the theatre's income is earned through sales to the performances, totalling more than $33 million. The broader economic impact of spending in the region attributable to the Stratford Festival is $125 million with more than 3,000 jobs created either directly or indirectly. Estimated attendance at 2008 performances was 528,000 people.

Stratford has a wide range and a large number of shops and services, due to its size. Because of its reputation as an arts centre, many shops sell a variety of antique and contemporary art products, locally made pottery and small giftware. 'Gift and specialty shops' is the largest category, with 35 listed businesses. Stratford has a roughly even mix of fine and casual dining (overall around 60 restaurants and dining options). For visitors who choose to stay overnight or longer, there are more than 70 accommodation providers. These consist of B&Bs, camping areas, hotels and inns, motels and resorts and suites and apartments. There are as many as 53 B&Bs, which is the largest accommodation category, targeting the main visitor groups.

(continued)

Case Study 7.1 (continued)

Figure 7.2   Family and Co. Toy Store and the Amazing Clayworks.

History of the Stratford Festival Theatre

That Stratford, Ontario, is the home of the largest classical repertory theatre in North America is ultimately attributable to the dream of one man, Stratford-born journalist Tom Patterson.

In the early 1950s, seeing the economy of his home town endangered by the withdrawal of the railway industry that had sustained it for nearly 80 years, Patterson conceived the idea of a theatre festival devoted to the works of William Shakespeare. His vision won the support not only of Stratford City Council and an enthusiastic committee of citizens but also of the legendary

(continued)

Case Study 7.1   (continued)

British actor and director Tyrone Guthrie, who agreed to become the proposed festival's first Artistic Director. The Stratford Shakespearean Festival of Canada was incorporated as a legal entity on October 31, 1952; a giant canvas tent was ordered from a firm in Chicago; and in the parklands by Stratford's Avon River work began on a concrete amphitheatre at the centre of which was to be a revolutionary thrust stage created to Guthrie's specifications by internationally renowned theatrical designer Tanya Moiseiwitsch.

From that stage, on the night of July 13, 1953, actor Alec Guinness spoke the opening lines of Richard III: *Now is the winter of our discontent / Made glorious summer by this son of York.* Those words marked the triumphant end of what had sometimes seemed a hopeless struggle against the odds to turn Patterson's dream into a reality and the beginning of an astonishing new chapter in Canadian theatre history.

In the years since its first season the Stratford Festival of Canada has set benchmarks for the production not only of Shakespeare, Molière, the ancient Greeks and other great dramatists of the past but also of such ninetheen century masters as Samuel Beckett, Bertolt Brecht, Anton Chekhov, Henrik Ibsen, Eugene O'Neill and Tennessee Williams. In addition to acclaimed productions of the best in operetta and musical theatre, it has also showcased and in many cases premiered works by outstanding Canadian and other contemporary playwrights. Its artists have included the finest actors, directors and designers in Canada, as well as many from abroad.

Drawing audiences of more than 600,000 each year, the Festival season now runs from April to November and includes a full program of fringe activities, including concert recitals, discussion sessions and readings by celebrated authors. It offers an extensive program of educational and enrichment activities for students, teachers and other patrons, and operates its own in-house school of professional artist development: the Stratford Festival Conservatory for Classical Theatre Training. The Festival is currently building a $50 million Endowment Foundation to ensure that its founder's dream remains a reality for all time.

Case Study Sources:

http://www.stratfordfestival.ca/about/history.cfm (accessed May 2010)
http://www.city.stratford.on.ca/ (accessed May 2010)

dozen spectacles and extravaganzas. However, because Disney structures the consumer experience so carefully, it is often difficult to 'own' one's encounter with a Disney theme park. When guests arrive at Walt Disney World they know what to expect, what they will do, what they will videotape and photograph and what they will talk about upon their return home. For example, to ensure amateurs take home good-quality photos and videos, helpful signs to the best vantage points in Disney Parks are provided courtesy of Kodak. Disney provides a totally scripted consumer experience. They have even created a totally planned community called Celebration— where property owners can take up residence in a utopian version of an

American Town. While there is much to learn from the Disney approach to experience management, there are many critics of this staged approach to service delivery in that it creates an artificial version of reality, or 'hyper-reality' (Giroux 1994, 1999; Holbrook 2001; Kline 1995; Kunster 1993). The critics argue that Disney has created an idealised version of reality and its Main Street USA is a utopian and sanitised version of small town America. Indeed, Pine and Gilmore have moved on to write about 'authentic' experiences and argue that, because Disney has been part of our culture for so many years it has become authentic, claiming that in a world increasingly filled with deliberately and sensationally staged experiences—an increasingly unreal world—consumers choose to buy or not buy based on how real they perceive an offering to be. They claim that successful business today, therefore, is all about being real, original, genuine, sincere and authentic (Gilmore and Pine 2007).

The lesson for tourist shopping villages is to recognise the need to provide visitors with a satisfying leisure experience, both within individual shops and within the broader context of the village and its surrounds. This experience should not be one that is perceived as contrived or manufactured but should be rooted in the local culture and character that is distinct to that region and its resources. This requires creativity and cooperation on the part of the local businesses and tourism authorities to develop a more organic visitor experience that can be engaged in at different levels by different visitor markets. The main lesson from the experiential marketing literature is that the most satisfying experiences are the ones in which the visitor feels involved and immersed and in which their individual participation results in the experience being unique and personal to them.

Colonial Williamsburg provides a good example of an interactive visitor experience by creating a living history museum (see Case Study 7.2). Shopping and retail are imbedded both within the historic district itself and the adjacent Merchant's Square. Similar to St. Jacobs Mennonite village in Ontario, Canada, the shopping opportunities have diverged from those consistent with the ethnic or heritage appeal of the locations, to incorporate outlet shopping on a much larger scale in nearby precincts.

Closely aligned to this discussion of the experience design at TSVs is Richards and Wilson's (2006) discussion of creative tourism. They cite Richards and Raymond (2000: 18) who defined creative tourism as "tourism which offers visitors the opportunity to develop their creative potential through active participation in courses and learning experiences which are characteristic of the holiday destination where they are undertaken." According to Richards and Wilson (2006), creative tourism arguably has a number of potential advantages over 'traditional' tourism because creativity allows destinations to innovate new products relatively rapidly, giving them competitive advantage over other locations. Because creativity is a process, creative resources are generally more sustainable and more mobile than tangible cultural products. Creativity involves not just value creation (economic wealth) but the creation of values. The application of creativity

Case Study 7.2   Colonial Williamsburg, Virginia, U.S.

Colonial Williamsburg is the historic district of the city of Williamsburg, Virginia and consists of many of the buildings that, from 1699 to 1780, formed colonial Virginia's capital. Williamsburg, Yorktown and Jamestown make up the Historic Triangle of Virginia and are also well-represented by world-class accommodations, attractions, restaurants, and golf resorts. Colonial Williamsburg is the nation's largest living history museum, encompassing 301 acres including some 500 buildings, homes, stores and taverns reconstructed and restored to their eighteenth century appearances; tradesmen practising 30 historic trades and domestic crafts; historical interpreters and character actors; and 90 acres of gardens and greens, and now featuring the live action drama, Revolutionary City™, daily from mid-March to the holiday season. Colonial Williamsburg is owned and operated as a living museum by the Colonial Williamsburg Foundation, the non-profit entity endowed initially by the Rockefeller family. Central to the Rockefeller vision of Williamsburg was the need for retailing to not only pay for the upkeep of Williamsburg, but also to aid in educating visitors through affordable reproductions. Colonial Williamsburg is an open-air assemblage of buildings populated with historical re-enactors whose job it is to explain and demonstrate aspects of daily life in the past. The re-enactors work, dress and talk as they would have in colonial times. Items available for purchase include leather goods, jewellery, clothing and food.

Figure 7.3   The Colonial Williamsburg General Store (source: Wikimedia).

Over 4,000,000 people visit the Williamsburg area every year to experience the award-winning, authentic, interactive tours of the times and lives of colonial ancestors. Located adjacent to Colonial Williamsburg's Historic Area, Merchant's Square is a charming retail village featuring more than 40 shops, a variety of restaurants and even an art gallery. Adjacent to the interstate is Prime Outlets-Williamsburg, the largest outlet shopping facility in south-eastern Virginia with over 120 designer and brand name outlet stores.

Case Study Sources:

http://www.visitwilliamsburg.com/index.aspx (accessed 12 May, 2010)
http://commons.wikimedia.org/wiki/Image:Colonial_Williamsburg_Store_Interior_
   DSCN7245.JPG (accessed 25 January 2010)

in this process can be achieved by individuals or groups undertaking creative and innovative activities which then form the basis of more passive tourist experiences. This production of creative experiences for passive consumption by tourists might be termed 'creative spectacles' which are characteristic of much cultural tourism activity and can be equated with Pine and Gilmore's (1998) passive participation.

A second approach is the development of a spatially demarcated 'creative enclave' populated by cultural creatives (a term used to refer to groups of individuals with the talent or interest in participating in cultural activities). For example, TSVs can provide a platform for local artisans and craftspeople to not only sell their unique products but demonstrate their skills. These types of 'creative spaces' are often visually and emotionally seductive areas which may attract a wide range of tourists. Colonial Williamsburg provides an excellent example. Finally, when the tourists themselves participate in the creative activities being undertaken, skill development and/or creative challenge can form the basis of active tourist experiences. This participation is closer to the development of 'creative tourism' and can also imply a convergence of creative spectacles and creative spaces. Other examples that are applicable to TSVs include such activities and experiences as trying one's hand at painting, pottery, sculpture, perfume creation, candle making, tapestry, weaving, music making, ethnic dancing, cooking, acting, craft stitching and photography.

The success of Build-A-Bear Workshop, Inc. which offers an interactive make-your-own stuffed animal retail-entertainment experience is a good example of the potential of customer participation. Founded in 1997, the company and its franchisees currently operate more than 400 Build-A-Bear Workshop stores worldwide, including company-owned stores in the United States, Puerto Rico, Canada, the United Kingdom, Ireland and France, and franchise stores in Europe, Asia, Australia and Africa. Build-a-Bear Workshops encourage participation. Shopping is more than selecting a toy from a shelf and taking it to the cash register. The process involves choosing the outer casing for the animal, stuffing it, fluffing it and sewing it up. The final steps involve grooming the animal and dressing it. The toy leaves the store as a pet in a take-home decorated box with a birth certificate. In 2007, the interactive experience was enhanced—all the way to CyBEAR space—with the launch of buildabearville.com, the company's virtual world stuffed with fun. The company was named as one of the 2009 FORTUNE 100 Best Companies to Work For. Build-A-Bear Workshop posted total revenue of $468 million in fiscal 2008 (Kids Today 2009).

The remainder of this chapter will focus on highlighting examples from the Canadian village, Niagara-on-the-Lake, and specifically feature the food- and wine-related activities and the George Bernard Shaw Festival Theatre as a consistent theme used strategically throughout the year within an orchestrated series of events and activities.

The importance of the combination of shopping and dining as experience was evidenced in the research report earlier in this chapter.

Niagara-on-the-Lake, located at the mouth of the Niagara River on the south shore of Lake Ontario in Ontario Canada, just 15km from Niagara Falls, is an example of building a core theme around food and wine (see Profile 7.3). This region is well-known for its annual celebrations of terroir-focused foods and award-winning wines. The French concept of terroir focuses on the idea that the social-ecological context of food's production shapes its character. The Niagara Fruit Belt also produces 90 per cent of Ontario's tender fruit crop; extending from Hamilton to Niagara-on-the-Lake, it is one of the richest fruit-producing areas in Canada. A typical journey to Niagara-on-the-Lake would start at a charming inn, followed with a wine tour or two, a play at the Shaw Festival theatre, antique shopping, a local spa treatment and a gourmet meal.

Regular food- and wine-related events are held in the region annually, celebrating the four seasons of Niagara. The annual Icewine Festival is held in January, coinciding with Winterglow, which includes special events and activities—such as the ice sculptures which line the main street. The 'Days of Wine and Chocolate' event runs over three weekends in February and features stops at 20 wineries which feature decadent chocolate selections matched with a premium wine. 'Fabulicious' is a dining extravaganza in late February/early March during which a renowned and envied collection of Niagara-on-the-Lakes' finest establishments serve spectacular lunch and dinner fare at pre-set pricing seen only once a year in wine country (Wineries of Niagara-on-the-Lake 2010). In May a Wine and Herb Touring program features different herb and wine pairings at each winery and samples of herb-flavoured food delicacies. Visitors can collect a set of 21 recipe cards by visiting all the participating wineries. The strawberry, cherry and peach seasons are celebrated with festivals in June, July and August. In September the Annual Wine Festival is comprised of more than 100 events, including fine wine tasting, winery tours, concerts, Niagara cuisine, artisan shows and wine seminars. The annual 'Taste of the Season' tour is held in November as a celebration of the season's bounty. Visitors purchase a passport to 21 wineries offering delectable food and wine pairings available only to pass holders. Passes are valid only on the weekend on which they are purchased and also include a collectible holiday ornament. These food- and wine-related events are clearly positioned to extend the appeal of the destination beyond the traditional peak season and in particular provide a focus on the village in the traditionally slow post-Christmas winter months.

A very interactive experience is provided by the Wine Country Cooking School—located within Strewn, an estate winery minutes from Niagara-on-the-Lake. This unique culinary experience for recreational cooks is provided by Canada's first winery cooking school, which is focused on the relationship between food and wine and the abundance of fresh products grown in the region which are showcased in recipes and menus that reflect the seasons (Wine Country Cooking School 2010).

Figure 7.4   Themes in Niagara-on-the-Lake: wine tasting and George Bernard Shaw.

Another key focus of the Niagara-on-the-Lake experience is the George Bernard Shaw Festival Theatre from April to November each year which, like the Stratford Shakespearean Festival Theatre, has played a leading role in developing a strong 'summer theatre' presence throughout rural southern Ontario. This includes the St. Jacobs Country Playhouse Theatre which was opened by Drayton Entertainment when they took over the building vacated by the failed St. Jacobs Country Winery and Cidery (Mitchell and de Waal 2009). In addition to attending performances, visitors to Niagara-on-the-Lake can partake in backstage tours and creative workshops. For example, the Manners, Customs and Costumes package offered in 2010 includes a workshop that examines Victorian values and manners and relates them to the plays and passions of the day. It includes the workshop, a buffet lunch, a pre-show chat and the matinee performance of 'An Ideal Husband'. These limited-season theatre experiences provide a complementary attraction that both enhances the appeal of these villages to visitors as well as the experience itself. The strategic use of festivals and events consistent with the theme of a shopping village can be useful tools in attracting more visitors and extending the visitor season.

Case Study 7.3   Niagara-on-the-Lake, Ontario, Canada

Niagara-on-the-Lake, situated below the crest of the Niagara Escarpment and stretching to the Niagara River and the shores of Lake Ontario, is the heart of Ontario wine culture and a world-renowned wine country destination. It is less than two hours from Toronto and a short drive from Buffalo, New York. With a population of approximately 14,500, Niagara-on-the-Lake, often called the loveliest town in Ontario, has a long and distinguished history. The site of the old Neutral Indian village of Onghiara, it was settled at the close of the American Revolution by Loyalists coming to Upper Canada, many of whom had been members of the much feared Butler's Rangers based during the American Revolution at Fort Niagara, then under British control.

In 1781 the British Government purchased land from the Mississaugas and by 1782, 16 families had become established and had cleared 236 acres. In 1792, Newark, as it was named by Governor Simcoe, became the first capital of the newly-created colony of Upper Canada, and the legislature met there for five sessions, until Lieutenant-Governor John Graves Simcoe moved the capital to York. The physical appearance of the town, with the exception of the powder magazine at Fort George, was virtually erased by the burning of the town by the Americans during the War of 1812.

Rebuilt, Niagara became an active commercial centre, with a busy shipping and ship-building industry, as well as many shops and warehouses. The beautiful old homes lining the tree-shaded streets attest to the prosperity of its citizens.

Today, Niagara-on-the-Lake offers many tourism attractions including historic sites – Fort George and the Historical Society Museum, the Shaw Festival with its three theatres, the marina, the heritage business district for shopping, golf courses, parks and beautiful farmland, agricultural markets and the world-famous Niagara wineries.

Case Study 7.3   (continued)

Figure 7.5   Prince of Wales Hotel and specialty food in Niagara-on-the-Lake.

History of the Shaw Festival

The Shaw Festival was started in 1962 by Niagara-area lawyer and playwright Brian Doherty. During the summer, Mr. Doherty organized eight weekend performances of Don Juan in Hell and *Candida* by Bernard Shaw under the title "*Salute to Shaw*". For this event, the Assembly Room in the historic Court

---

Case Study 7.3   (continued)

House on Queen Street was converted into a small theatre. The following year, the Shaw Festival Theatre Foundation was established as a non-profit organization, with an elected volunteer Board of Governors whose mandate was to produce the dramatic works of Bernard Shaw and his contemporaries. In its first decade, the Shaw Festival enjoyed explosive audience growth, and the company toured extensively in the United States and Canada. Then on June 20, 1973, the Festival Theatre was officially opened by Her Majesty Queen Elizabeth II, enabling the Shaw Festival to mount large scale productions which drew national and international acclaim.

The company works in three theatres. The largest is the Festival Theatre, which at 856 seats is still intimate by most standards. The Court House Theatre, located where the Shaw Festival began in 1962, has 327 seats in a 'thrust' configuration. Each year The Shaw leases the Assembly Room in the historic Court House from the Town of Niagara-on-the-Lake and installs a theatre in the space. The Royal George Theatre, which seats 328, was built in 1915 as a little vaudeville house and acquired by the Shaw Festival in 1980.

The Shaw Festival is an art theatre rather than a commercial theatre – hence its status as a non-profit and charitable organization. Still, it is run in a very businesslike and efficient manner. Over 70 per cent of annual revenue comes from box office sales and other earned revenue. The Festival produces 10 to 12 plays each season, with over 800 performances in the three theatres, to audiences totalling about 300,000 people.

Case Study Sources:

www.shawfest.com (accessed May 2010)
http://www.niagaraonthelake.com/aboutnotl/jpage/1/p/About/content.do (accessed May 2010)

CONCLUSION

Much of the previous discussion can be summarised as a process of developing distinctive and engaging experiences which are linked by a strong theme. According to Stamboulis and Pantoleon (2003), the question of experience is related to the creation of myth (an organised, designed, experience and an accompanying narrative) in which the tourist will express the wish to live. The experience emerges from the interaction between destinations and tourists—with destinations as 'theatres' at which the experience takes place, and tourists as 'actors' who have to play their own role—depending on the extent of immersion. In developing this metaphor the owners and managers of tourist shopping precincts are effectively the script writers and directors. In this view and consistent with the perspectives adopted in this chapter it can be suggested that the first crucial step in designing an engaging experience is envisioning a well-defined theme. This social construction and labelling of the village—in effect the village story and the justification for its distinctiveness when compared to other locations—drives all the design elements and staged events of the experience toward a unified story line with the potential to engage the customer (Pine and Gilmore 1998). Stamboulis and Pantoleon (2003) see destination themes as being articulated as collective social artefacts involving both planned and haphazard elements. Tourists may be immersed in, and actively participate in, the myth as it unfolds through everyday life of local society. The authors emphasise that this is a highly tacit, knowledge-creating process, based on the interaction between place, theme and tourist.

While the theme provides the foundation, the experience must be rendered with indelible impressions which affirm the nature of the experience to the customer/visitor by being consistent with the theme. Unplanned or inconsistent visual and aural cues can leave a customer confused or lost. Therefore, according to Pine and Gilmore (1998) ensuring the integrity of the experience requires more than the layering on of positive cues. More specifically, experience stagers must eliminate anything that diminishes contradicts or distracts from the main theme. Additionally, the more senses an experience engages the more effective and memorable it can be. Like the glamorous theatres of the world, the best shopping villages not only have to be designed imaginatively but the performances and experiences on offer in these settings have to engage the minds of visitors and generate excitement.

8 Information, Support Services and Facilities

INTRODUCTION

This chapter explores the interactions between TSV shopping and the provision of support services and facilities. The particular amenities to be considered are information services, accommodation, transport and parking, restrooms and public spaces. These amenities are highlighted in the TSV Visitor Experience Model presented in Figure 8.1. Many of these amenities can be regarded as 'hygiene factors' (Herzberg 1968). If they are provided or delivered effectively they are unlikely to be memorable items defining the visitors' experience. On their own they may not even contribute to visitor satisfaction. If these amenities are lacking in any way they are likely to become a major source of visitor dissatisfaction. In terms of the key perspective guiding this volume the failure to provide these facilities will undermine visitor mindfulness with broad ranging and negative consequences for the trip to the TSV.

INFORMATION SERVICES

Visitors to TSVs are likely to require information at various stages of their journey, from the initial decision to visit a particular destination through to their arrival and experience of the village. Some visits may be the part of a larger touring itinerary and may be the result of considerable pre-trip planning, while others might be represent more impulsive detours which occur in response to road signs encountered on a route. Findlay and Southwell (2004a: 3) propose a sequence of visitor information needs that fall into four distinct decisional stages. These are described in Table 8.1 and form the basis for further discussion.

The following discussion examines the role of visitor information centres, and considers orientation aids such as signage and maps. The role of interpretation is also briefly reviewed.

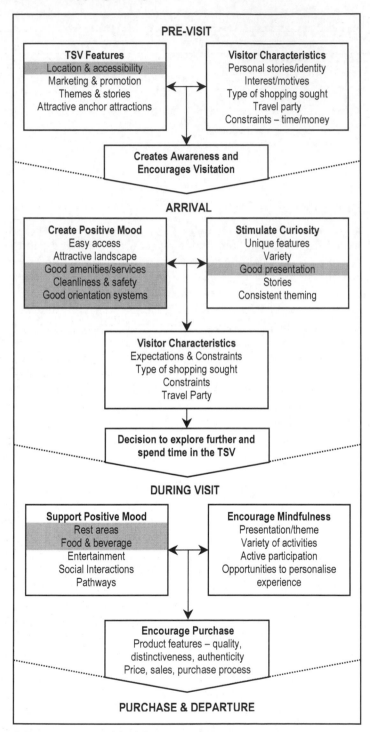

Figure 8.1   A model of the TSV visitor experience.

Table 8.1   A Sequence of Visitor Information Needs

Decision Stage	Information Need	Information Provision
Pre-arrival	The decision to visit a site for a particular experience or activity	Brochures, advertisements, websites, word of mouth, tourist road signs
Transit	Choice of transport and route to the destination	Signs, road maps, visitor centres, verbal and written directions, landmarks
Arrival	Local approach journey to site, orientation, traffic and pedestrian management	Signs, staff, locals, following other users, environmental cues (e.g. car parks)
Onsite experience	Achieving recreational goal: where to go and what to do on site, opening hours, facilities, interpretation and education, site regulations	Signs, information boards, visitor centres, brochures, local maps, staff, locals, interpretation, watching other users, environmental cues (e.g. sounds from café).

Adapted from Findlay and Southwell, 2004b.

Visitor Information Centres

The marketing of villages and the design of experiences for visitors to these settings (see Chapter 7) are supported in many instances by visitor information centres both within and outside the village. Pearce (2004: 8) defines the visitor information centre as "a clearly labelled, publicly accessible, physical space with personnel providing predominantly free of charge information to facilitate travellers' experiences." He also points out that the nomenclature used to refer to visitor centres varies and may include: welcome centres, tourist information centres, interpretive centres and visitor resource centres.

Visitor information centres can influence visitors to spend more money than planned, to extend their stay or to visit additional attractions not planned prior to visiting the information centre (Fesenmaier and Vogt 1993). However, increasing expenditure and altering the places visited appears to be somewhat easier to influence than delivering longer stays (Fesenmaier, Vogt and Stewart 1993). Fesenmaier, et al. (1993) also found that visitors are highly likely to use the information obtained at information centres to plan future trips, suggesting that information is often collected and then stored for future use.

The functions of many visitor information centres extend beyond promotion. Pearce (2004) proposes a 'four plus' model in which all visitor centres undertake the following multiple functions to differing degrees:

1. Promotion: the active promotion of the region to stimulate tourist demand and increase visitor expenditure. Despite this economic development agenda, this function is viewed by visitors as providing an explicit, induced information source which is trustworthy and not excessively self-serving.

2. Orientation and enhancement: the provision information to support quality visitor experiences. This includes the provision of maps and displays that identify key locations, activities and features of the destination. The enhancement function might also involve shaping visitor demand for certain activities to encourage sustainable behaviour.
3. Control and filtering: influencing the flow and movement of visitors to manage visitor density and pressure on key resources and settings. This function may include suggestions about the best time of day to undertake various activities or alternative locations for less crowded experiences.
4. Substitution: providing a substitute for some tourist experiences and perhaps also acting as a substantial visitor attraction. This is most commonly an interpretive function used to describe places, their history and the people who live and work there.
5. The plus functions: visitor centres can also act as community facilities for a range of local cultural and social events. These additional functions often serve the community rather than visitors by providing a community centre and a place for volunteers and locals to meet, displaying the pride and political achievements of the area and serving as the administrative centre for coordinating local tourism activities.

All of these functions would seem to be relevant to tourist shopping villages, although the key function observed in many village visitor information centres is focussed on promotion and orientation. Many successful villages include a visitor information centre prominently located on the main shopping strip. These centres play a critical role in providing basic information such as village maps, accommodation options, tours and activities.

This is consistent with findings that maps and advice about attractions are the most common types of information obtained from visitor centres (Fesenmaier and Vogt 1993). In some cases the centres may also have a commercial role by acting as booking agents for tours and accommodation. The control and filtering function does not seem common but there is some opportunity for villages with heavy visitation to use their visitor centres as tools to disperse visitors throughout the shopping precinct, particularly at peak periods that coincide with coach tours. The substitution function is particularly pertinent in rural destinations like tourist shopping villages where many of the attractions are historical or scattered and hard to appreciate (such as agricultural activities or heritage sites). Information centres in rural locations are often the focal point for Destination Management Organization (DMO) or convention and visitors bureau efforts and are commonly staffed by volunteers from the local community. Information is usually available for a range of experiences and support services available not only in the village but also the surrounding countryside.

It is essential for effective information centres to be easy to access (Pearce 2004; Perdue 1995). In successful villages visitor information centres are often located in refurbished historic buildings or are designed to blend seamlessly with the streetscape by adopting a locally distinctive architectural style. Effective centres are usually found in prominent locations along the main retail strip or close to major car parks. Pearce (2004) suggests that a signage plan is necessary to help visitors find the centre, and that signage should be used near the entrance as well as along key roads and other entry points to the village to help visitors find the centre. It is important to have advance warning signs advising visitors where and when they need to turn off the road. Figure 8.2 provides some good examples of visitor centres with these characteristics. Access to the visitor centre should be facilitated by

Figure 8.2   Visitor centres at Kuranda (top) and Cheddar showcase regionally distinctive architectural styles and are clearly marked with signs and *i* symbols.

turning lanes on adjacent roads and car park entries should be clearly visible. Visitors are likely to arrive by car in the first instance and it is important that car parking areas are large enough to accommodate private vehicles as well as coaches and RVs.

Orientation and Circulation Devices

The role of visitor information centres in aiding visitor orientation has already been discussed above, but the important role of signs and maps in TSVs warrants further attention. Bitgood (1994) observes that visitor orientation and circulation is one of the most neglected areas of visitor studies. He argues that orientation and circulation may be one of the most important areas because it influences whether or not people actually visit various attractions, whether or not visitors see particular areas, what they learn from their experience, what they tell friends and relatives and whether they will return.

The provision of services and facilities that aid orientation and circulation is frequently described in the literature on wayfinding. This literature draws on a variety of disciplines, including environmental and cognitive psychology and geography. Moscardo (1996) argues that orientation devices play a critical role in helping visitors to be more mindful because people who have difficulty orienting themselves experience feelings of anxiety which prevents them from appreciating their surroundings. The literature suggests that visitors to a new location use a variety of devices to assist with wayfinding, including landmarks, maps and signs (Bitgood 1994). The use of maps and signs are particularly pertinent to this discussion because they can be controlled by destination managers to improve visitor orientation.

While some shopping villages follow a simple linear pattern, as discussed in Chapter 5, many historic shopping villages are organic and spatially complex, with hidden laneways, arcades and courtyards. Maps are particularly important devices for helping visitors get the most out of their experience by understanding these complex settings. TSV visitor maps are typically found in handheld and fixed formats. Handheld maps are reported to be the most frequently used orientation devices in visitor settings (Bitgood and Richardson 1987; Hayward and Brydon-Miller 1984). Handheld road maps are useful in the first instance in directing visitors to the village. Once visitors arrive, more detailed village maps play an important role in activity planning and helping visitors find useful amenities such as attractions, visitor information centres, car parks, restrooms, resting places, transport nodes, disabled facilities and phone booths. In the visitor studies field, the provision of handheld maps has been found to increase the number of exhibits visitors viewed (Bitgood and Richardson 1987) so it could be concluded that handheld maps may increase the number of attractions and shops visited in a TSV. An issue for further attention and research is to consider the importance and role of maps downloaded from the Internet. The influence of map types on the shops visited and the purchases made would be an interesting avenue of inquiry. Warnaby (2008) also points out that maps are used as a promotional tool to highlight key destination attributes. It is not unusual to see maps displayed quite prominently in the marketing of destinations.

The literature dealing with the design of effective visitor maps is quite extensive and will only be discussed briefly. Some of the key guidelines for designing effective TSV maps are summarised in Table 8.2.

Table 8.2   Features of Effective Visitor Maps

Feature	Summary of Literature
Detail	Simple maps are more effective because visitors are easily overwhelmed by large amounts of information. Maps should indicate the key features likely to be required by visitors but should minimise the amount of information and unnecessary detail (Talbot, et al. 1993). Strategies for minimising detail include: • simplification by excluding other land uses not deemed relevant to visitors, such as non-retail/leisure sites; • smoothing minor bends in roads, railways and pathways; and • exclusion of minor or secondary locations (Warnaby 2008)
Colour	While visitors appear to prefer colour maps, there is limited evidence to suggest that they are actually more effective in visitor orientation. Colours used for decorative purposes should therefore be avoided because they may distract or confuse visitors (Devlin and Bernstein 1997). Colour can, however, be used effectively to distinguish between: • different districts/quarters that comprise the town centre; • areas that are primarily shopping-oriented and those where other land uses are predominant; • areas where access may be restricted (i.e. between areas that are for pedestrians and those that are not); and • area that is parkland and/or green space, and built up areas (Warnaby 2008).
Labels	Map labels are more effective and recalled more easily when integrated in situ on the map, rather than in a separate list of labels (Devlin and Bernstein 1997; Schwartz and Kulhavy 1981).
Directions	Maps should be accompanied by written directions to the destination (Devlin and Bernstein 1997; Warnaby 2008)
Scale	Visitor maps are often figurative representations and scale and spatial accuracy are of less importance (Warnaby 2008)
Projection	Most town centre maps use an oblique projection which provides visitors with a three dimensional representation of the site (Warnaby 2008). Oblique projections allow for landmarks to be more easily incorporated into the map.

In terms of reducing detail, it is useful to consider precisely what features should be included on a visitor map for a TSV. In his study of visitor maps and the representation of urban shopping precincts, Warnaby (2008) suggests that maps of town centres aimed at shoppers should include:

- Visitor services and amenities (visitor information centres, car parks, restrooms, resting places, transport nodes, disabled facilities and phone booths);
- Retailers (possibly in directory format);
- Attractions (such as heritage, entertainment and cultural attractions); and
- Descriptive content relating to the town (i.e. history, transport facilities, hinterland, contact telephone numbers, etc.).

The work of Lynch (1960) is particularly useful in understanding the components visitors use in constructing mental maps of their surroundings (see also Chapter 4). These components are described as landmarks, paths, boundaries (edges), districts and nodes (intersections). Many successful visitor maps contain these five components. The importance of prominent landmarks has already been mentioned but their inclusion on maps can help visitors to establish a sense of direction and to understand their position in relation to key site attributes (Southworth and Southworth 1982). The inclusion of landmarks may be particularly important for female visitors, who process spatial information differently to male visitors (Devlin and Bernstein 1997). Such landmarks may be natural (e.g. a rock outcrop or large stand of trees) or artificial (e.g. a building or street corner) (Xia, et al. 2008). Well-known or distinctive architectural buildings should be included on maps because they may be used as symbolic landmarks by visitors, especially if they can be sighted from a long distance away.

Maps can also be used to manage the circulation of visitors. The use of direction arrows, for example, can encourage visitors to follow a particular pathway through the village to experience the various elements in a specific sequence. Alternately a map may be used to highlight different walking itineraries in larger villages. The decision to exclude certain pathways on a visitor map may assist in keeping visitors away from quiet backstage or residential areas of the village. The indication of boundaries, such as rivers, railway lines, parks and gardens can assist visitor movement. The use of colour to indicate different thematic elements of districts may be used for distinguishing between different land uses. Nodes are perhaps the most important features on TSV visitor maps, and would typically include the various facilities and amenities mentioned above.

An effective orientation system includes not only maps, but signs which ultimately enhance visitor experiences. In fact, research suggests that a lack of signs can seriously diminish the quality of the visitor experience (Laws 1998). It appears that maps and signs play different roles in visitor orientation (Bitgood 1994). Fixed maps are useful for conceptual orientation; in the case of shopping villages this includes information about what there is to see and do, orientation to the broader village setting, different spatial elements and land uses. Directional signs on the other hand are more useful for wayfinding, or being able to locate specific places and features. For example, a visitor might use a map to locate the general vicinity where restrooms can be found, but might then use signs to identify the correct building and appropriate entrance. Handheld maps are important devices for both wayfinding and conceptual orientation.

Signs play a number of important roles which are at the same time promotional and informational. Like maps, signs also have the potential to be used as a form of social control to constrain visitor movements and behaviour (Dann 2003). Interestingly, the presence of the signs in a non-tourism setting has also been found to significantly reduce perceived crowding, discomfort, anger and confusion (Wener and Kaminoff 1983). The importance of signs in attracting visitors is recognised by Leiper (1990), who builds on the work of MacCannell (1976) to identify three categories of 'markers'. These include generating markers, transit markets and contiguous markers and correspond with different trip phases. Similarly, Dann (2003: 466) argues that:

> [S]igns have to contain sufficient details to lead people in the right direction and, on arrival, by means of "reassurance signs", to confirm their belief that they have reached the designated place. Ancillary information, such as the location and price of lodging facilities and eating establishments, can also be transmitted through a variety of logos and other brand images. If any of these *vade mecum* data are missing, such a situation can produce anxiety in the subject.

Directional signage also plays an important role in helping visitors locate the village while in transit. Dornbusch and Kawczynska (1992) found that tourist-oriented directional signs (TODS) were by far the most popular method of locating tourist attractions and businesses, followed by brochures and personal directions. Such signs also play an important role in influencing visitors to make unplanned stops. In the UK it has been reported that a lack of signs and directions was a significant barrier for visitors to the countryside (Countryside Agency 1998). Similarly, there are some challenges for TSV managers and businesses. A number of countries, including the U.S., Australia and the UK limit the amount of commercial signs and directional information along major arterial roads (Dornbusch and Kawczynska 1992). In Australia and the UK directional information about tourist sites is often provided using standard white on brown road signs but these signs are erected and vetted by main roads authorities. The challenge for emerging TSVs and attractions is to convince main roads authorities that the village or attraction is worthy of such signage.

Once visitors arrive at a village, there is a need for signage to reassure them that they are in the right place and how they can go about accessing key facilities such as restrooms, parking and visitor information centres. Drivers will need to know where to park and whether they need to pay (Findlay and Southwell 2004b). Findlay and Southwell (2004a) identify a number of different types of sign messages from the literature:

- Site promotion and directions;
- Visitor welcome;
- Information about the site and its facilities;
- Visitor orientation;
- Education and interpretation;
- Advisory and warning signs; and
- Commercial signs.

While signs may be present, there are a number of problems which can be easily avoided through careful planning. Two of the most common problems are a lack of signs when they are expected and the visibility of signs (Findlay and Southwell 2004a). For example, visitors leaving a car park might expect a directional sign for support facilities but such signage is not always provided. Likewise, visitors reaching a junction might expect a sign to provide them with more information about which path to take. Signs may also be obscured by topography or roadside vegetation. Similarly, visual clutter on the streetscape can distract visitors and prevent them from noticing signs. Another problem with signs occurs when there is an inconsistency in the names and labels used for the site, its facilities or directions (Findlay and Southwell 2004b). The problem occurs most commonly in shopping villages when new signage systems are installed without removing older signs. Sometimes this problem can also occur when signs, symbols, names or landmarks are identified differently on the initial information source (e.g. a website brochure or map) used by visitors. Confusion may result when the names, symbols and appearance of information subsequently encountered are different.

An integrated signage and mapping approach is a sensible strategy for assisting visitors with orientation. Unfortunately very few villages excel at the use of both signage and maps. An exception is the rainforest village of Kuranda, which provides visitors with particularly good orientation including a fixed map as well as extensive and distinctive themed signage. The fixed map provides visitors with several walking itineraries distinguished by different colours (see Figure 8.3). The directional signage uses the same consistent eccentric design cues as benches, rubbish bins, lamp posts and other street decorations and includes not only directional signage but also street signs (see Figure 8.4). A handheld map of the village is also available from the visitor centre. Niagara-on-the-Lake also provides a number of effective orientation devices which

Figure 8.3   Fixed map with various walking itineraries at Kuranda.

largely follow the guidelines discussed in this section. Consistent directional signs are supported by handheld and fixed maps.

It is common to find fixed maps in most villages, although there are some
exceptions. Many of the shopping villages in England provide a handheld
village map. These are usually available at the visitor information centres
(sometimes for a small charge) and in some cases are also provided online
for pre-trip planning. It is not uncommon to find that the maps exhibited on fixed signs differ in style to handheld maps, creating the potential
for visitor confusion. Villages such as Niagara-on-the-Lake and St. Jacobs
also make handheld maps available to visitors but this approach appears
to be uncommon in villages in Australia and New Zealand. Some villages
provide no maps (fixed or handheld) at all and rely instead on limited signage to orientate visitors. Consistent with the view expressed by Moscardo
(1996), it seems likely that villages with ineffective or non-existent maps
and signage will be more likely to induce mindlessness in their visitors than
those with effective orientation systems. Some visitors are also likely to be
annoyed by having to pay for maps which may be of low quality.

There is an opportunity for many villages to develop an integrated map
and signage strategy. While there is some need to avoid street clutter in
heritage streetscapes there is room for tasteful heritage signs which adopt
design cues from the surrounding streetscape and architecture. The use of

Figure 8.4 Examples of consistent, themed directional signage at Kuranda

colour and symbols or icons on these signs can be transferred to maps so there is consistency in the communication of various features.

Interpretation

The role of interpretation has already been alluded to in the discussion about visitor information centres and signage. The discussion about signage and maps is often included in the broader interpretation literature. Interpretation had been described as an educational activity which aims to reveal meanings and relationships (Tilden 1977). Interpretation can be an important medium for increasing the educational and recreational experiences of visitors. Moscardo (1996) also proposes that effective interpretation can encourage sustainable behaviour and can play an important role in the management of visitors in built heritage sites. In addition to the use of orientation and circulation devices discussed earlier, interpretive displays can influence visitor behaviour in more subtle ways by providing cues about appropriate behaviour and by fostering an appreciation of the environment, local population or heritage of a village.

Moscardo (1996) argues that effective interpretation plays an important role in mindful visitor experiences. She suggests that mindfulness can be encouraged by:

- Using a variety of media including multisensory exhibits and exhibits with extreme physical properties;
- Creating content which is perceived by the visitors to be personally relevant, vivid or affectively charged;
- Using media or content that is novel, unexpected or surprising;
- Posing questions to create conflict or ambiguity;
- Providing opportunities for visitors to control the information that they receive (for example interactive or participatory tours);
- Ensuring interpretive devices are dynamic or animated;
- Designing exhibits or tours that give visitors the opportunity for direct contact with objects/topics; and
- Developing a structure that underlies the organisation of interpretive content.

However, Moscardo cautions that too much novelty, conflict or information in a setting may not result in mindfulness because visitor efforts will be directed towards trying to develop some system to deal with the information overload. This perspective provides an important and generic link with the approach to tourist shopping village studies in this volume. The support services reviewed constitute predisposing conditions affecting the visitors' mental readiness to enjoy the shopping experience. Distractions provided by ineffective visitor centres, inadequate signage, poor interpretation and confusing maps hinder the well-being of shoppers, retailers and residents.

ACCOMMODATION

Accommodation in or near a tourist shopping village can be an important extension of the tourism experience (Wight 1998). Accommodation is arguably less important in the early stages of TSV evolution but its importance grows as villages offer more activities. For many visitors a trip to a TSV is a half or full day excursion, but for some it is part of a short break holiday in the countryside. The desire to seek out rural settings, to recharge and to escape for a short time from an urban lifestyle creates demand for accommodation in and near TSVs. The social, economic and environmental contexts of many rural destinations mediate the scale and type of accommodation. Indeed, it is likely that different patterns of accommodation are suitable for different regions (Moscardo, Morrison and Pearce 1996).

The style of accommodation most frequently associated with rural areas can best be described as 'specialist' or 'boutique' accommodation (Emerick and Emerick 1994; Morrison, et al. 1996). The term 'specialist' is used specifically as a generic, integrative and non-elitist term to cover a broad range of accommodation styles in a variety of locations (Morrison, et al. 1996). From a definitional perspective, Morrison, et al. (1996: 24) suggest that specialist accommodation establishments should exhibit the following five characteristics:

1. Personal interaction between the guests and the owner hosts.
2. A special opportunity or advantage for guests afforded by the location, physical structure or services offered.
3. Special activities offered to guests.
4. Owner operation.
5. Small guest accommodation capacity (generally less than 25 rooms).

Typical examples of specialist accommodation include bed and breakfast (B&B) inns, country inns, guest houses, commercial cottages or cabins, farm stays and dude ranches (see Figure 8.5). Guest quarters are frequently found in restored old houses or new houses constructed respecting traditional architecture and materials (Emerick and Emerick 1994). In some locations guests may be accommodated in renovated mills, barns, dairies, shearing sheds or workers quarters. The use of heritage buildings in particular may contribute to visitors' understanding of the history of the destination as well as providing an affective experience which is different to accommodation housed in purpose-built or modern buildings (McIntosh and Siggs 2005).

As already discussed in Chapter 4, when considering lifestyle entrepreneurs and small business development relevant to TSVs, multiple economic and social motives drive the establishment of these businesses. A number of researchers have confirmed that economic motives are often the major reason for establishing B&Bs and farm stays (Evans and Ilbery 1992; Frater 1983; McGehee and Kim 2004; Nickerson, Black and McCool 2001; Ollenburg and Buckley 2007; Pearce 1990; Sharpley and Vass 2006; Weaver and Fennell 1997). As

Figure 8.5   Examples of B&B accommodation found in Niagara-on-the-Lake and Bayfield, Canada.

noted earlier, specialist accommodation does fill a niche that may not be economically feasible for traditional providers. However, some researchers have also found that these styles of accommodation are not hugely profitable, are prone to seasonality and have lower occupancy rates than traditional accommodation (Emerick and Emerick 1994; Morrison, et al. 1996; Nilsson 2002). While many of these establishments have a lower break-even point in terms of room capacity it has already been established that other motives may prompt the provision of accommodation in or near TSVs.

To summarise, it can be said that that specialist accommodation establishments are in demand in rural locations because they offer comfort, luxury, uniqueness, history, host-guest interaction and a more personal touch (McIntosh and Siggs 2005). The profile of B&B guests in particular suggests that they tend to be couples without children who have higher than average incomes. They are often better educated and are quite likely to be experienced travellers (Lee, Reynolds and Kennon 2003; Morrison, et al. 1996; Pearce 1990; Warnick and Klar 1991). In many parts of the world they are also older travellers (Pearce and Moscardo 1992), however in some parts of the U.S. young couples have been reported as the key market segment (Rowe 1991). Guests appear to favour non beach-related outdoor recreation activities (Morrison, et al. 1996). These motives and characteristics seem to align well with the overall holiday motives of visitors to TSVs.

As a result of the personal relationship between hosts and guests, specialist accommodation providers are in the unique position to identify, promote and provide tourists with a range of experiences. Hosts are able to influence visitors' experiences of TSVs and the surrounding landscape in a wider spatial and temporal sense because many specialist accommodation establishments tend to be located in small towns and rural landscapes where having local insights is invaluable (McIntosh and Siggs 2005).

TRANSPORT AND PARKING

The management of transport and parking is a serious challenge for shopping villages as visitor numbers grow. There are three dimensions to the provision of transport in successful tourist shopping villages:

- Adequate parking located close to the shopping streetscape;
- Access to public transport to move visitors around the village; and
- Management of traffic flow and congestion to preserve the village atmosphere.

The provision of parking spaces is a major management issue for many TSVs. Historic shopping villages are often characterised by narrow streets, which were not built with on-street parking in mind. Local governments and entrepreneurs have also placed further pressure on-street parking by widening sidewalks to accommodate street displays, alfresco dining and

Figure 8.6 Narrow streets and sidewalks in Kinsale (top) and use of the village square for parking in Stow-on-the-Wold.

increasing numbers of pedestrians. In some older European villages the streets and pedestrian walkways are so narrow that the road often becomes a de-facto pedestrian space to be shared with vehicles. An example of this issue is illustrated by the Irish village of Kinsale in Figure 8.6. In other older villages traditional village squares have been converted to parking lots. Stow-on-the-Wold provides a good example of this approach. This use of valuable public space raises some questions about the opportunity costs of providing central parking infrastructure.

Fluctuations in visitor numbers to TSVs further compound the problems of parking and traffic management. Many villages experience seasonal fluctuations as well as weekly fluctuations, with weekends being a particularly busy time in most villages. It may not be feasible to set aside large areas of land for parking when this parking is only used for two days of the week. Villages also face fluctuations in numbers during the course of the day, with 11 a.m. to 3 p.m. generally being the peak time. This period also coincides with tour coach itineraries.

The presence of on-street parking, modern vehicles and tour coaches have an undesirable visual, auditory and olfactory impact on a streetscape otherwise characterised by picturesque old-world buildings. Traffic noise and vehicle emissions in particular have the potential to overpower the soundscape and aromas associated with rural village environments (see Chapter 5 for a fuller discussion). The presence of on-street parking, particularly on the main retail streetscape, also contributes to traffic flow problems as visitors and workers search for available parking spaces.

Many successful villages have developed strategies to cope with the provision of parking. These generally include some or all of the following:

- Provision of public car parks;
- Provision of off-street parking behind shops;
- Planning ordinances and by-laws requiring new developments to provide off-street parking; and
- Encouraging visitors to stay overnight in the village, using off-street parking facilities at accommodation providers.

In instances where large car parks cannot be located close to the main tourist areas of the village it may be necessary to provide public transport for visitors. Public transport is also used to move visitors around shopping villages that are larger or more dispersed and is a particularly useful service for elderly or disabled visitors. Climatic conditions may also necessitate the use of public transport to protect visitors from the elements. Several shopping villages in the U.S. and Canada, including Sedona, Gatlinburg and Niagara-on-the-Lake use vintage trolley buses to transport visitors between key sites (see Figure 8.7). In some instances these buses also fulfil visitor interpretation and orientation roles by providing local tours and commentary. More antiqued novelty forms of transport, such as horses and carts also play a small role in facilitating the

Figure 8.7 Examples of trolley buses in Sedona (top) and Niagara-on-the-Lake.

movement of visitors within the village as discussed in Chapter 5, however public transport is generally underutilised in most TSVs.

In the wider spatial setting, many shopping villages are served by bus, rail and cable car routes that connect them to nearby urban areas. The use of heritage trains appears to be a particularly compatible mode of transport that has less impact on the heritage theme of many villages. These rail connections play an important role in bringing visitors to villages such as Kuranda, Williams and St. Jacobs. The mountain village of Kuranda can be reached from the tourist centre of Cairns by Kuranda Scenic Railway as well as the Skyrail Rainforest Cableway. While these experiences are managed by different operators, cooperative packaging allows visitors to travel to the village on one mode while using the other on their return trip. This substantially reduces the number of cars and buses required to transport visitors and impacts positively on the 'village in the rainforest' environment. A few villages are accessible using the public transport networks of adjacent metropolitan areas. For example, Hahndorf can be accessed using the Adelaide urban bus network.

The management of traffic flow and congestion is the third transport dimension discussed in this chapter. Riganti and Nijkamp (2008) contend that traffic congestion at destinations can cause an accumulation of negative impacts which reduce visitors' enjoyment and appreciation of the site. The challenge of managing traffic flow and congestion is partly facilitated by the well-planned placement of parking facilities. If vehicles can be captured by car parks before they enter the main tourist thoroughfare then this will dramatically reduce the level of congestion and associated unpleasant externalities. However, additional steps can be taken to manage traffic flow. The most successful approaches observed in shopping villages involve strategies to divert traffic from the main shopping area. Such strategies include:

- Signposting and engineering of alternate routes, including realignment of roads and intersections to divert traffic away or around the shopping precinct;
- Traffic calming devices such as speed bumps, chicanes, chokers, raised pedestrian crossings and textured pavements which compel drivers to slow down, thereby making alternative routes faster and more attractive;
- Introducing one-way traffic flow;
- Prohibiting on-street parking along the main shopping streetscape;
- Prohibiting turning across oncoming traffic;
- Limiting car park entrances along the main shopping strip so that vehicles have less incentive to travel down the street;
- Access to service areas and private car parks from parallel streets where possible; and
- Encouraging visitors to use substitute modes of transport, such as bicycles or public transport.

Bourton-on-the-Water illustrates the first of these approaches. Visitors travelling along the Fosseway are diverted onto Station Road by the use of signage and traffic signals. A large car park then captures traffic before it reaches the village high street. The aim is not to completely remove traffic from the road, but to reduce the amount of traffic to the extent that it does not overwhelm other enjoyable aspects of the streetscape.

In the future, it is likely that intelligent transport systems (ITS), which optimise traffic flow by using intelligent technologies, may be used by TSVs (Mrnjavac and Marsanic 2007). The increasing adoption of in-car navigation systems will allow visitors to receive information about parking, weather and traffic conditions. Parking guidance and information systems (PGI) could be used to feed information to navigation systems or to electronic roadside signs advising travellers of car parking capacity and availability. The ability to guide vehicles to the closest vacant parking space reduces traffic congestion and the time spent in searching, while also increasing the occupancy rate of parking lots. Such systems could also assist in managing visitor fluctuations by directing travellers to secondary overflow car parks during peak visitation.

PUBLIC SPACES AND AMENITIES

Successful shopping villages seem to pay particular attention to the provision of additional amenities and public space for visitor enjoyment. Such amenities include:

- Rubbish bins located at convenient intervals along major pedestrian routes;
- Public restrooms located close to car parks and shopping facilities. Larger villages may require several of these facilities dispersed throughout the setting;
- Places for people to rest, including benches, ledges and lawns for picnics;
- Shelter or shade to protect visitors from the elements;
- Lighting and lamp posts for night-time activities; and
- Safe parks and playgrounds to cater for families with children.

While the need for these amenities is obvious they are surprisingly absent in some villages or are located in the most unlikely places. Sometimes these facilities are hidden or tucked away so that their utilitarian appearance does not distract from the heritage streetscape. Several villages have turned mundane amenities such as bins and seats into attractive features which are designed to blend with the theme of the village. Kuranda employs a distinctive, possibly eccentric, design to all of its street furniture, including signs, bins, seats, bollards and barriers. Montville likewise has attractive bins, lamps and seating which follow the same design and are all coloured in bronze metallic heritage hues (see Chapter 5). Many of the English Cotswold village streetscapes follow the traditional black heritage style commonly seen in London for street amenities. The styles adopted by all of these villages are noteworthy.

The location of restrooms often presents town planners with challenges. In addition to sanitary considerations, restrooms are all too often poorly designed and presented and this can detract from the theme of the village. However these amenities can also be designed with care to ensure that they blend in to the streetscape. Directional signage and maps become critical in helping visitors locate restrooms because ironically many well-designed restrooms do not look the way people expect restrooms to look. Well-designed and located restrooms can also provide tour coaches with an incentive to stop at the village, thereby delivering additional visitors, albeit for a short visit.

CLUSTERING OF VISITOR SERVICES

The clustering of visitor facilities and services is a strategy employed successfully by a number of villages. The co-location of information centres with large parking facilities would seem sensible. Visitors who arrive by private car or coach are able to immediately locate the information centre when they arrive and are then able to access important activity information at the start of their experience. Several authors have reported that visitors to information centres in the U.S. often stop for convenience reasons, such as stretching, buying refreshments or using the restroom facilities (Fesenmaier and Vogt 1993). Many of these visitors subsequently collect information to assist them with their trip, but this behaviour illustrates the importance of co-locating visitor centres with restroom facilities. While this research relates mainly to highway welcome centres, it seems appropriate to suggest that many visitors will arrive at a tourist shopping village having spent an extended amount of time in a car or on a coach. For some of these visitors the relief offered by restrooms is likely to be an immediate priority, with information needs being of secondary importance. Moreover, when visitors return to their transport at the end of a productive shopping day, a quick comfort stop may be desirable before embarking on the long road trip home. Access and facilities for the elderly and disabled are also important considerations.

9 Evolution, Challenges and Information Needs

INTRODUCTION

This chapter explores again the challenges associated with the sustainable development of tourist shopping villages. These concerns were raised in Chapter 2 in a generic fashion but the issues are dealt with again in this chapter in the light of the research and ideas presented about tourist shopping villages throughout the previous chapters. More specifically, this chapter will explore the challenges and barriers faced by villages at different stages of development. Key challenges to be considered include the management of capacity since the very the popularity of some villages can arguably lead to their demise if growth is not carefully managed. A second and widespread challenge to consider lies in resident attitudes and perceptions. The influx of visitors can create serious issues in tourist shopping villages and can lead to negative resident attitudes and a loss of community, especially where visitor volume exceeds the physical capacity of small villages. Notwithstanding capacity issues, some villages evolve to the stage where they are extremely desirable tourist destinations but have very little value for local residents. Essentially the services and facilities required by locals are replaced by tourist shopping and dining opportunities—a process which has been described and discussed previously as creative destruction (Mitchell 1998). Just as small villages have inherent physical limits to growth or redevelopment, social capacity must also be considered, as villagers are likely to be more aware of, and concerned about, change in general and tourism developments in particular. The impact of these changes on local residents, as well as the impact of increased visitation, congestion and crowding will be a key focus of this chapter.

There are also planning challenges associated with the presentation and product mix of villages as they evolve. Getz (2000) notes that adaptive reuse for retail functions has preserved many historic buildings. In many cases deliberate architectural and historical theming is an entrepreneurial tool used to develop tourist attractiveness. There remains a risk however that not all will appreciate such re-use of facilities. The charges of inauthenicity or touristification which have been raised in previous chapters can lead to perceptions that the village can no longer provide what visitors and residents alike seek.

The challenges discussed in this chapter do not manifest themselves in all villages. In particular the concerns and management dilemmas faced by some villages tend to vary according to the evolution and life cycle stage of the village. In order to recognise these varied concerns the sustainability of tourist shopping villages in this chapter will be explored according to the different development characteristics of the villages. The perspective of various stakeholders will be considered systematically for each level of tourist shopping village growth. The chapter will conclude by considering the information needs of researchers, planners and policy makers interested in tourist shopping villages. It will present a research agenda to improve our understanding of this form of tourism.

STAKEHOLDERS IN TOURIST SHOPPING VILLAGE DEVELOPMENT

It is useful to recognise at the outset of any discussion about the challenges faced by TSVs that there are a number of stakeholders in the social arena who may be affected by the growth of tourism in a village. Mitchell's (1998) initial work on the postmodern community development of rural Canadian villages identifies entrepreneurs, residents and visitors as important stakeholders. The roles of residents and visitors are reasonably clear, although it is recognised that both groups are sometimes not homogenous. Residents can be divided into long term residents and more recent arrivals, so called 'sea changers' and 'tree changers' (Tonts and Greive 2002). A distinction may also be made between residents who have a vested interest in increasing visitor numbers to a village (e.g. local entrepreneurs, employees of visitor-oriented services, local property owners, local government representatives) and residents who do not derive any close or tied benefit from visitors.

Entrepreneurs are an interesting stakeholder group. In Mitchell's work they appear to be the individuals responsible for initiating new tourism developments in villages. However, a distinction can be made here between entrepreneurs, property owners and personnel who work in visitor-oriented services within a village. These three groups are often treated as a homogenous group when their interests may in fact vary quite significantly. For example, property owners may support a streetscaping project which results in higher rental yields, while entrepreneurs may oppose such developments because of the potential disruptions to business and the need to pay ongoing improvement levies. As already observed, employees working in the village stores are often residents and may have a different agenda to residents who do not derive any benefit from visitors.

In addition to these stakeholders, Mitchell and Coghill's (2000) study of Elora identifies two additional stakeholder groups: the preservationists and the producers. The preservationists are motivated by a desire to retain and enhance the historical environment of the village. The producers/creators are the artisans, crafts people and workers who create the regionally distinctive products found in many tourist shopping villages. Further work has identified government agencies and civic leaders as another significant stakeholder group in some locations (Fan, Wall and Mitchell 2008). Local municipal authorities and civic leaders have played a particularly important role in securing funding and support for streetscape improvements. In some parts of the world this role tends to be played by Chambers of Commerce or local business development associations.

Evans (1997) provides a useful framework for organising these various stakeholders into groups. He views the different stakeholders as:

- *Producers* of the retail setting (i.e. property owners, entrepreneurs, retailers, construction and design professionals etc.);
- *Intermediaries* in the retail setting (i.e. local and national government, estate agents/property managers, amenity providers, preservationists etc.); and
- *Users* of the retail setting (i.e. building tenants/occupants, residents, visitors etc.).

These stakeholder groups are not mutually exclusive and there is often considerable overlap between stakeholder groups as illustrated in Figure 9.1. In addition, not all of these groups may be present or active in every village and the power of different stakeholders is often unequal (Bramwell and Sharman 1999).

Moscardo (2005b) identified three pre-requisites for effective tourism development in rural and regional areas: tourism leadership, community understanding of tourism and effective coordination mechanisms to guide tourism development. Effective tourism leaders are often entrepreneurs but it is important to note that effective leadership may emerge from a number of the stakeholder groups that have been identified. These leaders are knowledgeable and enthusiastic about tourism, have strong community networks and the ability to include a wide range of people in tourism decisions (Moscardo 2005a).

The various stakeholders who may play a role in the development of TSVs have different agendas and priorities. It is the interaction of these stakeholders that necessitates the need for effective coordination mechanisms. Bramwell and Sharman (1999) note that there are many benefits and opportunities when stakeholders in a destination are able to collaborate and build consensus. Yet the various priorities of different stakeholder groups create a number of the challenges faced by TSVs, as well as the impacts explored in an earlier chapter of this book.

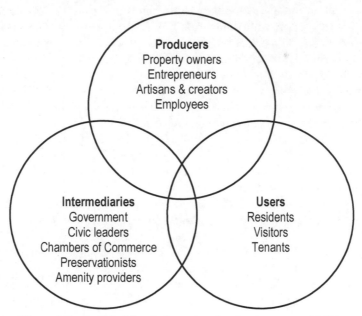

Figure 9.1   Stakeholders influencing the development of TSVs.

STAGES OF TOURIST SHOPPING VILLAGE DEVELOPMENT

The challenges faced by tourist shopping villages tend to vary according to the level of development. Embryonic shopping villages face quite different challenges to those that are well-developed and heavily visited. Several models of tourism development could be used to explore these challenges as shopping villages develop. Three models that are particularly useful are Butler's (1980) tourist area life cycle (TALC), Mitchell's (1998) model of creative destruction and Snepenger, Reiman, Johnson and Snepenger's (1998) downtown tourism life cycle model. While all three models can be criticised for being deterministic, they do provide a useful framework for understanding TSV challenges.

Butler's (1980) TALC model is well-known and frequently cited in the tourism literature. The basic premise is that tourism areas typically develop through a number of stages: exploration, involvement, development, consolidation and stagnation. Following stagnation, a destination may start a new development phase (rejuvenation), may continue to stagnate or may decline. Baum (1998) observes that the TALC has been subject to extensive scrutiny, application and criticism and is one of the most robust conceptual and managerial frameworks in the tourism area.

Snepenger, et al.'s (1998) premise of a downtown tourism life cycle model is based on the work of Butler. The downtown tourism life cycle model proposes that urban shopping areas move through Butler's five stages of development depending on the number and purchasing power of tourists and locals using the retail area.

Mitchell's (1998) model of creative destruction draws on an established body of literature in economic and rural geography and was developed to describe the evolution of rural towns based around the commodification of heritage. It has been considered in earlier chapters of this volume, notably in Chapter 3. The model is concerned with the creation of landscapes based on a rural idyll and their eventual destruction through over-development. Mitchell argues that if the creation of a commodified rural landscape is not managed carefully then the pre-existing rural idyll may be destroyed. The process of creative destruction has five phases: early commodification, advanced commodification, pre-destruction, advanced destruction, post-destruction.

The model has been tested and refined over the last 10 years and has been applied to villages in Canada (Mitchell 1998; Mitchell and Coghill 2000; Mitchell, Atkinson and Clark 2001), Australia (Tonts and Greive 2002) and China (Fan, Wall and Mitchell 2008). The work of Mitchell and her colleagues in Canada is based on several well-known TSVs profiled in this book, including Niagara-on-the-Lake, St. Jacobs and Elora.

There is some alignment between these stages of development but the stages do not correspond directly with each other. Table 9.1 provides a summary of the alignment between the models formulated from Butler's work and the approach adopted by Mitchell and colleagues. The tables also include examples of villages that show some of these characteristics although there is an element of subjectivity in the placement of villages. It is important to recognise that there are various stakeholder perspectives regarding the evolution of specific villages.

The way in which the development of the village is managed through the various stages is crucial in determining the impacts of change. For example, many of the Cotswold shopping villages in the UK can be described as being in a mature consolidation phase. In these settings building covenants and municipal ordinances have restricted the styles, sizes and types of building and businesses that are able to operate within the tourist precinct of these villages. This has essentially preserved the heritage streetscape of these villages, despite increased levels of visitation and entrepreneurial investment.

The Butler(1980)/Snepenger, et al. (1998) life cycle concept will be used as a framework to discuss the challenges faced by shopping villages as they develop. While Mitchell's model is useful, the nomenclature and focus on 'destruction' carries negative connotations which do not necessarily fit well with the evolution of some well-developed shopping villages. The creative destruction model was also developed for heritage villages and while most TSVs are heritage villages, not all fit this description. Some TSVs which have been created entirely for the tourist market, such as Ngong Ping Village, do not follow a Mitchell like trajectory of development.

Table 9.1   Application of Key Life Cycle Models to TSVs

Butler/ Snepenger et al.	Mitchell and Colleagues	Description	Examples
Exploration	-	Shopping precinct mainly serves residents, some incidental tourists. Buildings may be antiquated and less well-maintained due to lack of rural economic growth	Cromwell, New Zealand Woodford, Australia
Involvement	Early commodification	Tourism increases as result of rural idyll, business start to target tourists while still serving locals. Initial investment from local and non-local entrepreneurs in buildings and maintenance. Retail space still belongs to residents	Geraldine, New Zealand Eumundi, Australia Shere, England
Development	Advanced commodification	Tourist-focussed businesses displace local stores. Entrepreneurial investment escalates. Tourists actively targeted and retail space belongs to visitors. Redevelopment of renewal of buildings. Gentrification of village. Cooperative approach to marketing village.	Montville, Australia Arrowtown, New Zealand
Consolidation	Pre-destruction	Reinvestment of profits to meet needs of expanding visitor market. Some cultural activities and businesses become contrived or deviate from heritage theme, shopping district no longer serves everyday needs of residents	Niagara-on-the-Lake, Canada Bourton-on-the-Water, UK Volendam, Holland Sedona, U.S.
Stagnation	Advanced destruction	Outflow of local residents – social and demographic change in resident population. Crowding, congestion, large-scale developments (e.g. resorts and hotel developments). Substantially weakened theme. Less distinctive products or mass-produced products	Kuranda, Australia
Decline	Post-destruction	Development of chain stores, factory outlets and/or franchises. Visitors view village as a contrived commercial experience, no longer authentic, rural idyll completely lost. New types of tourists may be attracted by significantly altered landscape	Gatlinburg, U.S.

The geography and town planning literature provides a number of models and frameworks that are relevant to the planning and development of TSVs. The most pertinent is the concept of Town Centre Management (TCM), which emerged during the late 1980s in England (Reeve 2004). Warnaby, Alexander and Medway (1998: 18) define TCM as "the search for competitive advantage through the maintenance and/or strategic development of both private areas and interests within town centres, initiated and undertaken by stakeholders drawn from a combination of public, private and voluntary sectors". A central focus of TCM is collaboration between the public and private sectors—most notably between entrepreneurs and local government authorities. The idea of public and private 'partnership' is a defining characteristic of TCM rather than a convenient addition (Reeve 2004).

The Town Centre Management approach shares some similarities with the *Mainstreets* and *Downtown* programmes from the U.S. but its evolution is quite different. TCM emerged in the late 1980s as a response to the economic decline of rural town centres in England. It was originally initiated by national chain retailers, led by *Marks & Spencer* and *Boots the Chemists*, who sought to protect the value of their property portfolios by promoting retailing activities on the high street. The economic decline of town centres was attributed to the growth of purpose-built shopping malls and the direct threat they represented to the traditional high street as a retail location (Reeve 2004). Some researchers have observed that TCM replicates the management practices of shopping centres in order to attract shoppers back to town centres (Pal and Sanders 1997).

While early approaches to TCM were almost solely focused on retailers' interests, more recent definitions have embraced the physical and socio-economic contexts of town centres, thus including the public realm as part of the concern of town centre management. It has also been argued that in recent years the focus of some TCM initiatives have shifted from a predominantly managerial focus towards a focus on regeneration and entrepreneurial investment (Otsuka and Reeve 2007). The English Tourism Board (1995: A-24) recognised the synergies between tourism and TCM when it stated that "there is a vital role for visitor management plans, tourism and economic development strategies and local (land use and transport) plans to complement and work with TCM to ensure that the full benefits of tourism are achieved with a minimum negative impact on the immediate environment and local communities". The concept has also gained some traction in the tourism literature, particularly in the context of place marketing (Page and Hardyman 1996).

A number of Town Centre Management schemes start with small scale works related to the environment, such as the provision of benches, planters, graffiti removal and local marketing and promotion campaigns (Pal and Sanders 1997). The TCM approach will be used to assist the understanding of activities in the phases of tourist shopping village change and growth.

The Exploration Phase

Previous chapters have discussed the potential for rural villages to reinvent themselves by providing authentic and unique shopping experiences. Jansen-Verbeke (2000) identifies shopping as one of the best alternative economic sectors for declining rural areas. Some rural villages wishing to establish themselves as tourist destinations may find themselves in the exploration stage. These tend to be small rural towns, close to major capital cities or tourist destinations that benefit from small numbers of tourists transiting through the town and perhaps purchasing incidental products.

In the exploration stage many villages are likely to be dominated by businesses which service the local population. These might include fuel supplies, agricultural products, local produce, pubs and bars, groceries, hairdressers, banks, automotive repairs and local eateries. In some cases villages seeking to use tourism as an economic growth strategy may be doing so because of declining economic opportunities and net outflow of residents to larger cities (Powe and Shaw 2003). Many small town centres are facing serious challenges as residents are diverted elsewhere for shopping and employment (Powe 2006). Retail opportunities in rural towns are further disadvantaged due to geographic isolation, unfavourable cost structures and restricted population catchments (Paddison and Calderwood 2007). This is a pattern that has certainly been common in rural Australia and the United Kingdom through the last few decades. Such towns may be characterised by a failing local economy exemplified by vacant commercial property and declining services. The key challenge for villages in this category is to develop the profile necessary to attract visitors.

An initial challenge in developing the profile of a village is the need to identify a clear theme which capitalises on the distinctive and valued characteristics of the countryside, amenity landscape and local identity (Anderson and McAuley 1999). As noted throughout earlier chapters, most successful villages have a strong theme created around heritage, food and wine, ethnicity, local produce, arts and crafts, antiques, performing arts or environmental/natural features. While visitors are likely to seek out the rural idyll, the village needs to identify something distinctive to set it apart from other surrounding rural villages. For example, a village which can be classified as an emerging location is Woodford, Australia. This village is located in a farming community and is building its profile through an annual large scale folk music festival. To prevent the theme from appearing contrived, it is important that it emerges from the unique characteristics of the village and is congruent with resident representations of their community. Initial starting points for defining a theme might include the following:

- Events and festivals: some villages have successful annual festivals and events and this might provide the impetus for a theme that could be developed further;

- Distinctive product categories: a number of villages have specialised in distinct product categories, for example Hay-on-Wye is well-known for its book shops, while Cheddar is well-known for...well, cheddar cheese! The attraction and clustering of similar retailers may allow a village to differentiate itself by providing a competitive edge and promotional angle (Paddison and Calderwood 2007); and
- Architectural heritage: many rural villages invariably have historical importance and the architectural heritage of the buildings is sometimes a point of distinction (Powe and Shaw 2003). The distinctive architectural style of the Cotswolds shopping villages, with their shingle and thatched roofs atop Cotswold stonework, provide an excellent example.

Earlier chapters have discussed the importance of variables such as amenity landscape, anchor attractions and the presence of artisans and crafts people. The presence of a critical mass of 'producers', such as visual, performing, literary artists or culinary producers who contribute to both tangible and intangible heritage within a community can be a powerful asset upon which to build a successful TSV (Fan, Wall and Mitchell 2008; Morris and Buller 2003). Bunting and Mitchell (2001) suggest that the attraction of producers and tourists to villages evolves through a symbiotic relationship. Producers gain inspiration from the natural setting or ready availability of raw materials or produce and view the village as a pleasant and relatively inexpensive place to live. Visitors are attracted initially by the amenity landscape but this is augmented by the opportunity to purchase a tangible but authentic reminder of the experience. As this relationship evolves, the producers become part of the landscape and the relationship becomes mutually beneficial as producers derive income from visitors. Attracting a critical mass of artists and producers is therefore a necessary precursor to further development of many rural towns into shopping villages. The presence of an entrepreneur too may be crucial, because these entrepreneurs often create the anchor attractions that draw visitors. This issue has been discussed in some detail in Chapter 4.

Fan, et al. (2008: 648) observe that successful shopping villages have the following characteristics:

1. They are accessible to a large and relatively affluent population.
2. An amenity heritage environment, including an attractive physical setting, such as a river, appealing local culture and heritage, and the presence of a rural or small town atmosphere.
3. An entrepreneurial spirit along with the availability of capital must be present.

Even at an early stage of development it is useful for a range of stakeholders to be involved in discussions about the future of the village. Most entrepreneurs are likely to be focussed on generating a return from their investment. In villages with a strong heritage focus, local preservation groups are likely to have some views about the presentation and use of buildings in the village streetscape. Local government, civic leaders and chambers of commerce can play an important role in lobbying regional tourism organisations and government agencies to secure support for developing a village. Residents should be consulted about the impacts increased visitation is likely to have on their town, and should be active participants in steering initial efforts to attract visitors. Unfortunately the coordination of various stakeholder groups is often lacking. Problems with coordination and communication between private and public stakeholders has been identified as a major barrier to tourism development in rural areas (Moscardo 2005a). The development of partnerships and alliances to foster community input and control over tourism development as well as ownership of tourism enterprises should be a key priority in the exploration stage.

Visitor numbers in the exploration stage will be low and the funding of infrastructure, such as car parks, road improvements, streetscaping and restrooms is unlikely. The exploration phase does however provide an opportunity for various stakeholders to work together to plan the development and growth of the village. A plan which details the type, style, size and location of tourist shops is likely to be useful. Projections of visitor numbers, strategies for managing resident impacts and the preservation of heritage facades are important considerations.

The Involvement Phase

The involvement phase is characterised by a discernable shift in the provision of services to tourists. While still serving locals, some retailers begin to augment their product mix with authentic items targeted at the tourist market (Snepenger, et al. 2003). These products might include local produce, food, wine, arts, crafts, antiques, collectables and local souvenirs. Tourists may become a more visible part of the streetscape and are likely to have an increased presence at events and festivals formerly dominated by locals. The length of stay, is however, likely to be only a few hours due to the lack of a variety of activities for visitors. The greatest number of visitors is likely to occur during weekends.

One of the factors that may trigger the involvement stage is the movement of people from urban areas to rural towns. This phenomenon, which in Australia has been dubbed 'tree change', has also been observed in other developed countries like the U.S. (Tonts and Greive 2002; Wolff 1999). Wolff (1999) describes the phenomenon as the 'Fifth Migration' and observes that the movement of people to smaller communities is driven by a desire for improved lifestyle, personal safety and health. Towns that are able to offer a mix of amenity landscape, heritage architecture and good access to urban centres have been the focus of attention for people seeking out the countryside ideal (Tonts and Greive 2002). Many of the people who settle in smaller rural communities are well-educated and some are successful entrepreneurs. These entrepreneurs are more likely to identify opportunities for lifestyle investments in the community which lead to the generation of profit (Mitchell 1998). Additionally, entrepreneurial investment may also emerge from long term local residents who perceive new opportunities to diversify their income in response to the growing numbers of tourists. In some cases the emergence of local entrepreneurs may be associated with conflict and negative competition, with tourism development favouring those local families who already had capital and expertise (Moscardo 2005a).

Tonts and Greive (2002) observe that the arrival of new residents from urban areas results in a number of changes to the rural landscape. The concerns of tourists, second home buyers and urban refugees become increasingly prominent, partly because they make an important economic contribution. The demand for land and housing is likely to lead to the sub-division of larger rural properties into 'hobby farms' (Tonts and Greive 2002). The purchase of farmland by these new residents results in changes to the landscape. Uncleared land is likely to be preserved while elevated, non-arable land becomes prime real estate for 'statement homes' (Barr, Wilkinson and Karunaratne 2005). These homes are built on hilltop or hillside positions with commanding views and often send messages across the landscape about the owner's social position. While these properties are used for housing, they are also often also utilised for small scale agricultural production. Examples depend on the local climate and acceptable rural conditions but may include specialised crops, boutique wineries, alpaca studs, ostrich farming, goats, boutique diaries, hydroponics or organic produce. Some primary producers who continue to farm their land may also diversify into tourism by providing farm stays and accommodation for tourists.

Several challenges become apparent in the involvement stage. Retailers may find it increasingly challenging to serve the needs of both tourists and locals. For example, stores that were previously only open during weekdays may find that they have to extend their opening hours to weekends. Stores in traditional rural towns are often not open on Sundays, are rarely open late and usually close for half a day during the week (Powe 2006). In some countries Sunday trading is a particularly contentious issue and may be strongly regulated by local by laws which only permit trading in tourist areas. This is a considerable barrier because business opportunities will be missed if shops are not able to open during peak visitor times (Getz 1993). More broadly, it is desirable at this stage of development for all entrepreneurs and shop owners to agree on common opening hours which can then be promoted through marketing campaigns. Entrepreneurs and chambers of commerce will most likely need to lobby for a change in the designation of a village which has not been previously regarded as a tourist area.

As the tourism presence grows, entrepreneurs and chambers of commerce are also likely to start pushing for TCM schemes to provide the basic infrastructure needed by visitors, such as public restrooms, additional parking bays, interpretation and visitor information. There will be pressure to present the village in a more professional and sophisticated manner and changes in presentation are likely to be welcomed by locals as evidence of the economic well-being of the community (Fan, Wall and Mitchell 2008).

Historic or architecturally significant buildings are likely to be purchased and renovated to create retail and dining opportunities for tourists. In St. Jacobs, for example, the former mill and storage silos were converted into retail spaces. Getz (2000) notes that adaptive reuse for retail function has preserved many historic buildings. In many cases deliberate architectural and historical theming is an entrepreneurial tool used to develop tourist attractiveness. Since such efforts are a visible statement of change in small towns it is reasonable to suggest widespread and participatory consultation to prevent perceived inauthentic re-creations or inappropriate new designs.

The involvement phase is therefore largely one of renewal and transformation of dilapidated and run down facilities. Some early tensions are likely to begin to emerge between entrepreneurs and preservationists but for residents there is still a sense of community and ownership of shopping and leisure spaces. Minor impacts, such as the increasing presence of litter and a lack of parking during peak holiday periods might be noted by some residents. Using the language to describe the phases of development developed by Mitchell and colleagues the rural idyll remains in place in this evolutionary phase.

The Development Phase

The development phase, as the name suggests, is a time of dramatic development and change, fuelled by escalating levels of entrepreneurial investment. This is an energetic time for entrepreneurs, employees, property owners and others providing services for the tourism industry. A range of new businesses will be established, while existing local stores will either be displaced or will increasingly service visitors rather than locals. The village streetscape is likely to undergo dramatic changes. Major developments may include the establishment of new anchor attractions and retailers. The development phase is also likely to include the entry of new accommodation providers and growth in the provision of boutique and bed and breakfast establishments. The presence of these businesses, along with the escalating number of stores and other tourist activities is likely to increase length of stay. The village itself will become the main purpose for visitation rather than a place to visit as part of a day out in the countryside. It is important to note that as a result of careful management, many mature shopping villages do not progress past this stage of development.

The expansion of accommodation options is likely to put pressure on businesses to open after hours to service the needs of overnight visitors.

This is particularly the case for cafés, restaurants, bars and entertainment venues. Like theme parks, many successful shopping villages essentially shut down in the evenings. The rainforest village of Kuranda is an excellent example. All commercial businesses except for the local hotel close at about 5 p.m. every evening. Public transport, including the cableway and train, which run to the village, cease operating late in the afternoon. There is nothing to do and nothing to see after the village closes. Attempts to extend visitor access into the evening hours are likely to result in some opposition from residents because the evenings provide a respite from the visitor presence.

As the tourist precinct of a village expands, some thought needs to be given to managing the interaction between hosts and visitors. Residents who do not benefit from the tourism industry are likely to perceive a decline in their quality of life and sense of community. Mitchell and Coghill (2000), in their evaluation of the Canadian town of Elora, suggest that the maintenance of a spatially separate central business district which caters to local residents may minimise resident-visitor interaction and promote relatively amicable relationships between the two groups. At a broader regional scale the maintenance of a hierarchy of regional centres becomes relevant (Davies, Townshend and Ng 1998). It may be acceptable for an entire village to evolve as a TSV if other nearby regional centres are maintained for more traditional rural and local roles. A risk associated with this strategy is that the TSV does indeed become increasingly like a theme park, a place where locals go to work but one in which few actually reside. Entrepreneurs may find it challenging to recruit employees. Montville village certainly exhibits some of these characteristics. Many entrepreneurs live on larger properties and small farms surrounding the village rather than in the village itself. The town of Maleny, located about 14 km from Montville, acts as the regional service centre for local residents. This arrangement does appear to minimise resident dissatisfaction because few residents actually live in the village. In addition, locals do benefit from the restoration of local buildings and the provision of specialty stores and high quality restaurants which were previously not available in the local area.

The village will increasingly be marketed as an experience, rather than just a shopping trip as visitors become more demanding. This requires a collaborative approach to place marketing involving a number of stakeholders, including entrepreneurs, chambers of commerce, tourism and community associations. Many villages will develop a sophisticated branding strategy that includes the use of various marketing channels, as well as the branding of products that originate from the village. This marketing approach will in turn attract even more visitors. Cheddar Gorge offers an example of a tightly branded destination experience. The Cheddar Gorge brand is managed by the company which dominates most of the tourist experiences in the gorge. This brand and its style of information provision is prominently displayed at the site, on brochures, maps, tour busses and products.

The village streetscape is likely to be altered by the addition of new buildings and businesses. Art galleries, upscale coffee shops, eateries and boutiques are likely to displace traditional stores. If appropriately managed, new shops and buildings can be designed to blend in with existing heritage facades. This approach has been used successfully in villages like Arrowtown, Montville and Niagara-on-the-Lake, where new buildings are often indistinguishable from older heritage buildings. In some cases local authorities have introduced building covenants and municipal ordinances which provide some control over the style, size and type of buildings. However, if this aspect of presentation is not well-managed there is a considerable risk that the 'village atmosphere' and rural idyll will be partially destroyed by uncontrolled development.

Major tensions are likely to erupt between entrepreneurs and preservationists as the former seek to develop more of the heritage streetscape. The preservation and maintenance of heritage buildings is often more costly than demolition and construction of modern structures. In some cases the layout of heritage properties may not be suitable for tourist activities and renovations are likely to be constrained by architectural conservation programs or protected through listings on heritage registers. There may also be considerable opposition to the redevelopment of some culturally significant sites from long term residents of a village. According to Mitchell and Coghill (2000) a strong local body of presentationists serves to limit the profit-driven activities of entrepreneurs.

An increase in property values is another challenge that may emerge during the development phase. As property and rental prices increase, some of the original artisans and producers which attracted visitors in the first place are likely to be displaced. Higher prices also reduce the economic attractiveness of land purchase for more traditional rural uses, such as agriculture. This problem has been observed in Montville, which initially provided a retail outlet for the work of a sizeable 'alternative lifestyle' commune located in a nearby valley. The community produced a range of handmade arts and crafts, clothing and home wares which were then sold in stores in the village. As property values increased, many moved away from the area because they were no longer able to afford increasing rental costs. Other artists not affiliated with the commune similarly found that their profit margins were being eroded by increasing rental prices. The departure of some of these original artists and crafts people has in some ways changed the village, which now offers more expensive home wares and artworks and targets economically advantaged shopping clientele.

Funding for streetscaping is likely to be a major challenge as the village develops and Town Centre Management schemes become more grandiose. The pressure to improve the outdoor environment to create a more aesthetic streetscape is likely to increase as the village becomes more competitive with other retail destinations. As visitor numbers increase, physical changes to the streetscape will also be necessary to accommodate growth.

Local government authorities, property owners and chambers of commerce are all likely to initiate TCM schemes which may involve substantial changes to the structure of the streetscape. Such changes might include the de-cluttering of the streetscape, widening of pedestrian walkways, the introduction of pedestrian crossings and traffic calming devices, extensive landscaping, introduction of street furniture and street art. These aspects are discussed in detail in Chapter 5 and 8. The funding of these changes is often a source of controversy. While most TCM schemes are supported by some type of contribution from retailers, some are reluctant to contribute to streetscaping improvements. The most common sources of funding are government grants for urban renewal, or the payment of a levy by retailers for the construction and maintenance of the streetscape. Medway, Warnaby, Bennison and Alexander (2000) found that retailers were reluctant to support streetscaping improvements for a range of reasons. Firstly, many retailers felt that it was someone else's job (i.e. local government) rather than their responsibility. Similarly, many retailers already make a contribution to the local chamber of commerce, and felt it was the responsibility of the chamber to initiate streetscaping projects. Secondly, many retailers are sceptical or cynical about the benefits that improvements will deliver for their business. An absence of proven benefits and the reluctance of other retailers to get involved can exacerbate this issue. Thirdly, some retailers simply did not have the time or money to devote to improvements, even when they supported them in principle. There is also likely to be tension between entrepreneurs, local government, civic leaders and residents over the impact of streetscape construction work on aesthetics and accessibility to business premises. In the spirit of TCM, it is therefore essential that local entrepreneurs, government, residents and preservations play a central role in the planning and redevelopment of the streetscape.

The growth of visitation that accompanies the development stage is likely to exert some pressure on transport infrastructure. While the provision of transport infrastructure has been discussed in Chapter 8, it is noted again here as a challenge confronting most villages as they expand. During peak periods, parking is likely to be a major challenge for both visitors and residents. Most villages traditionally offer on-street parking but as visitation increases the need to widen pedestrian pathways and the provision of landscaping is likely to put pressure on parking bays. A higher number of parked cars will also have a negative impact on the village's character. An increase in visitor numbers is also likely to result in the growth of road traffic and congestion through the village. This not only affects the tranquillity of the village by elevating noise levels, it also makes the pedestrian experience less enjoyable. This is a particularly pertinent point because many heritage villages, especially in Europe, have narrow laneways and streets with small building setbacks. Some planning and coordination will be required to remove traffic from the main village thoroughfare and to find space for off-street parking which is within comfortable walking distance of the shopping precinct but does not detract from its aesthetic presentation. Strategies that have been employed successfully by villages in various countries are summarised in the previous chapter.

The Consolidation Stage

The consolidation stage eventuates when the village streetscape and product mix starts to become contrived. Of course, some villages that are completely fabricated immediately reach this stage and may continue to be very successful. Ngong Ping Village, mentioned several times in this book, provides a fine example of a completely planned experience. Ngong Ping Village has been designed to reflect the area's cultural heritage and spiritual history but the village includes international brands such as Starbucks and 7-Eleven housed behind 'traditional' Chinese shopfronts. Despite this contrived environment, the village has been a popular Hong Kong attraction since its inception in 2006. Since the village does not have a local resident population the impacts of visitors are minimised. Other villages moving through the consolidation phase, or 'early destruction' as Mitchell (1998) calls it, face greater challenges.

Ngong Ping is an unusual example. Most villages evolve to the consolidation stage when activities and products become contrived. In many villages this happens when local crafts people and artisans leave the area and the void is filled by stores selling more readily available tourist paraphernalia. International fast food chains such as McDonalds, Denny's, Taco Bell and Starbucks may establish themselves in the village. Some villages may also see the arrival of hotel chains and in some cases this may be accompanied by the development of substantial resorts. The village of Sedona has some of these characteristics, with several spa resorts and time-share developments, complete with lush golf courses and swimming lagoons close to the village. Another example is the development of a Harrah's Cherokee Casino and Hotel in Cherokee, North Carolina. This development may bring substantially more visitors to the town but it is not clear whether these visitors engage in shopping in the village itself.

The increasing scale of development is not inevitable in TSVs. In the case of Montville an AUD$250 million residential golf course development was rejected by the state premier on the grounds that it was inconsistent with the state's regional plan. The development would have more than doubled the village's current development footprint and population with up to 500 residences, 150 villas, a boutique hotel and commercial space.

The consolidation stage is likely to see the development of a number of contrived retail experiences. As the heritage core of the village becomes increasingly saturated and available space is occupied, entrepreneurs may start to consider larger developments on adjacent sites. In St. Jacobs this resulted in the construction of a factory outlet mall three kilometers from the village (as described in Chapter 5). The villages of North Conway and Williamsburg have followed a similar development pattern, with factory outlet malls located away from the traditional village areas. This separates modern developments from the heritage streetscape but may impact more broadly on the amenity landscape of the surrounding rural area.

Unless the interaction between visitors and residents is carefully managed, the consolidation stage is likely to result in increased resident dissatisfaction. This discontent may be caused by a variety of factors, including increasing litter, crime, crowding, traffic flow, slow drivers and parking difficulties as well as the loss of a sense of community. Some residents may leave the village in search of other locations that provide a quieter rural lifestyle. These residents may be replaced by new residents who are attracted by opportunities in a more developed tourist village. The population structure of the village therefore changes as a result of this process. Newer residents are more likely to work within tourism and have more frequent contact with tourists, and as a result are more likely to express a desire to share the community with non-locals (Weaver and Lawton 2001).

The consolidation stage is also likely to highlight more clearly the distinction between residents who benefit from the growing tourism industry and those who feel that their rural way of life is being eroded by the influx of visitors. Madrigal (1995) identified three distinct resident groups in his study of attitudes toward the growth of tourism in Sedona.

1. Realists: residents who acknowledged both the positive and negative consequences associated with tourism development. These residents recognised that tourism helps the local economy and provides jobs, but also believed that tourism is responsible for increased traffic and litter.
2. Haters: residents who believed that not only did the negative aspects of tourism outweigh the benefits, they also believed that tourism did not provide good jobs and that it contributed to increased traffic congestion and litter.
3. Lovers: residents who agreed with the positive dimensions and strongly objected to the negative aspects of tourism development. This group most strongly believed that the benefits of tourism outweighed the negatives and that tourism provided good jobs to local residents.

Weaver and Lawton (2001) also identify three similar groups of residents in a more recent study of attitudes toward tourism in the village of Mount Tamborine. The main tourist shopping precinct is itself now so successful that few stores servicing the needs of the local population remain. Products are no longer relevant to the daily lives of locals and the cost of many goods and services may be beyond the means of most residents (Snepenger, et al. 1998). In the case of some villages, local residents may not be physically displaced, but may start to use other regional service centres. Some residents may feel that they have been displaced by visitors in their own town and choose to shop in other locations.

The product mix provided by various stores in the village may also change. As original residents and producers move away from the area in search of more peaceful rural locations, the authentic handmade products and homemade produce may be replaced by mass-produced tourism paraphernalia. These changes are difficult to manage. Chambers of commerce or local authorities cannot force businesses to sell particular types of products. There is a substantial risk that the original theme of the village may be diluted by a broader range of products. This problem has occurred to some extent in the village of Hahndorf, which originally had a strong German ethnic theme. While German food, music and architecture can still be found in the village, the potency of the theme has been weakened by new buildings and the introduction of stores that sell a broader range of products.

The consolidation stage may also be triggered by major new transport developments. In the case of Kuranda, visitation was boosted by the construction of a cable car service from the coastal city of Cairns, dramatically altering accessibility as well the experience of reaching the village. Mitchell (1998) suggested that the development of a heritage railway between St. Jacobs and the nearby population centre of Waterloo would dramatically increase the number and type of visitors to the village, thereby contributing to its creative destruction. The railway commenced operation following the publication of Mitchell's work but ceased running in 1999 due to high maintenance costs. A heritage rail service was revived in 2007 and operates on a limited schedule during peak tourist demand. Rather than causing the 'creative destruction' of some villages, these transport developments may in fact ease traffic congestion and parking issues in villages, as discussed in Chapter 8.

Stagnation and Decline

According to Snepenger, et al. (1998) the stagnation stage is accompanied by a change in the mix of visitors. Many local residents may resent new types of visitors and reject the shopping precinct that is no longer genuinely theirs. According to Mitchell, this stage will occur only if residents resign themselves to the inevitability of ensuing change. New settlers may be attracted by the gentrification of the village and are likely to replace substantial numbers of departing residents who perceive a total disintegration of the sense of community. The village may increasingly attract a transient workforce. Residents who remain are likely to be involved in the lucrative tourism industry. Major retail, transport and accommodation developments are likely to divert trade away from smaller established retailers and their settings (Coles 2004b).

If poorly managed, such villages may deteriorate as visitor destinations. Visitors seeking the rural idyll or a distinctive atmosphere may be unwilling to visit a TSV which they perceive as closely mirroring the urban retail environment which they have tried to escape (Mitchell 1998). The outcome is likely to be a decline in visitation resulting in diminished retail opportunities, reduced investment, vacant stores and declining property values. Unless other industries take the place of tourism such villages are likely to experience contracting economic conditions, resulting in a decline in the local population as residents search elsewhere for employment and economic opportunities.

Given the close proximity of some TSVs to major urban areas, there is a risk that urban sprawl will eventually devour the village and its surrounding rural landscape. At the very least, some villages may eventually become commuter suburbs for vast metropolitan areas, completely altering the population structure as well as the characteristics that draw visitors to the village. At the outset this book has proposed that TSVs are successful because they offer visitors something different, an escape from the ordinary and a place where life is simpler and moves at a slower pace. This point of differentiation is lost as the urban fringe encroaches on rural villages. Arguably the urban sprawl of Sydney has impacted negatively on the success of TSVs in the Blue Mountains region, including villages like Leura. The development of a dual carriage motorway and regular commuter rail services have destroyed the rural amenity landscape and many of these villages are now perceived as being on the outer fringe as opposed to offering a distinct rural escape from the city.

In other cases, the growth trajectories of villages may lead to the introduction of attractions and experiences which diverge significantly from the original theme. In some cases, this amounts to the virtual cloning of urban tourist shopping strips replete with chain food and accommodation outlets. For example, Gatlinburg, Tennessee has grown from a base serving outdoor recreation experiences in the Great Smoky Mountains to a heavily commercialised destination which includes inconsistent attractions such as the Ripley's Aquarium of the Smokies. The accommodation and food outlets are typical of those found throughout the rest of the country and substantial outlet shopping in neighbouring Pigeon Forge attracts new visitor markets to the area.

The villages which have been established for an extended period of time raise some interesting questions. While these villages may be described as stagnant or declining, there are a number of important stakeholder perspectives and questions to consider. When visitor numbers have levelled out this may be considered by some stakeholders to be a successful balance between competing interests. Some villages may choose to pursue continuous growth through outlet malls, resorts and casinos, while others will make a conscious decision to place limits on development in order to retain their distinctive characteristics. The profile of visitors is likely to change as those villages seeking higher levels of growth evolve, with new markets and types of tourists likely to patronise these villages. At the same time, in villages where the balance of power in the community opts for limiting growth the story and theme becomes a central marketing tool to attract a sustainable base of visitors and encourage repeat visitation because stories and themes can continue to evolve to create new experiences.

FURTHER RESEARCH AND INFORMATION NEEDS

Several preceding chapters have alluded to the scarcity of information dealing with tourist shopping villages and tourist shopping more generally. The purpose of the final section of this chapter is to consider what we do not know about TSVs in order to develop an agenda for further research. It is acknowledged that while the information needs presented here do consider multiple stakeholder perspectives, discourses and levels of relevance, they are strongly focussed around the academic perspectives presented in this book. Although multiple stakeholders will be discussed, the research agenda that is presented focuses on longer term, international and more holistic issues. The concluding remarks of this chapter will briefly discuss the relevance of these perspectives.

Tourist Shopping

It has been argued at the outset of this volume that shopping in general is a significant but poorly researched visitor activity. It would be useful to explore why tourist shopping is such a neglected area, both within the tourism and retail literature. Chapter 1 proposes three key dimensions of motivation, spatial location and phase of the travel experience as a basis for a new typology of tourist shopping. This typology identifies six main forms of tourist shopping. There is a need to explore whether this typology is suitable for describing the different types of tourist shopping across a range of settings. The typology offers the ability to predict different shopping behaviours and purchases but this capacity needs to be verified and substantiated by further research in various tourist shopping contexts. Although this research agenda is not specifically focused on TSVs, an understanding of these broader issues would assist in understanding TSV visitors and experiences more specifically.

Planning TSV Experiences

The discussion of the evolution of tourist shopping villages in this chapter indicates that there are many routes to a successful TSV. Some villages appear to emerge in an environment of very little planning, while others are deliberately planned or managed by entrepreneurs, local government, tourism marketing organisations or other groups. It is clear that at some point in the growth or evolution of a shopping village a more coordinated and integrated approach becomes necessary. Yet it is unclear how the dynamics of this coordination works. Like allied areas such as town planning and urban renewal, the coordination, management and presentation of entire villages suffer from a number of tensions and challenges. More work is needed to understand the political environment and power plays that occur between various actors involved in the governance of these villages. Such work might make use of social networking theory to identify the leading actors and followers and the influence of various actors. The role of entrepreneurs has been extensively discussed in this chapter as well as in Chapter 4. A study of biographical accounts by these entrepreneurs has some potential to better understand the factors that influence key decisions about planning and development. The issue of capacity building in rural and regional locations is also an important consideration for research exploring these issues.

In many villages there is a great deal of ambiguity and difference of opinion about who should be responsible for staging experiential elements that encompass the entire village, rather than individual in-store experiences. These concerns have practical implications, including who should be responsible for the funding and management of both tangible and intangible aspects of staging a successful experience for visitors.

Precursors to TSV Experiences

There are opportunities to further explore the characteristics, behaviour and decision making processes of TSV visitors. Tracking the extent of preparation, planning and information search behaviours undertaken by visitors would provide interesting insights that have implications for village marketing and onsite orientation. More information is needed to understand whether visitors target particular stores and cafés prior to their visit. Do anchor attractions or the village theme influence tourist decision making? Such questions could be assessed by gathering direct feedback from visitors as well as examining visitor comments posted online on blogs and discussion boards.

Onsite TSV Experiences

The onsite experiences of tourists in shopping villages are poorly understood. There is a temptation to draw conclusions about TSV visitor behaviour from research conducted in other settings such as tourist attractions, urban retail precincts and heritage sites, but are such comparisons valid? Shopping villages are complex environments in which the visitor experience is influenced by both tangible and intangible elements. More work is needed to understand the linkage and integration of experience elements that are consistent with the overall theme of the village. How important are elements of the streetscape and servicescape in providing cues and tangibles that support the themed experience? Much of the servicescape research is conducted on interior urban shopping malls and there is an opportunity to examine the relevance of this work to TSVs and other outdoor shopping precincts. On the other hand, it is equally useful to consider how intangible elements such as service quality, meeting new people, discovering distinctive local products, experiencing other cultures or simply doing something different influences the experience in these unique environments.

One of the major trends observed in some villages is a shift from passive consumerism to visitor activities that are participatory and interactive. Increased participation in activities such as learning how traditional handicrafts are made, getting involved in cooking and wine appreciation courses or designing custom-made products moves the village towards an experience economy model. But what is the pay-off of this approach? Do visitors have better experiences? Are they willing to pay more for participatory and interactive experiences and do these activities increase visitation and profitability for businesses?

At the individual business level, there are questions about the product mix and purchase behaviour of visitors. Many shop keepers interviewed during the course of preparing this book expressed their frustrations about visitors who seemed content to browse rather than purchase products. The barriers to purchasing therefore need further exploration. TSV products and motives for purchasing these are likely to be quite different to more utilitarian shopping environments. Are visitors reluctant to buy products they admire because of cost, transport constraints or other reasons? Are visitors more interested in the shopping environment and village theme rather than the products on offer? What product mix is likely to be more profitable for shop keepers and how can we anticipate what goods will be fashionable?

The role of ancillary and support services and their contribution to the overall village experience should not be overlooked. How does the style and character of accommodation influence the experience and length of stay? What is the relationship between transport access and TSVs? Do certain modes of transport detract from the village theme? What interpretive tools are used to help visitors understand the village, its history and its cultural and heritage elements? What wayfinding approaches are used to orientate visitors and to help them manage their time? It is not clear whether the absence of some support services and facilities impacts on the visitor experience and success of the village.

The temporal aspects of the TSV experience also requires further attention. Does the presence of accommodation in a village create demand for night-time activities? Many villages seem to operate on a 10 a.m.–4 p.m. schedule but can villages extend the visitor experience and increase their success by offering night-time activities? Can villages increase their profile and viability by catering for niche activities such as weddings, film sets or other leisure experiences and events?

Any discussion about the onsite TSV experience also needs to recognise that these experiences do not occur in a vacuum. TSV experiences are often linked with other activities and in some cases, may form part of an extended trip itinerary. There is not much information available about what other activities people combine with a TSV visit.

Impacts of TSV Experiences

The challenges associated with the evolution and development of TSVs have been explored in this chapter, while earlier chapters provide insights into the impacts of visitation to small regional and rural villages. It would be interesting to explore in more detail resident perspectives and impacts in TSVs. Several studies have examined the concept of creative destruction in Canadian and Chinese villages, but can these findings be generalised to other locations? Given the diversity of TSV development models, sizes and themes, there is some scope to examine in more detail how various impacts are related to different types of villages and village experiences. Further work could focus on the characteristics and dynamics between various stakeholders. There are multiple points at which a village may undergo change and it is important to understand the dynamics of change and the way in which stakeholders, markets and characteristics of the village itself combine to determine outcomes. Detailed historical analysis of the histories of shopping villages may prove useful in understanding the dynamics of change. Likewise, forward looking systematic analyses of alternative futures, including multiple stakeholders, represent a form of action research which may guide the trajectories of villages.

TSV Evolution and Futures

TSV visitation, like most forms of tourism, is essentially driven by discretionary time and money. The next chapter provides some insights into how external trends such as the Global Financial Crisis may impact on TSVs but more work is needed to understand the influence of broader political, economic, environmental social and technological drivers. Several commentators have discussed the growing trend toward second homes, while demographers and geographers have examined issues such as amenity migration. It is not clear how these developments influence the growth and development of TSVs in regional areas that might otherwise remain quiet backwaters.

Research Relevance

Identifying research topics in response to varied information needs requires multiple levels of analysis. However, there is always a risk that the etic approach adopted in much of this volume is constrained by the academic discourse and subsequently has little relevance for the planners, shop keepers, tourism organisations and associations involved in the day to day operation of shopping villages. There are multiple stakeholders involved in tourist shopping villages and each of these stakeholder groups have different information needs and priorities. The motives of these stakeholders are varied and information needs may be influenced by competing agendas including commercial viability, development, preservation and presentation.

Pearce (2005) discusses the question of research relevance and suggests that a framework that considers relevance to whom, in what tourism or development sector, at what scale, over what time period and with what themes? Using this framework, the information needs associated with tourist shopping villages derive from the various structures presented in Table 9.2.

A discussion of these multiple stakeholder information needs and perspectives is well-beyond the scope of this chapter but the framework presented in Table 9.2 does provide additional levels of analysis that may be helpful in better understanding the TSV phenomenon.

Table 9.2   A Framework for Conceptualising TSV Information Needs

Relevance	*Levels of Analysis*
To whom?	Retailers, entrepreneurs, developers, regional and state government, planners, preservation groups, special interest groups, residents, visitors, marketing organisations, academics
In what sector?	Transport, retail, attractions, accommodation, public sector, events
At what scale?	Shop, village, region, state, national, international
Over what time period?	Past, present, short term future, long term future, generational change, longitudinal perspectives
With what themes?	Economic, socio-cultural, environmental, governance

10 The Future of Tourist Shopping Villages

INTRODUCTION

The previous chapters in this book have systematically explored a range of factors influencing the state and the characteristics of a broad cross section of international tourist shopping villages. In particular the studies have attempted to consider the contextual, emic and dynamic nature of tourism settings using rich and novel methods as well as emerging theoretical schemes (Cohen 1979; Dann, Nash and Pearce 1988; Harris 2005).

This final chapter adds another broad perspective to the existing work by considering key global tourism trends of relevance to the future of tourist shopping villages. These issues are drawn from the concerns expressed by the leading international and regional industry bodies and organisations as well as contemporary writing by tourism scholars and futurists. The issues to be considered, at least succinctly, are the Global Financial Crisis, recurring global crises, predicted global problems, alterations to transport operations, changing technologies, generational changes, emerging Asian markets and accreditation and certification processes at destinations. Following these key considerations the final section of the chapter provides some key conclusions from this entire research investigation.

THE GLOBAL FINANCIAL CRISIS

The 15 years leading up to 2007 were characterised by one of the most sustained periods of economic growth and wealth creation in recent history. This resulted in higher amounts of discretionary consumer spending and was accompanied by strong growth in international tourist arrivals to most destinations. Economic growth slowed in late 2007 as a result of a liquidity crisis in the United States banking system. As the liquidity crisis worsened throughout 2008, a number of developed economies followed the U.S. into recession. These events have now become known as the Global Financial Crisis (GFC). In contrast to former economic downturns, the GFC has had a global and all-encompassing impact that has hit the tourism industry particularly hard (Smeral 2010). Most of the major international tourism source markets originate from developed countries and the economic downturn resulted in a four per cent decrease in international arrivals in 2009 (UNWTO 2010).

Although the impact of the GFC on international arrivals has been sharp and severe some countries have fared better than others. For example, the outlook in the U.S., UK and other European countries remains uncertain, while countries such as Canada and Australia have fared much better, largely due to more conservative lending practices and buoyant commodity exports. There are also indications that domestic and short-haul travel has not suffered to the same extent as long-haul trips (Smeral 2010). Several analysts have predicted a return to positive growth in international visitor arrivals and spending in 2010 (Papatheodorou, Rossello and Xiao 2010; Song and Lin 2010; UNWTO 2010). However, recent economic events in Greece, and high debt levels in several other European economies suggest a more complex 'W' shaped recovery rather than the simple 'V' shaped rebound that many commentators initially anticipated.

According to Sheldon and Dwyer (2010), tourism spending has experienced greater declines during the GFC than other consumer spending and that this has affected outbound, inbound and domestic tourism flows and the economic contribution of tourism to destinations worldwide. Broad increases or decreases in international visitor arrivals are difficult to link with TSV trends because only a small proportion of travellers to most villages are international visitors. It has also been argued that during economic crises visitors tend to substitute longer, more expensive international travel for shorter holidays closer to home (Papatheodorou, et al. 2010; Smeral 2010). This behaviour would appear to favour increased domestic visitation to TSVs, which are typically located close to major urban centres.

There is a general lack of knowledge regarding visitor behaviour during times of economic recession. While consumers may spend or travel less, the extent to which they shift to other products, reduce debt or increase savings is not well-known (Sheldon and Dwyer 2010). In general, it would appear that the GFC has had a greater impact on business travellers rather than the leisure market on which TSVs rely (Smeral 2010). Additionally markets such as those visiting friends and relatives, repeat visitors, special-interest tourists and independent travellers are expected to be more resilient (Papatheodorou, et al. 2010).

Despite this optimism, it is possible to identify several challenges that may emerge in TSVs as a result of economic downturns such as the GFC:

1. Consumer confidence and discretionary spending: consumer confidence is one of the key indicators of the overall well-being of the economy. When consumer confidence is high consumers make more purchases, but if confidence is low consumers tend to save more of their discretionary income. The result may not be a reduction in TSV

visitor numbers but reduced length of stay and a reluctance to purchase local goods and services. There is significant evidence that the GFC has resulted in a decrease in tourism spending for many of the countries examined in this book (Ritchie, et al. 2010). Nevertheless, a survey of 900 regional tourism businesses in Australia revealed that regional tourism fared better than expected during the economic downturn (Lewis 2009).

2. Declining asset prices and wealth: reductions in the value of assets such as property and real estate can have powerful implications for TSVs, particularly if assets are locally owned. A decline in property prices, coupled with decreased discretionary consumer spending, affects the ability of entrepreneurs to fund debt or to invest in new developments. Additionally the decline in wealth has substantial implications for some market segments important to TSVs, such as senior travellers.

3. Credit availability: a notable outcome of the GFC is that most lenders have adopted much more conservative lending practices in order to reduce their exposure to risk. Tourism, with its notoriously low profit margins, is likely to be perceived as a more risky investment during an economic downturn. This makes it difficult for entrepreneurs to raise the necessary capital to invest in tourism, resulting in fewer opportunities for growth, product renewal and employment within the industry.

4. Government spending: at a local government level, authorities have responded to the GFC by cutting back on infrastructure spending and employee numbers while spending less on tourism and visitor servicing (King 2009). However, several national governments have responded to the GFC by introducing economic recovery legislation and economic stimulus measures to create jobs and promote investment and consumer spending. In the short term, some of this funding is invested in regional areas and it is possible to identify several benefits for TSVs, including new infrastructure projects and funding of public sector activities such as marketing. The implications for new product development, investment, marketing, and staffing are not clear once the benefits of this spending start to fade.

It is difficult to conceive that any of these impacts have long term consequences because economic downturns typically last for only two to three years. In the long term, the tourism industry appears to be resilient and has recovered from many crises. A sense of perspective is also important. As Ritchie, et al. (2010) note, while the current crisis has been significant other past events such as natural disasters, pandemics and terrorist attacks have had an even more significant impact. Indeed, a recent academic forum on tourism and the GFC concluded that the economic downturn presented opportunities for tourism operators and destination managers to enhance their competitive advantage over the longer term (Sheldon and Dwyer 2010).

While economic downturns are disruptive, buoyant economies can also have a detrimental impact on TSVs. One of the most notable effects is the impact of economic growth in property prices. As the previous chapter highlights, TSVs often emerge in locations where there is a large concentration of artists or crafts people. These people provide the unique products and services that may transform a village into a popular destination. However, in times of economic prosperity visitor growth may make real estate attractive for external investors. These investors primarily acquire property in TSVs because of potential capital gains and as landlords may not be particularly interested in the retail mix or thematic aspects of the village experience. One of the challenges is that rising property prices and rental costs can force smaller pioneering businesses and artisans out of the village.

CRISES AFFECTING TOURISM

The Global Financial Crisis is not the only kind of dynamic and volatile force in the contemporary world with implications for tourism. Several debilitating issues repeatedly affect tourism activity. Some of these forces have powerful implications for the operation and future of tourist shopping villages although not all of these implications are negative. Tse (2006) labels these forces as the crises of tourism and four broad categories may be distinguished. There are extreme and well-recorded challenges to tourists and tourist destinations arising from (1) natural catastrophes; (2) terrorism and civil unrest; (3) life and health threatening epidemics; and (4) technical problems such as airline crashes and disasters (Beirman 2003; Timothy 2006). The scale of these problems can vary from global impacts to events with a more localised set of implications.

For the present interest in tourist shopping villages several kinds of outcomes of these tourism crises and catastrophes can be highlighted. First, there is a problem that the largest crises can deny travellers access to the whole region where there are villages. For example, the eruption of the Eyjafjalla volcano in Iceland (April 15, 2010) and the subsequent ash cloud caused the cancellation of 95,000 flights across the globe in a six day period (Tourism Emergency Response Network 2010). The ensuing travel chaos halts the flow of visitors to most locations including of course shopping villages. Immobility can also arise due to restrictions on access to specific rural locations caused by any of the various forms of crises.

Since tourist shopping villages depend on the positive appeal of the rural settings as documented in earlier chapters, disruptive forces to rural life and its attractiveness can overwhelm business. In the 2001 foot and mouth crisis in Britain two million animals from flocks and herds were killed and their carcasses burned (Beirman 2003; Coles 2003; Timothy 2006). The movement of citizens and visitors alike was curtailed and many rural attractions and walking trails closed. In addition to the restrictions on moving around the country it is easy to appreciate that the attraction of the rural settings and related shopping is limited when the countryside is blighted by the mandatory slaughter and incineration of farm animals. Myths and misinformation are a problem too, with epidemics such as Asian bird flu causing some to think that the consumption of poultry products was not only dangerous but also that rural areas should be avoided when this was unnecessary (Rittichainuwat and Chakraborty 2009).

Arana and Leon (2008) document the phenomenon of the public perception of crises. They observe that countries and regions culturally allied to or geographically near crisis locations also suffer from the travelling public's mounting disinclination to travel. Indeed much of the literature in tourism concerned with the various forms of crises pursues this very issue of providing accurate information about which specific parts of destinations are problematic for tourists and tourist activity since without this precise detail larger areas may be assumed to be affected than may actually be the case (Prideaux, Laws and Faulkner 2003).

A more localised but still very severe impact in rural areas is caused by floods and fires. In particular, rural areas are often subjected to destructive forest fires or bushfires (Ciocco and Michael 2007; Hystad and Keller 2008). Some of the Australian tourist shopping villages in the state of Victoria considered in this volume were damaged by the country's most severe fires in 2009, raising doubts that they can be rebuilt in a way that will attract visitors again. The village of Marysville in Victoria is a particularly tragic example of the devastation that accompanies bushfires. A bushfire struck the town in February 2009 killing 34 people and destroying all but 14 out of the approximately 400 buildings in the village (Victorian Bushfire Royal Commission 2009). For Marysville a major challenge in recovering from this tragedy has been convincing tourists to return so that the remaining businesses can operate (Legge 2010). Clearly one of the specific challenges for TSVs is to develop effective plans for restoring tourism business after a natural disaster.

Not all of the consequences associated with the negative forces affecting tourism work against the tourist shopping villages. There have been several studies documenting that after the September the 11th terrorist attacks there was considerable increased travel to destinations within the United States which were closer to home and seen as safe. Specific studies in North Carolina (Gut and Jarrell 2007) and in Hawaii (Bonham, Edmonds and Mak 2006) provide evidence that attractions and locations such as tourist shopping villages and rural attractions were seen as unlikely targets for terrorism. This perceived immunity may ensure the continued viability of tourist consumption in some villages despite a more threatening wider environment. The notion that there is a shift in the choice of destinations such as rural villages following crises is linked to shifts in the ways different markets respond to the unrest or crises. Fuchs and Reichel (In Press) note that repeat visitors to volatile destinations are driven by different needs than first time visitors and can be more easily persuaded to come to problem areas. This kind of analysis is borne out in several other settings with Bhattari, Conway and Shrestha (2005) noting the resilience of Asian pilgrimage visitors in Nepal compared to western travellers and Rittichainuwat and Chakraborty (2009) observing that the knowledge base of experienced backpackers in Thailand facilitates their ability to select safe options. Going back to well-known places inherently suits villages which have large and stable repeat visitor markets.

As Paraskevas and Arendell (2007) argue it is a notable feature of many tourist settings that they are open access public areas and hence inherently a soft target for terrorists (see also Pizam and Mansfeld 1996). Yet, despite these difficulties many would also argue that shopping villages are relatively safe destinations and this feature may be a powerful force in ensuring their strong future in the face of the larger crises of tourism. In the response to the foot and mouth epidemic in Britain the marketing slogan used in the recovery plan was "UK-OK" (Tse 2006). It can be suggested that OK is an apposite designation for the safety and crises positioning of tourist shopping villages. This comparative strength may be a major factor if the world of tourism is disrupted by more and more extreme crises.

CLIMATE CHANGE AND PEAK OIL

In every era there are prophecies of doom and destruction. At the present time there are three related prophecies—climate change, natural disasters and peak oil. Like all such prophecies there is considerable debate about the likelihood, extent, severity and risks involved in each case. What is clear, however, is that the existence of the prophecy itself has real consequences through government policies, business practices and consumer belief and behaviour (Moscardo, Laws and Faulkner 2001). In other words the predictions alone will have implications for TSVs.

Climate change has been the centre of much public, political and scientific debate in both the international arena and within many countries. The fundamental argument proposed is that the burning of carbon-based fuels to support energy needs, transport systems and the production of food, goods and services generates carbon emissions or greenhouse gases. In turn these emissions then alter the climate resulting in changed weather patterns and rising sea levels (Desjardins 2007). It is proposed that one way to slow or halt this process of climate change is to cut carbon emissions (Rainey 2006). To achieve this many governments either have already developed or have proposed various policies to reduce carbon emissions. These include emissions trading schemes, taxes on certain activities and goods, subsidies and grants for the adoption of practices and/or technologies to limit energy use or emissions and switching to alternative types of energy (Dovers 2005). In addition to these attempts to limit or reduce climate change processes, there is also increasing attention being paid to how governments, businesses and residents can adapt to the predicted consequences of climate change (Lobell, et al. 2008).

Businesses, managers and planners in TSVs have to be aware of both these aspects of climate change:

- The contributions that their operations make to climate change and how these can be limited; and
- How they can adapt to the predicted changes in weather.

In the former case it seems likely that there will be increasing pressure from governments on businesses to cut their energy use and carbon emissions. There is also likely to be increasing consumer pressure from visitors who are concerned to limit their own carbon emissions (National Geographic 2009). For TSVs this will mean that attention needs to be paid to adopting energy efficient practices across all aspects of their operations. This creates both opportunities and challenges for TSVs. In terms of opportunities it is likely that adopting community wide initiatives to cut energy use and carbon emissions could be a competitive advantage in attracting increasingly environmentally aware visitors. In this context it may be challenging to convince visitors to participate in some environmentally responsible practices and programs. Also it must be remembered that a major contributor to greenhouse gas emissions in tourism is long-haul travel, either by road or air (Hall 2005). If these forms of transport become more heavily taxed to reduce emissions this could significantly alter the number and type of visitors coming to TSVs. The predicted changes to weather patterns, such as increasing temperatures and changes to rainfall (Hall 2005) also offer both challenges and opportunities for TSVs depending on their locations and the activities currently offered or available for visitors. One of the predictions associated with climate change is that there will be more frequent and extreme weather-related natural disasters including storms, hurricane, floods and droughts and bushfires (Hall 2005). For some TSVs, warmer, wetter weather or alternatively cooler, drier weather may extend the desirable times to visit thus offering more stable business opportunities. For other TSVs, changes to resource dependent activities such as winter ski seasons may require a significant change in the nature of the experience offered to the visitors.

Another environmental challenge is peak oil. The notion of peak oil refers to the point at which global oil production reaches its maximum point. After that point production begins to decline (Swallow 2009). The critical consequence of reaching or passing the peak oil point is that the price of oil will continue to increase until it reaches a point where it is no longer possible to sustain current business practices (Swallow 2009). The implications of peak oil for TSVs are essentially the same as those for climate change as they centre on reducing the use of, and reliance on, oil for energy.

TRANSPORT AND AVIATION

The transport sector is likely to be significantly influenced by fossil fuel scarcity in coming decades as noted in the previous section. The importance of transport links and accessibility to TSVs has also been discussed in some detail in earlier chapters. The consequences of fossil fuel scarcity and climate change are likely to result in increasing levels of attention, planning and investment in transport technologies and network planning. In terms of surface transport, some countries are already investing in public transport systems and programs designed to provide greater incentives for commuters to rely less on private vehicles. Many TSVs, as defined in this book, are within an hour or two of major metropolitan areas and as urban areas continue to spread and sprawl, some of these villages are moving into the catchment areas serviced by new public transport networks. This has a number of impacts. Firstly, these villages become more attractive living areas for urban commuters, potentially changing their population structure and affecting demand for real estate and changes in land use. Secondly, connections to public transport networks enhance visitor accessibility but are likely to change the experience. There is a risk of dramatic rises in visitor numbers, leading to problems such as crowding and congestion and negative impacts on the host community. Thirdly, access to urban public transport networks may not be in keeping with the rural ideal and idyll that visitors seek. Mass public transport systems may also interfere with elements of the streetscape as well as more traditional forms of transport used in the village. Some villages have overcome this issue by using more traditional forms of transport such as steam trains and trolley buses to transport visitors from urban centres to the village.

While people will undoubtedly continue to rely on private travel to access many villages, private vehicles are increasingly likely to rely on electricity or renewable energy. There are some positive benefits for village streetscapes and environments, which should be quieter and less polluted. It is highly likely however that the provision of parking spaces will continue to be a major logistical transport problem for a number of villages.

Trends in the aviation sector are also affecting the development of TSVs. Deregulation and privatisation of the aviation sector have resulted in the most significant structural changes in air transport over the last 20 years. One of the results has been the emergence of low cost carriers (LCCs) in North America and Europe, and more recently in Asia (Francis, et al. 2006). LCCs tend to operate point to point services to secondary airports rather than hub and spoke networks and this has brought new kinds of visitors to previously less accessible destinations. This increased access may result in the development of villages close to major new regional tourism aviation nodes. Shannon airport in Ireland illustrates this process with the village of Adare benefiting from the arrival of international flights and tours from a newer nearby hub. The opportunity to see this process repeated in Eastern Europe and Asia is particularly deserving of further research attention. Nevertheless, while the development of low cost air travel has been spectacular, future growth may be impeded by fossil fuel scarcity and increasing costs of air travel.

ELECTRONIC COMMERCE, THE INTERNET AND NEW TECHNOLOGIES

In discussions of tourism futures, technology is frequently described as a key driver for increasing the mobility of tourists, and therefore, for sustaining the growth of the tourism industry (Rayman-Bacchus and Molina 2001). Despite the potential widespread impact of technology on tourism, research into this phenomenon has been restricted to studies of "technology as a tool of the tourism industry" (Stipanuk, 1993: 267). In particular this research has focussed on the use of technology in the operational divisions of tourism businesses such as hotels (O'Connor and Frew 2002), mobile technologies (Kim, Park and Morrison 2008), information search (Xiang, Wober and Fesenmaier 2008), online distribution and marketing (Buhalis and Law 2008; Frew 2008; Litvin, Goldsmith and Pan 2008) and more recently social media (Xiang and Gretzel 2010). Somewhat earlier, Stipanuk (1993) provided a useful holistic framework to illustrate the developing roles of technology in tourism. This framework is presented in Table 10.1, along with some examples of applications in TSVs.

Within this broader framework the role of technology in TSVs extends well-beyond marketing and distribution, although technologies such as the Internet have perhaps had the most dramatic impact on TSVs. The Internet offers a new form of independence for travellers and while travel agents and tour operators continue to exist and, in some markets flourish, the ability of Internet-connected consumers to have more pre-departure information and different kinds of information about their destination is of considerable consequence for those who manage their onsite experience. However, even the most cursory review of TSV websites indicates that while most villages have a basic Internet presence, the vast majority have failed to capitalise on the interactive nature of the web. There is a great deal of scope for villages to better use the Internet to help visitors plan aspects of their visit (e.g. activities, food and parking) and to include the village as part of a wider customised itinerary. Likewise, there is some potential for villages to use social media to connect with visitors and to build relationships which encourage return visits. The same technologies may also be used to update past and potential visitors about forthcoming events, new products and new store openings.

The development of Web 2.0 technologies such as blogs provides unprecedented opportunities for electronic word-of-mouth communication (Litvin, Goldsmith and Pan 2008). The power of deciding what travellers read, listen to and watch has spread from a handful of media companies to anyone with a camera, a connection and a computer. The communication

Table 10.1   The Role of Technology in TSVs

Role of Technology	TSV Applications
Contributing to tourism growth	· Transport technologies are closely linked to growth in tourism; · Media technologies expand knowledge create demand for travel to TSVs; and · Information and communication technologies support the exchange of vast amounts of information about TSVs
Creating the tourism experience	· Architects, engineers, builders use technology to construct TSV infrastructure; and · Technology used as the basis for tourist attractions, activities and experiences in TSVs
Protecting the tourism experience	· Protecting tourists (e.g. closed circuit cameras, secure access, explosives detection, airport security, biometrics, alarms, GPS tracking); and · Protecting & preserving destinations & resources (e.g. dehumidifiers, site hardening, energy conservation, waste management, renewable energy)
Enhancing the tourism experience	· Orientation (e.g. GPS SatNav); · Comfort & convenience (mobile technologies, digital cameras, Wi-Fi, electronic pocket translators, food and beverage storage and preparation); and · Interpretation (e.g. information kiosks, holograms, podcasts, virtual tour guides, film and multimedia displays of TSV heritage, motion/voice activated displays)
Focal point of the tourism experience	· Industrial and agricultural attractions (e.g. breweries, factories, farms, mills, arts & crafts); and · Re-enactment and recreation of environments/ activities that are too fragile, too expensive or no longer exist
Tool of the tourism industry	· Communication, marketing & distribution (e.g. Internet, booking systems, onsite); Management of visitors/guests (e.g. managing queues, visitor flows, access, visitor tracking, traffic management);· · Management of facilities (e.g. property management systems); and · Decision making & back office systems (e.g. inventory, recipe costing, accounting, HR systems)
Destroying the tourism experience	· Technology failure: inconvenience (e.g. failure of booking systems, power outages, climate systems) and safety & security (e.g. failure of smoke alarms, warning systems, traffic lights); · Technology interference – noise or visual pollution (e.g. cell phones, audio guides, tour buses); and · Resource destruction, climate change·

pathways involved may include sharing knowledge using micro-blogs, blogs and wikis (e.g. WikiTravel, twitter), writing reviews on TripAdvisor, adding photos to Flickr and creating 'mashups' on Google. Many commercial tourism operations have used various approaches to influence this new form of communication, including establishing their own blogs and offering visitors incentives to post their positive entries and reviews. It has become important too for managers to respond rapidly and convincingly to negative reviews. Those responsible for the promotion of tourist shopping villages need to consider adopting some of these strategies and some business operators may need to develop a better understanding of the electronic distribution environment.

A final note about technology concerns the potential to improve onsite visitor experiences. The increased use of digital technologies such as GPS SatNav devices, smart phones and iPods are likely to provide travellers with onsite information in ways which will change travellers' use of guidebooks and local information sources. Websites optimised for smart phones could allow visitors to download useful information such as visitor maps and menus from restaurants in the village. Self-guided podcast tours depicting the heritage or thematic elements of the village could be used to enhance the experience for some market segments. GPS devices coupled with audio and video streaming create further potential to design site-specific multimedia presentations that are triggered when visitors enter particular zones within the village. There are many future possibilities which hitherto appear to have been largely ignored in TSVs.

CHANGING TOURISM MARKETS: EMERGING AND AGING GENERATIONS

Global trends and future predictions are often organised under the macro-categories of political, economic, social and technological (Hall 2005). Within the social realm two major trends dominate—the ageing population and the rise of new generations, especially Gen Y.

There has been considerable government attention paid to the challenges associated with an aging population. As a consequence of improvements to health care and decreasing birth rates most countries in the world, especially those that are the primary generators of tourists, have a population in which the fastest growing segment are those over 55 years of age. In many places the proportion of the population in this cohort is, or soon will be, the largest (Moscardo 2006). Researchers and social commentators generally agree that these 'senior citizens' will live longer in retirement, and be healthier and more active than previous people in these age groups (Kim, Wei and Ruys 2003). There are also claims that these seniors will be wealthier are more difficult to sustain (Moscardo 2006), especially in light of the recent GFC. What is not contested is that these seniors are currently playing and will continue to play a significant role in travel and tourism (Moscardo 2006).

The existing research into senior travellers can be summarised around three key themes of importance to TSVs:

- The strong interest of senior travellers in travel focussed on nostalgia, education and self-development and cultural activities;
- The need to provide additional facilities and services that recognise some of the physical constraints that emerge with age; and
- The problems of providing these facilities and services without isolating seniors and treating them according to ageist stereotypes which may portray them as less capable (Moscardo 2006).

In general TSVs are and will continue to be popular destinations for senior travellers and it can be argued that the development of activities around education, self-development and creativity are likely to be important methods for retaining this market. TSVs will also need to recognise the need to incorporate physical facilities and services to support this group including considerations such as the size of text on signage, the provision of space for recreational vehicles in some countries, the supply of rest areas within the village and access for visitors to health care. But it is important to recognise the potential for ageist stereotypes to become embedded in our thinking about seniors and to continue to question the extent to which decisions made about senior visitors are based on poor assumptions rather than a genuine desire to provide appropriate service.

The potential dominance of negative stereotypes is also a problem for tourism industry members and planners in dealing with the second major social trend—the emergence of Gen Y as consumers, employees, entrepreneurs and policy makers. Gen Y, also known as millennials, echo baby boomers and the digital generation, are generally defined as people born between 1977 and 1995 (Donnison 2007) which means that in the year 2010 they are aged between 15 and 33 and are spread across adolescence and early adulthood. This is a generation that has been much discussed in the public arena and typically these discussions have focussed on negative attributes that are claimed to be associated with this generational cohort. A more detailed and critical analysis of these claims suggests that many are contradictory and few are based on sound evidence (Moscardo and Benckendorff 2010).

The available reliable evidence suggests that key characteristics of Gen Y are:

- That information and computer technology (ICT) dominates their world;
- That they actively seek and value social interaction and shared family experiences,

- That travel is important and that they particularly seek to use travel to maintain a positive work-life balance; and
- That they are concerned about social and environmental sustainability (Moscardo, Murphy and Benckendorff In Press).

The major implication for TSVs is that Gen Y represents a potentially important market worthy of substantial attention. To respond effectively to this market though TSVs will need to focus on how they use ICT in their marketing and in the support of the experiences they offer. This group will also add pressure to TSVs to improve their environmental and social performance.

EMERGING TOURISM MARKETS: GLOBAL CONSIDERATIONS

With international travellers projected to almost double by 2020, to approximately 1.6 billion, the most significant increases are expected to take place in the emerging markets of Brazil, China, Eastern Europe (specifically Belarus, Bulgaria, Czech Republic, Hungary, Moldova, Poland, Romania, Slovakia and the Ukraine), India, Russia, South Africa, and The United Arab Emirates (Tourism Intelligence International 2010). According to a report published by PATA (Monthievichienchai 2010), in terms of source markets, there is no doubt that India and China will continue to be the two countries to watch as their growing middle-classes exercise their desire to see the world. By 2020, the UNTWO expects India will account for 50 million outbound tourists, while China will contribute 100 million travellers.

The Chinese Outbound market is one of the few source markets which continued to grow during the global economic crisis. China is predicted to be the fastest growing outbound tourism market in the world over the next 12 years. The number of Chinese travelling abroad has nearly tripled in the past five years to over 34 million—making China the fastest growing tourism market in the world. Because they are in the early stages of outbound travel, and also because in many cases they are required to do so, Chinese tourists tend to travel in tour groups. They have other characteristics as well—they like to shop, they tend to stay in budget hotels and they often pack as many sights into their itineraries as possible (Gunasekara 2010).

An article in the Singapore Straits Times comparing the shopping habits of Chinese and Indonesian visitors claimed that Chinese tourists tend to be very loud, more demanding, and sometimes rude. Indonesians were described as being more fashionable as they often request exclusive or limited-edition designs and big-ticket spenders, whereas the Chinese want to see everything and tended to buy in bulk—10 to 20 pieces at a time. Indonesians spent S$2.1 billion in Singapore in 2008, S$702 million more than tourists from China, according to the Singapore Tourism Board (Pang, Ying and Qing 2010). The Chinese Communist Party has acknowledged the ambassadorial role of Chinese tourists abroad and recognised that systematic misbehaviour of Chinese tourists could tarnish the image of the country. To this end the 'official etiquette watchdog', the Communist Party's Spiritual Civilization Steering Committee developed a guidebook which promoted 'queuing days' to encourage the formation of orderly lines, and waged war against spitting and littering to heighten awareness and correct some embarrassing habits in the lead up to the Beijing Olympics (Chen 2008).

The 2008 Visa and PATA Asia Pacific Travel Intentions Survey of 5,554 respondents from Australia, China, France, Hong Kong, India, Japan, Korea, Singapore, Chinese Taipei, the United Kingdom and the United States provides some insight into the travel and shopping preferences of some key emerging markets. While the popularity of independent travel is growing, Chinese and Indian respondents were most likely to take part in tour group travel. Importantly, people from India, Singapore, and China were more likely to pay extra for convenient and hassle free service. Good customer service was also particularly important to respondents from India, China and Chinese Taipei. Local department stores were the most popular place to shop for Chinese (94 per cent), Indian (93 per cent) and Singaporean (98 per cent) respondents. Local bazaars/markets were also popular for respondents from Singapore (96 per cent), Hong Kong (94 per cent), China and India (both with 87 per cent) (PATA 2009).

A report prepared for the Royal Norwegian Embassy explored the outbound tourism potential of India and identified that, although there is now an increasing range of goods available in India compared with a few years ago, Indians still relish the opportunity to shop away from home. There has, however, been a shift in tastes of late and what used to be a preference for low cost items has now moved towards more expensive electronic gadgets, jewellery and designer goods. Indians can be very high spenders—in Singapore, for example, this market spends the largest amount per head of all visitors (Times Research Group 2004). This report also points out that many Indians, particularly those from rural areas, are very conservative and familiar food is very important to them. Many Indians are strict vegetarians and do not drink alcohol, in addition some sects have strict food preparation rules based on their religious beliefs. It is important, therefore, for Indians to be able to find food which is familiar to them and which has been prepared in the correct fashion.

The behavioural implications of large groups of international tourists in small regional towns are obvious and problematic. Is the product sold in TSVs appealing to these markets? What are the service implications in terms of food, information and accommodation? The local and regional tourism associations will need to utilise the market intelligence available to them from state and national tourist offices to develop an in-depth understanding of these emerging markets. While China and India are at the forefront, many of the other emerging markets, particularly from the Middle

East and Eastern Europe, will all have specific implications as well. The decision to make concerted efforts to attract visitor from these markets is not one to be taken lightly. The ability of the villages to offer an experience, in terms of shopping, dining and accommodation, which meets the unique needs of these markets must first be assessed. Any ill-prepared attempts to attract visitors could have long term detrimental impacts to the reputation of the TSV. A further consideration is the most desired overall visitor mix. While the visitor and spending power of these emerging markets might seem appealing, it is important that the overall visitor profile to any TSV is one that is consistent and compatible with the core experience and with other visitors.

QUALITY STANDARDS AND DESTINATION MANAGEMENT

It is widely accepted that today's consumers are more sophisticated and well-travelled, and demand increasingly higher standards of service. In order to remain competitive, businesses must focus on achieving consistent service excellence. Industry recognition of the need to provide some guarantee of quality tourism experiences is evidenced by the announcement on May 11, 2010 by Australia's federal government that it will spend $5.5 million over four years to implement and operate a National Tourism Accreditation Framework (NTAF). This initiative was introduced in an effort to better position Australia's tourism industry to compete on the basis of quality and reliability. The main purpose of quality accreditation programmes is to give visitors and the travel industry assurance that they are working with reputable operators who are serious about providing customers with good-value, high quality experiences (Department of Resources Energy and Tourism 2010).

Under Australia's proposed NTAF, high quality tourism businesses will carry a quality mark or logo which will be promoted to tourists and those businesses will be required to continually improve their products and services in return for global promotion, including listing on Australia.com and in the Australian Tourism Data Warehouse where wholesalers will have online access to accredited businesses. The government has emphasised that Australia has 580,000 tourism businesses, of which 1/3 are in regional Australia and 93 per cent are small. It claims that the NTAF will help promote market confidence in regional and small businesses that lack the advertising capacity or brand reputation of iconic destinations and bigger operators. The NTAF will bring together more than 20 existing rating and accreditation programs under one governance framework and each one will fund and manage their program within the guidelines of the proposed NTAF. New programs entering the NTAF will be required to meet their own costs, with the federal funding commitment going towards the development of a common mark for the NTAF, the marketing and promotion of the mark or brand and staff for administrative and policy support (Department of Resources Energy and Tourism 2010).

Of course Australia is not the first or only country to adopt such an accreditation program. The announcement of the program was made with particular reference to the success of Tourism New Zealand's marketing and promotion of a quality tourism brand using Qualmark as a guarantee of '100% Pure Assurance' since 2005 (New Zealand Tourism Board 2010). The Qualmark endorsement for accommodation and other tourism businesses, such as adventure and cultural activities, means that those businesses have been independently assessed against a set of national quality standards. Qualmark assurance identifies professional and trustworthy businesses and the scheme has been extended to include Qualmark Green accreditation for businesses assessed on their environmental performance.

In practical terms, the Qualmark assessments are completed once a year by business experts at the location of the business and can take from three hours to one day to complete. This includes assessment in customer service, standard of facilities, overall business operations, environmental business practices and general safety. Feedback cards are provided by Qualmark assured businesses to allow customers the opportunity to provide comments on their experience. A mystery shopper programme also provides a quality check. The assessment checks that the business has met the necessary legal, insurance and health and safety requirements and the system is regularly reviewed to ensure it adapts to changing industry standards and customer expectations. If a Qualmark business does not meet accepted quality standards the business can be withdrawn from the system (Qualmark New Zealand 2010).

Singapore Service Star is another accreditation scheme. It was developed by the Singapore Tourism Board to help businesses achieve service excellence with the ultimate goal of greater consumer spending, benefiting industry players and enhancing Singapore as a tourist destination. The scheme is designed to boost tourists' confidence in shopping in Singapore by delivering a truly unique experience for visitors (Singapore Tourism Board 2006). Singapore Service Star welcomes businesses from retail, food and beverage and nightspot industries to join the scheme. Of particular relevance to tourism shopping villages is the retail program which uses mystery shopping assessments to provide reports to business that will identify service gaps and the need for improvements. To obtain and retain membership in the scheme retail businesses must obtain a service mark above 70 or the industry average, whichever is higher (Singapore Tourism Board 2008).

So what is the relevance of these sorts of programs to tourist shopping villages? The importance of maintaining quality standards for TSVs is evident if they are to continue to attract both domestic and international visitors. There is scope for not only individual businesses to take advantage of accreditation schemes as a mechanism to both communicate a 'quality' message to visitors and to leverage the promotional benefits provided by inclusion in such schemes. It could also be possible that there is benefit for the villages as a whole to be proactive in adopting quality accreditation and perhaps even spearheading a push for entire villages to be evaluated. A clear 'stamp' of approval from accrediting bodies could be used by villages to assist in attracting organised tour business, particularly those catering to international tourists. This 'quality brand' recognition can be used not only in marketing activities, but also as a tool by local business associations and local and regional tourism organisations to encourage improvement in the standards and quality of service provided by local tourism operators and retail businesses.

Also of relevance is Australia's $20m project to create a national brand—Australia Unlimited—that goes beyond tourism and which will be used by the federal government's trade export arm to market Australia and its products to the rest of the world. According to Trade Minister Simon Crean, "Australia Unlimited has the breadth to market all of Australia's strengths—grounded in our commitment to innovation and quality" and "… is aimed at taking us beyond tourism messages. It will deliver a national brand for Australia through a consistent image and a consistent message" (Australian Minister for Trade 2010; Australian Trade Commission 2010).

While the current focus of the program is on 'branding' export products from Australia, similar to the use of '100% Pure' New Zealand to promote, among other things NZ honey, there might also be scope to use a broader 'Australia Unlimited' brand to designate uniquely Australian regional products produced and sold in TSV. The opportunity applies to other countries, given that one of the key attractors for the villages is the opportunity for visitors to purchase regionally distinctive and unique local products. The branding or designation of the 'authenticity' of products, whether at a national or regional level can also contribute to the ability of the villages to differentiate themselves in terms of the shopping experiences they provide. A relevant example is the Bandiere arancioni designation of rural villages in Italy (Touring Club Italiano 2010). The 'orange flag' accreditation scheme is administered by the Touring Club Italiano and publicly identifies villages throughout Italy which meet the following criteria:

- Population is less than 15,000 people;
- Located in the countryside;
- Accommodation has been star-graded;
- Distinguished by a unique or typical culture;
- Access to artistic, architectural, natural or folkloric resources;
- Sensitive to sustainability issues; and
- Pleasant ambience, scenery and a central historic region.

The combination of quality accredited regional villages and uniquely branded products might both help to differentiate the visitor experience offered by villages in any country. Additionally, accreditation processes are likely to increase the confidence of visitors to the region that a value for money experience is on offer. In particular such initiatives could facilitate the inclusion of the tourist shopping village experience in tour wholesaler and operator packages and itineraries.

CONCLUSION

As described in Chapter 1 this book has two stated goals. The first of these specified goals was to examine tourist shopping villages in order to understand how their performance can be enhanced for multiple stake-holders. The program of study directed at this goal had a strong focus on the management and production of the experience for visitors and consisted of undertaking some original research and closely examining existing literature. The second aim was to consider the tourist experiences in the shopping village context to augment the growing interest, both within and outside tourism, of the nature of contemporary experience. The pathways to reach this second goal included a focussed consideration of the literature on shopping markets, visitor motivation, theming of the village, the role of storytelling and interpretation and visitor activities.

It was established both in the introductory chapter and in subsequent consideration that tourist shopping villages are a complex topic of study and caution must be exercised in offering broad generalisations about the characteristics of villages, their futures and the markets they serve. Some generic features are apparent and if considered cautiously may be insightful in many instances. The first aim of the study focussing on the characteristics of villages which managers, government officials, retailers and some community groups favoured and which were supported by the detailed literature in numerous studies can be highlighted in the following points:

1. The Advantages of Accessibility and Links

   - Transport links to a major population base or touring route are a foundation for building a tourist shopping village.
   - Clear and compact shopping precincts that are integrated into the general layout of the village are desirable structural features enabling relaxed inspection of shops over a convenient distance.

2. Clear and Consistent Themes

   Combinations of themes appear to be effective.
   Heritage is a successful theme, particularly when combined with cultural ethnicity and/or arts and crafts.
   The environment setting or access to natural areas can be combined with health and recreation themes.

- Food and wine can be successfully combined with many other themes.

3. The Value of Tourist-focused Presentation of the Village

- Streetscaping is closely associated with perceptions of success.
- Signage which is both functional and aesthetically appealing is documented as a part of the appeal of villages.
- Visitor information and facilities apply not just to toilets, food, cafés and a centre for information but require some innovation and imagination to build the atmosphere of the setting.
- Immersive experiences developed through themes which enable stories to be constructed help define a memorable visit.
- Parking and its management are troublesome issues for many villages and heavy traffic areas and shopping streets are not compatible. Creative solutions include specialised parking areas with supporting transport links reinforced by clear directions and signage.

4. Communication and Presentation

- Clear and consistent imagery and branding separate the longer established villages from their emerging counterparts.
- The extension of the branding to regionally distinctive products and goods is a feature of the larger villages and this identity making represents a pathway for many developing destinations.
- High quality media communications represent an opportunity for tourist shopping villages, particularly in terms of the more extensive use of Web 2.0 technologies.

5. The Potential for Resilience

- The individual futures of shopping villages are closely tied to their age, state of development growth and national context.
- The conceptual arguments developed in this research program rejected a simple trajectory or path of evolution of tourist shopping villages, citing not only regional variation in these processes of change but also powerful examples of cases which did not fit creative destruction models or inevitable stages of evolution and transition.
- The broad set of considerations which frame tourism futures overall are somewhat in favour of the continuing positive future of tourist shopping villages which exhibit some advantages in the areas of more localised travel, some immunity to crises and a scale of operation permitting accreditation and quality control.

- Villages which have clear plans to manage crises and control their futures are likely to be successful into the future.
- Both older and younger markets as well as visitors from emerging economies may be drawn to imaginatively developed shopping villages.

These dominant themes represent key points in the findings about the management and future of tourist shopping villages. More specific recommendations and processes underlying successful management are documented in the preceding chapters, especially Chapters 1, 4, 5, 7, 8 and 9. Taken together and building on the key points summarised above, it is possible to suggest that a comprehensive scorecard of tourist shopping village functioning could be constructed from this extensive review of material. The formal development of that process may be a further future activity of the researchers in combination with village promoters, managers, retailers and communities.

The second aim of this volume and the presentation of information about visitors in the TSV settings involved reflecting on the nature of tourism experiences using this context as a touchstone for stimulating the development and application of ideas. This goal was realised by the detailed reviewing and some integration of multiple previous studies about shopping in general, as well as re-examining information drawn from the experience economy and postmodern appraisals of tourist shopping motivation. This component of the work was developed in particular in Chapters 1, 2, 3, 6, 7, and 10.

The following points highlight the conclusions drawn in relation to the nature of the tourist shopping village experience:

1. Motives: the motives for shopping in a tourist shopping village tend principally to involve purchasing discretionary, identity and relationship affirming goods and services rather than serving utilitarian goals. This includes a desire to understand and experience local people and places.
2. Visitor types: shopping in TSVs is an easy access activity often involving purposeful and focussed shoppers who can be termed specialist shopping enthusiasts but this group may be juxtaposed with visitors who are less directly interested in shopping and keener on experiencing the overall ambience and atmosphere of the villages.
3. Multiple roles: it is valuable to understand that purchasing for others as well as oneself is common in TSVs and that the purchasing process is often the mechanism to achieve an appreciation of the setting and its products, as a boost to remembering the visit and as a pathway to involve the shopper with local people and their world. These purchasing patterns are strongly underpinned by the sensory, emotional and activity based components of experience.

4. Self-directed pleasure: shopping as a destination enhancing experience is married with visitors' desire to satisfy internal motivations such as indulging in sensory experiences, buying luxury branded items, buying souvenirs for oneself, and collecting.

5. Changing Experiential provision: the kind of tourists welcomed in TSVs by local communities appears to depend on the stage of development of the TSV and as cheaper products appear in villages and more mass market visitors arrive the kind of experiences available to visitors alters. Those visitors seeking what are likely to be perceived as authentic, distinctive, locally produced products and experiences are more likely to find them in villages where the development process has been tightly controlled or the village is still emerging as a well-known entity.

6. Features supporting the performance: TSVs can be described as themed and managed stages for visitors to enact their shopping and entertainment roles. The well-defined features of what they seek to support their 'public' performances are:

   - Variety of stores and products;
   - Novel, unique, authentic and distinctive products, especially those not available at home;
   - Attractive prices/value for money;
   - Clean, well-lit, attractive stores with interesting window and product displays;
   - Easily accessible shopping areas in terms of location, having a pedestrian focus and extended opening hours;
   - Positive interactions with friendly, helpful and knowledgeable staff;
   - Safe and secure environments and transactions;
   - Opportunities to experience local culture;
   - Shops combined with leisure and entertainment activities;
   - Cheerful, colourful and lively settings;
   - Streetscapes with a variety of attractive facades; and
   - Attraction features and interactions which provide the basis for stories and narratives.

7. The TSV Visitor Experience Model: the integration and understanding of the TSV experience was facilitated in the research program by employing an adapted model of visitors' experiences. In particular mindfulness draws attention to the processes of capturing and retaining visitor attention while also emphasising the managerial need to eliminate distracting situational elements which draw the visitor away from focussed engagement on the experience itself. In essence this approach is repeated here in Figure 10.1 because the foregoing chapters have confirmed its usefulness and applicability as a convenient organiser of the stages and processes in conveying the experien'' nature of TSV shopping.

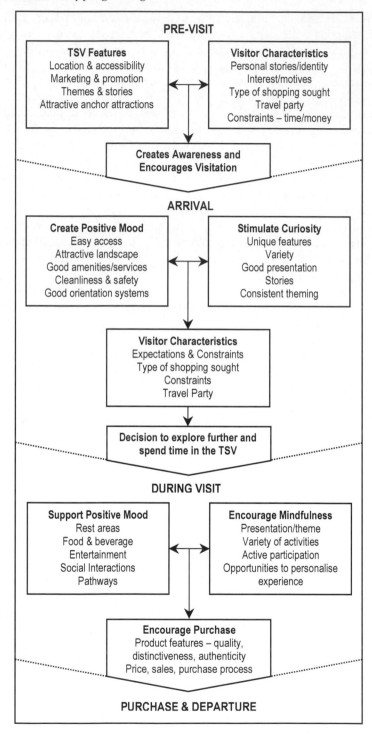

Figure 10.1   The TSV visitor experience model.

8. Extending the model: the applicability of the model in this context is a powerful argument for the further deployment of this approach in many analyses of tourists' experiences. It not only works in describing the individual's experience but offers an ontological position which links to what retailers and other experience designers can do to shape properties of the world to meet the visitors' psychological make up. In this way the study of visitors' experiences in the TSV context provides a stimulus to tourism practice and future study which reaches beyond the array of situations considered in this book.

This research journey commenced with the authors seeking to integrate their skills and efforts in a sustained endeavour to benefit both communities and the scholarship pertaining to experience design. We have engaged in much shop talk, we have been to many shops and we hope that the readers who have followed this tour can take away valued souvenirs from this study of tourist shopping villages.

References

Aaker, J. (1997) 'Dimensions of brand personality'. *Journal of Marketing Research* 34(3): 347–356.

Adaval, R. and Wyer, R. S. J. (1998) 'The role of narratives in consumer information processing'. *Journal of Consumer Psychology* 7(3): 207–245.

Akhter, S. H., Andrews, J. C., and Durvasula, S. (1994) 'The influence of retail store environment on brand related judgements'. *Journal of Retailing and Consumer Services* 1(2): 67–76.

Allen, F. (1999). The new old west. *American Heritage*, 50(5): 30.

Allport, D. (2005) 'The UK high street: current issues and their implications'. *Journal of Retail and Leisure Property* 5(1): 2–16.

Anderson, A. R. and McAuley, A. (1999) 'Marketing landscapes: the social context'. *Qualitative Market Research: An International Journal* 2(3): 176–188.

Anderson, L. M., Mulligan, B. E., Goodman, L. S., and Regen, H. Z. (1983) 'Effects of sounds on preferences for outdoor settings'. *Environment and Behavior* 15(5): 539.

Andrews, R., Baum, T., and Andrew, M. A. (2001) 'The lifestyle economics of small tourism businesses'. *Journal of Travel and Tourism Research* 1: 16–25.

Antupit, S., Gray, B., and Woods, S. (1996) 'Steps ahead: making streets that work in Seattle, Washington'. *Landscape and Urban Planning* 35(2–3): 107–122.

Arana, J. E. and Leon, C. J. (2008) 'The impact of terrorism on tourism demand'. *Annals of Tourism Research* 35(2): 299–315.

Areni, C. S. and Kim, D. (1993) 'The influence of background music on shopping behavior: classical versus top-forty music in a wine store'. *Advances in Consumer Research* 20(1): 336–340.

Areni, C. S. and Kim, D. (1994) 'The influence of in-store lighting on consumers' examination of merchandise in a wine store'. *International Journal of Research in Marketing* 11(2): 117–125.

Arnold, M. J. and Reynolds, K. E. (2003) 'Hedonic shopping motivations'. *Journal of Retailing and Consumer Services* 79: 77–95.

Arnold, M. J., Reynolds, K. E., Ponder, N., and Lueg, J. E. (2003) 'Customer delight in a retail context: investigating delightful and terrible shopping experiences'. *Journal of Business Research* 58: 1132–1145.

Arriaza, M., Cañas-Ortega, J. F., Cañas-Madueño, J. A., and Ruiz-Aviles, P. (2004) 'Assessing the visual quality of rural landscapes'. *Landscape and Urban Planning* 69(1): 115–125.

Asgary, N., de Los Santos, G., Vincent, V., and Davila, V. (1997) 'The determinants of expenditures by Mexican visitors to the border cities of Texas'. *Tourism Economics* 3(4): 319–328.

Asplet, M. and Cooper, M. (2000) 'Cultural designs in New Zealand souvenir clothing: the question of authenticity'. *Tourism Management* 21: 307–312.

Ateljevic, I. and Doorne, S. (2000) '"Staying within the Fence"': Lifestyle Entrepreneurship in Tourism'. *Journal of Sustainable Tourism* 8(5): 378–392.

Aubert-Gamet, V. and Cova, B. (1999) 'Servicescapes: From modern non-places to postmodern common places'. *Journal of Business Research* 44: 37–45.

Augoyard, J. F., Karlsson, H., and Winkler, J. (1999) 'Report and resolution of the Soundscape Research Study Group.' In: Karlsson, H. (ed.), From Awareness to Action, Conf. proceedings "Stockholm, Hey Listen!", Royal Swedish Academy of Music/World Forum for Acoustic Ecology, Stockholm, Sweden, 9–13 June 1998, 130–135.

Australian Minister for Trade (2010) *Australia Unlimited: The nation's new brand.* Available at: http://www.trademinister.gov.au/releases/2010/sc_100514.html (31 May 2010).

Australian Trade Commission (2010) *International launch of Australia Unlimited at Shanghai World Expo (Ministerial) Media Release.* Available at: http://www.austrade.gov.au/International-launch-of-Australia-Unlimited-at-Shanghai-World-Expo/default.aspx (28 May 2010).

Babin, B. and Attaway, J. (2000) 'Atmospheric affect as a tool for creating value and gaining share of customer'. *Journal of Business Research* 49(2): 91–99.

Babin, B., Darden, W., and Griffin, M. (1994) 'Work and/or fun: measuring hedonic and utilitarian shopping value'. *Journal of Consumer Research* 20(4): 644–656.

Babin, B. J., Hardesty, D. M., and Suter, T. A. (2003) 'Color and shopping intentions: the intervening effect of price fairness and perceived affect'. *Journal of Business Research* 56(7): 541–551.

Backstrom, K. (2006) 'Understanding recreational shopping: a new approach'. *International Review of Retail, Distribution and Consumer Research* 16(2): 143–158.

Baker, J. (1987) 'The role of the environment in marketing services: the consumer perspective'. In Czepiel, J., Congram, C. A., and Shanahan, J. (eds.) *The Services Challenge: Integrating for Competitive Advantage*, 79–84. Chicago: American Marketing Association.

Baker, J., Grewal, D., and Levy, M. (1992) 'An experimental approach to making retail store environmental decisions'. *Journal of Retailing* 68(4): 445–460.

Baker, J., Grewal, D., and Parasuraman, A. (1994) 'The influence of store environment on quality inferences and store image'. *Journal of the Academy of Marketing Science* 22(4): 328–339.

Baker, J., Parasuraman, A., Grewal, D., and Voss, G. B. (2002) 'The influence of multiple store environment cues on perceived merchandise value and patronage intentions'. *Journal of Marketing* 66(2): 120–141.

Banerjee, T. and Southworth, M. (Eds.) (1990) *City Sense and City Design.* Cambridge: MIT Press.

Baron, S., Harris, K., and Harris, R. (2001) 'Retail theater: The "intended effect" of the performance'. *Journal of Service Research* 4(2): 102–117.

Barr, N., Wilkinson, R., and Karunaratne, K. (2005) *Understanding Rural Victoria.* Victoria: Department of Primary Industries.

Baum, T. (1998) 'Taking the exit route: extending the tourism area life cycle model'. *Current Issues in Tourism* 1(2): 167–175.

Baum, T. and Lundtorp, S. (2001) 'Seasonality in tourism: an introduction'. In Baum, T. and Lundtorp, S. (eds.) *Seasonality in Tourism*, 1–4. Oxford: Pergamon.

Beirman, D. (2003) *Restoring Tourism Destinations in Crisis.* Crows Nest, Australia: Allen & Unwin.

Benckendorff, P., Moscardo, G., and Murphy, L. (2006) *Visitor perceptions of technology use in tourist attraction experiences*. Paper presented at the Cutting Edge Research in Tourism Conference, Surrey, UK, June 2006.

Berlyne, D. E. (1960) *Conflict, Arousal, and Curiosity*. New York: McGraw-Hill.

Bhattarai, K., Conway, D., and Shrestha, N. (2005) 'Tourism, terrorism and turmoil in Nepal'. *Annals of Tourism Research* 32(3): 669–688.

Bitgood, S. (1988). Problems in visitor orientation and circulation. In S. Bitgood, J. Roper, & A. Benefield (Eds.) *Visitor studies - 1988: Theory, research and practice*. Jacksonville, AL: Center for Social Design. pp. 155–170.

Bitgood, S. and Richardson, K. (1987) 'Wayfinding at the Birmingham Zoo'. *Visitor Behavior* 1(4): 9.

Bitner, M. J. (1992) 'Servicescapes: the impact of physical surroundings on customers and employees'. *Journal of Marketing* 56(April): 57–71.

The Blackall range. The Calm behind the Coast. http://www.brbta.com/history_montville.php. (accessed May 2010).

Blackman, A. (2008) 'Perspectives on leadership coaching for regional tourism managers and entrepreneurs'. In Moscardo, G. (ed.) *Building Community Capacity for Tourism Development*, 142–154. Wallingford: CABI.

Board, E. T. (1995) 'Town centre management'. *Insights* 7(1): A21–A25.

Bone, F. P. and Scholder, E. P. (1999) 'Scents in the marketplace: explaining a fraction of olfaction'. *Journal of Retailing* 75(2): 243–262.

Bonham, C., Edmonds, C., and Mak, J. (2006) 'The impact of 9/11 and other terrible global events on tourism in the United States and Hawaii'. *Journal of Travel Research* 45(1): 99–110.

Boswijk, A., Thijssen, T., and Peelen, E. (2005) *A New Perspective on the Experience Economy*. Available at: http://www.experience-economy.com/wp-content/UserFiles/File/Article%20lapland5.pdf (December 2007).

Bowring, J. (2006) *The smell of memory: sensorial mnemonics*. Paper presented at the IFLA Conference May 2006

Bramwell, B. and Sharman, A. (1999) 'Collaboration in local tourism policymaking'. *Annals of Tourism Research* 26(2): 392–415.

Brewer, W. F. and Lichtenstein, E. H. (1982) 'Stories are to entertain: a structural-affect theory of stories'. *Journal of Pragmatics* 6(5–6): 473–486.

Bryman, A. (2004) *The Disneyization of Society*. London: Sage.

Buhalis, D. and Law, R. (2008) 'Progress in information technology and tourism management: 20 years on and 10 years after the Internet–The state of eTourism research'. *Tourism Management* 29(4): 609–623.

Bunce, M. (1994) *The Countryside Ideal: Anglo-American Images of Landscape*. London: Routledge.

Bunting, T. E. and Mitchell, C. J. A. (2001) 'Artists in rural locales: market access, landscape appeal and economic exigency'. *The Canadian Geographer* 45(2): 268–284.

Butler, R. (1980) 'The concept of a tourist area cycle of evolution; implications for management of resources'. *The Canadian Geographer* 24(1): 5–12.

Butler, R. (Ed.) (2006a) *The Tourism Area Life Cycle Volume 1: Applications and Modifications*. Clevedon: Channel View.

Butler, R. (Ed.) (2006b) *The Tourism Area Life Cycle Volume 2: Conceptual and Theoretical Issues*. Clevedon: Channel View.

Caldwell, C. and Hibbert, S. A. (2002) 'The influence of music tempo and musical preference on restaurant patrons' behavior'. *Psychology and Marketing* 19(11): 895–917.

Cameron, M. A., Baker, J., Peterson, M., and Braunsberger, K. (2003) 'The effects of music, wait-length evaluation, and mood on a low-cost wait experience'. *Journal of Business Research* 56(6): 421–430.

Canadian Tourism commission (2007) Vaughan Mills as a 'shoppertainment' destination. *Tourism Online, 004(09)*. Available at: http://explore-canada.blog spot.com/2007/07/vaughan-mills-as-shoppertainment.html.

Carmichael, B. and Smith, W. (2004) 'Canadian domestic travel behaviour: a market segmentation study of rural shoppers'. *Journal of Vacation Marketing* 10(4): 333–347.

Carson, S. H. and Langer, E. J. (2006) 'Mindfulness and self-acceptance'. *Journal of Rational-Emotive and Cognitive-Behavior Therapy* 24(1): 29–43.

Caru, A. and Cova, B. (2003) 'Revisiting consumption experience: A more humble but complete view of the concept'. *Marketing Theory* 3(2): 267–286.

Cegielski, M., Janeczko, B., Mules, T., and Walls, J. (2001) *Economic value of tourism to places of cultural heritage significance: a case study of three towns with mining heritage.* Canberra: University of Canberra, Cooperative Research Centre for Sustainable Tours and Australian Heritage Commission.

Chang, J., Yang, B.-T., and Yu, C.-G. (2006) 'The moderating effect of salespersons' selling behaviour ion shopping motivation and satisfaction: Taiwan tourists in China'. *Tourism Management* 27(5): 934–942.

Chebat, J. C. and Michon, R. (2003) 'Impact of ambient odors on mall shoppers' emotions, cognition, and spending A test of competitive causal theories'. *Journal of Business Research* 56(7): 529–539.

Chen, W. (2008) *Olympic Cheerleaders Points New Direction for China's Diplomacy.* Available at: http://au.china-embassy.org/eng/xwfw/t516992.htm (01 June 2010).

Choi, T. M., Liu, S. C., Pang, K. M., and Chow, P. S. (2008) 'Shopping behaviors of individual tourists from the Chinese Mainland to Hong Kong'. *Tourism Management* 29(4): 811–820.

Ciocco, L. and Michael, E. J. (2007) 'Hazard or disaster: Tourism management for the inevitable in Northeast Victoria'. *Tourism Management* 28(1): 1–11.

City of Sedona (2010) Community Plan Update. http://www.sedonaaz.gov/ Sedonacms/index.aspx?page=613 (accessed May 2010).

Clawson, M. and Knetsch, J. L. (1966) *Economics of Outdoor Recreation.* Baltimore: John Hopkins.

Clegg, S. R., Hardy, C., and Nord, R. W. (Eds.) (1997) *Handbook of Organisational Studies.* London: Sage.

Cloke, P. (2006) 'Conceptualizing rurality'. In Cloke, P., Marsden, T., and Mooney, P. H. (eds.) *The Sage Handbook of Rural Studies*, 18–28. London: Sage.

Cloke, P. (Ed.) (2003) *Country Visions.* Harlow: Prentice Hall.

Cloke, P. and Milbourne, P. (1992) 'Deprivation and lifestyle in rural Wales. Rurality and cultural dimension'. *Journal of Rural Studies* 8(4): 359–371.

Cohen, E. (1979) 'Rethinking the sociology of tourism'. *Annals of Tourism Research* 6(1): 18–35.

Cohen, E. (2002) 'Authenticity, equity and sustainability in tourism'. *Journal of Sustainable Tourism* 10(4): 267–276.

Colclough, M. (2006) Fifty miles of track and ties. New Hampshire To Do Magazine. http://www.thesilentforest.com/journalism/stories_html_csrr.html (accessed August 2009)

Coles, T. (2003) 'A local reading of a global disaster: some lessons on tourism management from an annus horribilis in south west England'. *Journal of Travel and Tourism Marketing* 15(2–3): 173–197.

Coles, T. (2004a) 'Tourism and retail transactions: Lessons from the Porsche experience'. *Journal of Vacation Marketing* 10(4): 378–389.

Coles, T. (2004b) 'Tourism, shopping and retailing: An axiomatic relationship'. In Lew, A., Hall, C. M., and Williams, A. (eds.) *A Companion to Tourism*, 360–373. Oxford: Blackwell.

Conisbee, M., Kjell, P., Oram, J., Bridges-Palmer, J., Simms, A., and Taylor, J. (2004) *Clone Town Britain: The loss of identity on the nation's high streets.* London: New Economic Foundation.

Cooper, C., Fletcher, J., Gilbert, D., and Wanhill, S. (1993) *Tourism Principles and Practice.* London: Pitman Publishing.

Cooper, C. and Hall, C. M. (2005) *Oceania : A tourism handbook.* London: Channelview.

Costanza, R., Fisher, B., Ali, S., Beer, C., Bond, L., Boumans, R., Danigelis, N. L., Dickinson, J., Elliott, C., Farley, J., Gayer, D. E., Glenn, L. M., Hudspeth, T., Mahoney, D., McCahill, L., McIntosh, B., Reed, B., Riziv, S. A. T., Rizzo, D. M., Simpatico, T., and Snapp, R. (2007) "'Quality of life: An approach integrating opportunities, human needs and subjective well-being'." *Ecological Economics* 61(2–3): 267–276.

Countryside Agency (1998) *Barriers to Enjoying the Countryside.* Cheltenham: Countryside Agency.

Cox, A. D., Cox, D., and Anderson, R. D. (2005) 'Reassessing the pleasures of store shopping'. *Journal of Business Research* 58(3): 250–259.

Crick, M. (1989) 'Representations of international tourism in the social sciences'. *Annual Review of Anthropology* 18: 307–344.

d'Astous, A. (2000) 'Irritating aspects of the shopping environment'. *Journal of Business Research* 49(2): 149–156.

Dann, G., Nash, D., and Pearce, P. L. (1988) 'Methodology in tourism research'. *Annals of Tourism Research* 15(1): 1–28.

Dann, G. M. S. (2003) 'Noticing notices: tourism to order'. *Annals of Tourism Research* 30(2): 465–485.

Daugstad, K. (2008) 'Negotiating landscape in rural tourism'. *Annals of Tourism Research* 35(2): 402–426.

Davies, B. J., Kooijmanb, D., and Warda, P. (2003) 'The sweet smell of success: olfaction in retailing'. *Journal of Marketing Management* 19(5–6): 611–627.

Davies, W. K. D., Townshend, I., and Ng, L. (1998) 'The survival of commercial hierarchies: rural service centres in Western Victoria, Australia'. *Tijdschrift voor economische en sociale geografie (Journal of Economic and Social Geography)* 89(3): 264–278.

Davis, C. J. (2002) 'Street clutter: what can be done?'. *Municipal Engineer* 151(3): 231–240.

Davis, H. and McLeod, S. L. (2003) 'Why humans value sensational news: an evolutionary perspective'. *Evolution and Human Behavior* 24(3): 208–216.

Davis, J. S. and Morais, D. B. (2004) 'Factions and enclaves: small towns and socially unsustainable tourism development'. *Journal of Travel Research* 43(3): 3–10.

Davis, S. G. (1999) 'Space jam: media conglomerates build the entertainment city' *European Journal of Communication* 14(4): 435–459.

de Botton, A. (2002) *The Art of Travel.* London: Penguin.

de Figueiredo, J. M. and Kyle, M. K. (2004) 'Surviving the gales of creative destruction: the determinant of product turnover'. *Strategic Management Journal* 27(3): 241–264.

den Breejen, L. (2007) 'The experiences of long distance walking: A case study of the West Highland Way in Scotland'. *Tourism Management* 28(6): 1417–1427.

Dept. Environment and Heritage (2009) Hahndorf State Heritage Area. http://www.environment.sa.gov.au/heritage/shas/sha_hahndorf.html (accessed May 2010)

Department of Resources Energy and Tourism (2010) *Is Quality Tourism The National Tourism Accreditation Framework.* Available at: http://www.ret.gov.au/tourism/Documents/NTAF%20Fact%20Sheet%20for%20web%20changes.pdf (31 May 2010).

Desjardins, J. (2007) *Business, Ethics and the Environment*. London: Prentice-Hall.

Devlin, A. S. and Bernstein, J. (1997) 'Interactive way-finding: Map style and effectiveness'. *Journal of Environmental Psychology* 17(2): 99–110.

Dholakia, N. and Schroeder, J. (2001) Disney: Delights and Doubts. *Journal of Research for Consumers*, 1(2). Available at: http://www.jrconsumers.com/academic_articles/issue_2?f=5796. (5 December 07).

Di Domenico, M. (2005) 'Producing hospitality, consuming lifestyles: lifestyle entrepreneurship in urban scotland'. In Jones, E. and Haven-Tang, C. (eds.) *Tourism SMEs, Service Quality and Destination Competitiveness*. Oxford: CABI.

Diamond, J. (2006) *Collapse: How societies choose to fail or succeed*. U.S.: Penguin Group

Donnison, S. (2007) 'Unpacking the millennials: A cautionary tale for teacher education'. *Australian Journal of Teacher Education* 32(3): 1–13.

Donovan, R. J., Rossiter, J. R., Marcoolyn, G., and Nesdale, A. (1994) 'Store atmosphere and purchasing behavior'. *Journal of Retailing* 70(3): 283–294.

Dornbusch, D. M. and Kawczynska, C. J. (1992) 'Tourist oriented directional signs: a self-supporting program to promote rural business and economic development'. *Journal of Travel Research* 31(1): 3–9.

Dovers, S. (2005) 'Understanding the environment'. In Grafton, R. Q., Robbin, L., and Wasson, R. J. (eds.) *Policy Analysis, Environment and Sustainability*, 76–96. Sydney: University of New South Wales Press.

Dubé, L. and Morin, S. (2001) 'Background music pleasure and store evaluation: intensity effects and psychological mechanisms'. *Journal of Business Research* 54(2): 107–113.

Edwards, S. and Shackley, M. (1992) 'Measuring the effectiveness of retail window display as an Element of the marketing mix'. *International Journal of Advertising* 11: 193–202.

Emerick, R. E. and Emerick, C. A. (1994) 'Profiling American bed and breakfast accommodations'. *Journal of Travel Research* 32(4): 20–25.

English Tourist Board (1995) 'Town Centre Management'. *Insights*, 7(1): A21–A25.

Evans, G. (2000) 'Contemporary crafts as souvenirs, artifacts and functional goods and their role in local economic diversification and cultural development'. In Hitchcock, M. and Teague, K. (eds.) *Souvenirs: The material culture of tourism*, 127–146. Ashgate: Aldershot.

Evans, J. B. T. and Curtis-Holmes, J. (2005) 'Rapid responding increases belief bias: evidence for the dual-processing theory of reasoning'. *Thinking and Reasoning* 11(4): 382–389.

Evans, N. J. and Ilbery, B. W. (1992) 'Farm-based accommodation and the restructuring of agriculture: evidence from three English counties'. *Journal of Rural Studies* 8(1): 85–96.

Evans, R. (1997) *Regenerating Town Centres*. Manchester: Manchester University Press.

Fairhurst, A., Costello, C., and Fogle Holmes, A. (2007) 'An examination of shopping behavior of visitors to Tennessee according to tourist typologies'. *Journal of Vacation Marketing* 13(4): 311–320.

Falk, P. and Campbell, C. (1997) 'Introduction'. In Falk, P. and Campbell, C. (eds.) *The Shopping Experience*, 1–14. London: Sage.

Fan, C., Wall, G., and Mitchell, C. J. A. (2008) 'Creative destruction and the water town of Luzhi, China'. *Tourism Management* 29(4): 648–660.

Fesenmaier, D. R. and Vogt, C. A. (1993) 'Evaluating the economic impact of travel information provided at Indiana welcome centers'. *Journal of Travel Research* 31(3): 33–39.

Fesenmaier, D. R., Vogt, C. A., and Stewart, W. P. (1993) 'Investigating the influence of welcome center information on travel behavior'. *Journal of Travel Research* 31(3): 47–52.

Findlay, A. and Sparks, L. (2008) 'Weaving new retail and consumer landscapes in the Scottish Borders'. *Journal of Rural Studies* 24(1): 86–97.

Findlay, C. and Southwell, K. (2004a) ''I just followed my nose': Understanding visitor wayfinding and information needs at forest recreation sites'. *Managing Leisure* 9(4): 227–240.

Findlay, C. and Southwell, K. (2004b) *'You just follow the signs': understanding visitor wayfinding problems in the countryside.* Paper presented at the Open Space: People Space. An international conference on inclusive environments (27–29 October 2004)..

Framke, W. (2002) 'The destination as a concept: a discussion of the business-related perspective versus the socio-cultural approach in tourism theory'. *Scandinavian Journal of Hospitality and Tourism* 2(2): 92–108.

Francis, G., Humphreys, I., Ison, S., and Aicken, M. (2006) 'Where next for low cost airlines? A spatial and temporal comparative study'. *Journal of Transport Geography* 14(2): 83–94.

Frater, J. M. (1983) 'Farm tourism in England: planning, funding, promotion and some lessons from Europe'. *Tourism Management* 4(3): 167–179.

Frew, A. (2008) 'Information technology and tourism: a research agenda'. *Journal of Information Technology & Tourism* 3(2): 99–110.

Frost, W. (2006) 'From diggers to baristas: tourist shopping villages in the victorian goldfields'. *Journal of Hospitality and Tourism Management* 13(2): 137–143.

Fuchs, G. and Reichel, A. (In Press) 'An exploratory inquiry into destination risk perceptions and risk reduction strategies of first time vs repeat visitors to a highly volatile destination'. *Tourism Management* In Press, Corrected Proof.

Fukahori, K. and Kubota, Y. (2003) 'The role of design elements on the cost-effectiveness of streetscape improvement'. *Landscape and Urban Planning* 63(2): 75–91.

Furst, S. A. and Reeves, M. (2008) 'Queens of the hill: creative destruction and the emergence of executive leadership of women'. *The Leadership Quarterly* 19(3): 372–384.

Gentile, C., Spiller, N., and Noci, G. (2007) 'How to sustain the customer experience'. *European Management Journal* 25(5): 395–410.

Getz, D. (1993) 'Tourist shopping villages-development and planning strategies'. *Tourism Management* 14(1): 15–26.

Getz, D. (2000) 'Tourist shopping villages: development and planning strategies'. In Ryan, C. and Page, S. (eds.) *Tourism Management: Towards the New Millennium*, 211–225. Oxford: Elsevier Science.

Getz, D., Joncas, D., and Kelly, M. (1994) 'Tourist shopping villages in the Calgary region'. *Journal of Tourism Studies* 5(1): 2–15.

Getz, D. and Petersen, T. (2005) 'Growth and profit-oriented entrepreneurship among family business owners in the tourism and hospitality industry'. *Hospitality Management* 24(2): 219–242.

Geuens, M., Vantomme, D., and Brengman, M. (2004) 'Developing a typology of airport shoppers'. *Tourism Management* 25(5): 615–622.

Gilmore, J. H. and Pine, B. J. (2007) *Authenticity: what consumers really want.* Boston: Harvard Business School Press.

Giroux, H. (1994) 'Politics and innocence in the Wonderful World of Disney' *Disturbing Pleasures: Learning Popular Culture.* New York: Routledge.

Giroux, H. (1999) *The Mouse that Roared: Disney and the End of Innocence.* Lanham: Rowman and Littlefield.

Gober, P., McHugh, K.E. and Leclerc, D. (1993). Job-rich but housing-poor: the dilemma of a western amenity town. *Professional Geographer* 45(1): 12-20.

Goss, J. (1999) 'Once-upon-a-time in the commodity world: An unofficial guide to Mall of America'. *Annals of the Association of American Geographers* 89(1): 45–75.

Griffin, T. and Hayllar, B. (2006) 'Historic waterfronts as tourism precincts: an experiential perspective'. *Tourism and Hospitality Research* 7(1): 3–16.

Gunasekara, A. (2010) *Look towards Sri Lanka: A destination for Chinese travellers* Available at: http://www.sundayobserver.lk/2010/03/21/fea01.asp (31 May 2010).

Gut, P. and Jarrell, S. (2007) 'Silver lining on a dark cloud: the impact of 9/11 on a regional tourist destination'. *Journal of Travel Research* 46(2): 147–153.

Halfacree, K. (1997) 'Contrasting roles for the postproductivist countryside: a postmodern perspective on counterurbanisation'. In Cloke, P. and Little, J. (eds.) *Contested Countryside Cultures: Otherness, Marginalisation and Rurality*, 70–93. London: Routledge.

Hall, C. M. (2005) *Tourism: Rethinking the social science of mobility*. Harlow: Prentice-Hall.

Hall, C. M., Johnson, G., Cambourne, B., Macionis, R., and Sharples, L. (2000) 'Wine tourism: an introduction'. In Hall, C. M., Sharples, L., Cambourne, B., and Macionis, R. (eds.) *Wine Tourism around the World*, 1–23. London: Butterworth-Heinemann.

Hall, E. T. (1969) *The Hidden Dimension: Man's Use of Space in Public and Private*. London: Bodley Head.

Halme, M. and Fadeeva, Z. (2000) 'Small and medium-sized tourism enterprises in sustainable development networks'. *Greener Management International* 30: 97–113.

Ham, S. (2003) *Re: New Interpretation Article*. Available at: www.interp@lorenz.mur.csu.edu.

Harrell, G. D., Hutt, M. D., and Anderson, J. C. (1980) 'Path analysis of buyer behavior under conditions of crowding'. *Journal of Marketing Research* 17(1): 45–51.

Harris, D. (2005) *Key Concepts in Leisure Studies*. London: Sage.

Harris, R., Harris, K., and Baron, S. (2003) 'Theatrical service experiences'. *International Journal of Service Industry Management* 14(2): 184–199.

Hayllar, B. and Griffin, T. (2005) 'The precinct experience: a phenomenological approach'. *Tourism Management* 26(4): 517–528.

Hayward, D. G. and Brydon-Miller, M. L. (1984) 'Spatial and conceptual aspects of orientation: visitor experiences at an outdoor history museum'. *Journal of Environmental Education* 13(4): 317–332.

Haywood, K. M. (2006) 'Evolution of Tourism Areas and the Tourism Industry'. In Butler, R. (ed.) *The Tourism Area Life Cycle Volume 1: Applications and Modifications*, 51–69. Clevedon: Channel View.

Hedfors, P. (2003) *Site Soundscapes—landscape architecture in the light of sound*. Unpublished Doctoral dissertation, Swedish University of Agricultural Sciences.

Hennig, C. (2002) 'Tourism: enacting modern myths'. In Dann, G. M. S. (ed.) *The Tourist as a Metaphor of the Social World*, 169–188. Wallingford: CABI.

Herrington, J. D. (1996) 'Effects of music in service environments: a field study'. *Journal of Services Marketing* 10(2): 26–41.

Herzberg, F. (1968) *Work and the Nature of Man*. London: Granada Publishing.

Heung, V. and Cheng, E. (2000) 'Assessing tourists' satisfaction with shopping in the Hong Kong Special Adminstrative Region of China'. *Journal of Travel Research* 38(4): 396–404.

Hitchcock, M. (2000) 'Introduction'. In Hitchcock, M. and Teague, K. (eds.) *Souvenirs: The material culture of tourism*, 1–17. Ashgate: Aldershot.

Hoeffler, S. and Keller, K. L. (2003) 'The marketing advantage of strong brands'. *Journal of Brand Management* 10(6): 421–445.

Hogan, M. (2006). Thinking Outside the Big Box. Preservation Online.

Holbrook, M. (2001) 'Times Square, Disneyphobia, HegeMickey, the Ricky Principle and the downside of the entertainment economy'. *Marketing Theory* 1(2): 139–163.

Holbrook, M. and Hirschman, E. (1982) 'The experiential aspects of consumption: consumer fantasies, feelings and fun'. *Journal of Consumer Research* 9(2): 132–140.

Hollenbeck, C. R., Peters, C., and Zinkham, G. M. (2008) 'Retail spectacles and brand meaning: insights from a brand museum case study'. *Journal of Retailing* 84(3): 334–353.

Holloway, J. C. (2002) *The Business of Tourism*. Harlow, England: Prentice Hall.

Hopkins, J. (1998) 'Signs of the post-rural: marketing myths of a symbolic countryside'. *Geografiska Annaler: Series B, Human Geography* 80(2): 65–81.

Hsieh, A.-T. and Chang, J. (2006) 'Shopping and tourist night markets in Taiwan'. *Tourism Management* 27(1): 138–145.

Hsu, S.-Y., Dehuang, N., and Woodside, A. G. (2009) 'Storytelling research of consumer's self-reports of urban tourism experiences in China'. *Journal of Business Research* 62(12): 1223–1254.

Hu, B. and Yu, H. (2007) 'Segmentation by craft selection criteria and shopping involvement'. *Tourism Management* 28(4): 1079–1092.

Huang, H. Y. B., Wall, G., and Mitchell, C. J. A. (2007) 'Creative destruction: Zhu Jia Jiao, China'. *Annals of Tourism Research* 34(4): 1033–1955.

Hystad, P. W. and Keller, P. C. (2008) 'Towards a destination tourism disaster management framework: long-term lessons from a forest fire disaster'. *Tourism Management* 29(1): 151–162.

Ibrahim, M. F. and Ng, C. W. (2002) 'Determinants of entertaining shopping experiences and their link to consumer behaviour: case studies of shopping centres in Singapore'. *Journal of Leisure Property* 2(4): 338–357.

Institute of Tourism Poland (2008) *Tourism Sector—Data, analyses, forecasts*. Available at: http://www.intur.com (August 2010).

Ivakhiv, A. (1997). Red rocks, "vortexes" and the selling of Sedona. Social Compass, 44(3): 367–384.

Jackson, K. (1996) 'All the world's a mall: reflections on the social and economic consequences of the American shopping centre'. *The American Historical Review* 101(4): 1111–1121.

Jansen-Verbeke, M. (1991) 'Leisure shopping: a magic concept for the tourism industry?'. *Tourism Management* 12(1): 9–14.

Jansen-Verbeke, M. (1998) 'The synergism between shopping and tourism'. In Theobold, W. (ed.) *Global Tourism*, 428–446. Oxford: Butterworth-Heinemann.

Jansen-Verbeke, M. (2000) 'Leisure shopping: a magic concept for the tourism industry?'. In Ryan, C. and Page, S. (eds.) *Tourism Management—Towards the New Millennium*, 203–210. Oxford: Elsevier Science Ltd.

Johns, N. and Mattsson, J. (2005) 'Destination development through entrepreneurship: a comparison of two cases'. *Tourism Management* 26(4): 605–616.

Johnston, C. S. (2001) 'Shoring the foundations of the destination life cycle model Part 1: ontological and epistemological considerations'. *Tourism Geographies* 3(1): 2–28.

Jones, M. A. (1999) 'Entertaining shopping experiences: an exploratory investigation'. *Journal of Retailing and Consumer Services* 6(3): 129–139.

Jones, P. (1995) 'Factory outlet shopping centres and planning issues'. *International Journal of Retail and Distribution* 23(1): 12–18.

Josiam, B., Kinley, T., and Kim, Y.-K. (2005) 'Involvement and the tourist shopper: Using the involvement construct to segment the American tourist shopper at the mall'. *Journal of Vacation Marketing* 11(2): 135–154.

Kang, J. and Kim, Y.-K. (1999) 'Role of entertainment in cross-chopping and in the revitalization of regional shopping centers'. *Journal of Shopping Center Research* 6(2): 41–71.

Kaplan, R. (1985) 'The analysis of perception via preference: a strategy for studying how the environment is experienced'. *Landscape Planning* 12(2): 162–176.

Kaplan, R. (2001) 'The nature of the view from home: psychological benefits'. *Environment and Behavior* 33(4): 507–542.

Kemperman, A. D. A. M., Borgers, A. W. J., and Timmersman, H. J. P. (2009) 'Tourist shopping behaviour in a historic downtown area'. *Tourism Management* 30(2): 208–218.

Kids Today (2009) *Build-A-Bear Workshop becomes Santa's Workshop for the holidays: Retailer kicks off season with campaign to benefit Toys for Tots*. Available at: http://www.kidstodayonline.com/article/518991-Build_A_Bear_Workshop_becomes_Santa_s_Workshop_for_the_holidays.php (31 May 2010).

Kikuchi, A. and Ryan, C. (2007) 'Street markets as tourist attractions—Victoria Market, Auckland, New Zealand'. *International Journal of Tourism Research* 9(4): 297–300.

Kim, D., Park, J., and Morrison, A. (2008) 'A model of traveller acceptance of mobile technology'. *International Journal of Tourism Research* 10(5): 393–407.

Kim, J., Wei, S., and Ruys, H. (2003) 'Segmenting the market of West Australian senior tourists using an artificial neural network'. *Tourism Management* 24(1): 25–34.

Kim, S. and Littrell, M. (2001) 'Souvenir buying intentions for self versus others'. *Annals of Tourism Research* 28(3): 638–357.

King, C. (2009) *The Global Financial Crisis and Regional Australia / House of Representatives Standing Committee on Infrastructure, Transport, Regional Development & Local Government*. Canberra: House of Representatives Standing Committee on Infrastructure, Transport, Regional Development & Local Government.

Kline, S. (1995) 'The play of the market: on the internationalization of children's culture'. *Theory, Culture and Society* 12(May): 103–130.

Knutson, B. J. and Beck, J. A. (2003) 'Identifying the dimensions of the experience construct: development of the model'. *Journal of Quality Assurance in Hospitality & Tourism* 4(3–4): 23–35.

Kotler, P., Adam, S., Brown, L., and Armstrong, G. (2006) *Principles of Marketing* (*3rd ed.*). Sydney: Pearson Education.

Kozinets, R. V., Sherry, J. F., De Berry-Spence, B., Duhackek, A., Nuttavuthisit, K., and Storm, D. (2002) 'Themed flagship brand stores in the new millennium: theory, practice, prospects'. *Journal of Retailing* 78(1): 17–29.

Kunster, J. (1993) *The Geography of Nowhere: The Rise and Decline of America's Manmade Landscape*. New York: Simon & Schuster.

Langer, E. J. (1997) *The Power of Mindful Learning*. Reading: Addison-Wesley.

Laws, E. (1998) 'Conceptualizing visitor satisfaction management in heritage settings: an exploratory blueprinting analysis of Leeds Castle, Kent'. *Tourism Management* 19(6): 545–554.

Lazar, D. (2009) Mountain of opportunity. New Hampshire Troubadour. http://www.nhtroubadour.com/feature/mountain-of-opportunity/ (accessed August 2009).

Lee, S. Y., Reynolds, J. S., and Kennon, L. R. (2003) 'Bed and breakfast industries: successful marketing strategies'. *Journal of Travel and Tourism Marketing* 14(1): 37–54.

Legge, K. (2010) *A Year Later, Marysville awaits a Future The Australian, January 30*. Available at: http://www.theaustralian.com.au/news/nation/a-year-later-marysville-waits-for-a-future/story-e6frg6nf-1225824893878 (29 May 2010).

LeHew, M. and Wesley, S. (2007) 'Tourist shoppers' satisfaction with regional shopping mall experiences'. *International Journal of Culture, Tourism and Hospitality Research* 1(1): 82–96.

Lehto, X. Y. L., Cai, L. A., O'Leary, J. T., and Huan, T.-C. (2004) 'Tourist shopping preferences and expenditure behaviours: the case of the Taiwanese outbound market'. *Journal of Vacation Marketing* 10(4): 320–332.

Lehtonen, T.-K. and Maenpaa, P. (1997) 'Shopping in the East Centre Mall'. In Falk, P. and Campbell, C. (eds.) *The Shopping Experience*, 136–176. London: Sage.

Leiper, N. (1990) 'Tourist attraction systems'. *Annals of Tourism Research* 17(3): 367–384.

Leiper, N. (2000) 'Are destinations 'The Heart of Tourism?' The advantages of an alternate description'. *Current Issues in Tourism* 3(4): 364–368.

Lew, A. and McKercher, B. (2006) 'Modeling tourist movements: a local destination analysis'. *Annals of Tourism Research* 33(2): 403–423.

Lewis, R. (2009) *Regional Tourism faring better than expected in the face of economic slowdown.* Available at: http://www.visitvineyards.com/press/090301_regional_tourism_survey_march09.pdf (29 May 2010).

Lillebye, E. (1996) 'Architectural and functional relationships in street planning: an historical view'. *Landscape and Urban Planning* 35(2–3): 85–105.

Littrell, M., Paige, R., and Song, K. (2004) 'Senior travellers: tourism activities and shopping behaviours'. *Journal of Vacation Marketing* 10(4): 348–362.

Littrell, M. A., Anderson, L. F., and Brown, P. J. (1993) 'What makes a craft souvenir authentic?'. *Annals of Tourism Research* 20(1): 197–215.

Litvin, S., Goldsmith, R., and Pan, B. (2008) 'Electronic word-of-mouth in hospitality and tourism management'. *Tourism Management* 29(3): 458–468.

Lobell, D. B., Burke, M. B., Tebaldi, C., Mastrandrea, M. D., Falcon, W. P., and Naylor, R. L. (2008) 'Prioritizing climate change adaptation needs for food security in 2030'. *Science* 319(5863): 607–610.

Lohr, V. I., Pearson-Mims, C. H., Tarnai, J., and Dillman, D. A. (2004) 'How urban residents rate and rank the benefits and problems associated with trees in cities'. *Journal of Arboriculture* 30(1): 28–35.

Lowenthal, D. (1975) 'Past time, present time: Landscape and memory'. *Geographical Review* 65(1): 1–36.

Lowry, J. R. (1997) 'The life cycle of shopping centers'. *Business Horizons* 40(1): 77–86.

Lue, C., Crompton, J., and Fesenmaier, D. (1993) 'Conceptualization of Multi-Destination Pleasure Trips'. *Annals of Tourism Research* 20(2): 289–301.

Lumsdon, L. and Page, S. (2004) *Tourism and Transport: Issues and agenda for the new millennium.* Boston: Elsevier.

Lynch, K. (1960) *The Image of the City.* Cambridge: M.I.T. Press.

Lynch, K. and Rivkin, M. (1959) 'A walk around the block'. *Landscape* 8(3): 24–33.

MacCannell, D. (1976) *The Tourist: A New Theory of the Leisure Class.* New York: Schocken Books.

Machleit, K. A., Meyer, T., and Eroglu, S. A. (2005) 'Evaluating the nature of hassles and uplifts in the retail shopping context'. *Journal of Business Research* 58(5): 655–663.

Madrigal, R. (1995) 'Residents' perceptions and the role of government'. *Annals of Tourism Research* 22(1): 86–102.

Malkina-Pykh, I. G. and Pykh, Y. A. (2007) 'Quality-of-life indicators at different scales: theoretical background'. *Ecological Indicators.* Available at: http://www.sciencedirect.com (December 2007)

McEachern, M. G. and Warnaby, G. (2006) 'Food shopping behaviour in Scotland: the influence of relative rurality'. *International Journal of Consumer Studies* 30(2): 189–201.

McGehee, N. G. and Kim, K. (2004) 'Motivation for agri-tourism entrepreneurship'. *Journal of Travel Research* 43(2): 161–170.

McGoun, E. G., Dunkak, W. H., Bettner, M. S., and Allen, D. E. (2003) 'Walt's Street and Wall Street: theming, theater, and experience in finance'. *Critical Perspectives on Accounting* 14(6): 647–661.

McIntosh, A. J. and Siggs, A. (2005) 'An exploration of the experiential nature of boutique accommodation'. *Journal of Travel Research* 44(1): 74–81.

McKercher, B. (2001) 'A comparison of main-destination and through travelers at a dual purpose destination'. *Journal of Travel Research* 39(4): 433–441.

McKercher, B. (2004) 'The myth of the average tourist'. *Voice of TIC* 4: 19–23.

McKercher, B. and Lau, G. (2008) 'Movement patterns of tourists within a destination'. *Tourism Geographies* 10(3): 355–374.

Medway, D., Warnaby, G., Bennison, D., and Alexander, A. (2000) 'Reasons for retailers' involvement in town centre management'. *International Journal of Retail & Distribution Management* 28(8): 368–378.

Mehrabian, A. and Russell, J. A. (1974) *An Approach to Environmental Psychology.* Cambridge: MIT Press.

Michael, E. (2002) 'Antiques and tourism in Australia'. *Tourism Management* 21(3): 117–125.

Michalkó, G. (2001) 'Cross-border shopping in Hungary: causes and effects'. *Visions in Leisure and Business* 17(4): 32–49.

Michalkó, G. and Váradi, Z. (2004) 'Croatian shopping tourism in Hungary: the case study of Barcs'. *Turizam* 6(4): 351–399.

Miller, D. (1998) *A Theory of Shopping.* Cambridge: Polity Press.

Miller, D. (2001) *The Dialectics of Shopping.* Chicago: University of Chicago Press.

Miller, D., Jackson, P., Thrift, N., Holbrook, B., and Rowlands, M. (1998) *Shopping, Place and Identity.* London: Routledge.

Milliman, R. E. (1982) 'Using background music to affect the behavior of supermarket shoppers'. *Journal of Marketing* 46(3): 86–91.

Milliman, R. E. (1986) 'The Influence of Background Music on the Behavior of Restaurant Patrons'. *Journal of Consumer Research* 13(2): 286–289.

Mingay, G. (Ed.) (1989) *The Rural Idyll.* London: Routledge.

Mings, R. C. and McHugh, K. E. (1995) 'Wintering in the American Sunbelt: linking place and behaviour'. *Journal of Tourism Studies* 6(2): 56–62.

Mitchell, C. (1998) 'Entrepreneurialism, commodification and creative destruction: a model of post-modern community development'. *Journal of Rural Studies* 14(3): 273–286.

Mitchell, C. (2003) 'The heritage shopping village: profit, preservation and production'. In Wall, G. (ed.) *Tourism: People, Place and Products*, 151–176. Waterloo Ontario Canada: Dept of Geography, University of Waterloo.

Mitchell, C. and Coghill, C. (2000) 'The creation of a cultural heritage landscape: Elora, Ontario, Canada'. *The Great Lakes Geographer* 7(2): 88–105.

Mitchell, C. and de Waal, S. B. (2009) 'Revisiting the model of creative destruction: St Jacobs, Ontario, a decade later'. *Journal of Rural Studies* 25(1): 156–167.

Mitchell, C. J. A., Atkinson, G. R., and Clark, A. (2001) 'The creative destruction of Niagara-on-the-Lake'. *The Canadian Geographer* 45(2): 285–299.

Mitchell, D. J., Kahn, B. E., and Knasko, S. C. (1995) 'There's something in the air: effects of congruent or incongruent ambient odor on consumer decision making'. *Journal of Consumer Research* 22(2): 229.

Monthievichienchai, C. (2010) *PATA COMPASS: Insight March/April 2010.* Available at: http://www.pata.org/uploads/page/Insight%20Mar-Apr%2010. pdf (28 May 2010).

Morgan, M. (2006) 'Making space for experiences'. *Journal of Retail and Leisure Property* 5(4): 305–313.

Morin, S., Dubé, L., and Chebat, J. C. (2007) 'The role of pleasant music in servicescapes: a test of the dual model of environmental perception'. *Journal of Retailing* 83(1): 115–130.

Morris, C. and Buller, H. (2003) 'The local food sector'. *British Food Journal* 105(8): 559–566.

Morrison, A. (2006) 'A contextualisation of entrepreneurship '. *International Journal of Entrepreneurial Behaviour and Research* 12(4): 192–209.

Morrison, A. M., Pearce, P. L., Moscardo, G., Nadkarni, N., and O'Leary, J. T. (1996) 'Specialist accommodation: definition, markets served, and roles in tourism development'. *Journal of Travel Research* 35(1): 18–26.

Moscardo, G. (1996) 'Mindful visitors heritage and tourism'. *Annals of Tourism Research* 23(2): 376–397.

Moscardo, G. (2004) 'Shopping as a destination attraction: an empirical examination of the role of shopping in tourists' destination choice process and experience'. *Journal of Vacation Marketing* 10(4): 294–307.

Moscardo, G. (2005a) 'Peripheral tourism development: challenges, issues and success factors'. *Tourism Recreation Research* 30: 27–43.

Moscardo, G. (2005b). *Successful tourism development for regions.* Paper presented at the 2005 SEGRA Conference.

Moscardo, G. (2006) 'Third age tourism'. In Buhalis, D. and Costa, C. (eds.) *Tourism Business Frontiers*, 30–39. London: Butterworth-Heinemann.

Moscardo, G. (2008a) 'Community capacity building: an emerging challenge for tourism development'. In Moscardo, G. (ed.) *Building Community Capacity for Tourism Development* 1–15. Wallingford: CABI.

Moscardo, G. (2008b) 'Sustainable tourism innovation: challenging basic assumptions'. *Tourism and Hospitality Research* 8(1): 4–13.

Moscardo, G. (2008c) 'Understanding tourist experience through mindfulness theory'. In Kozak, M. and Decrop, A. (eds.) *Handbook of tourist behaviour*, 99–115. New York: Routledge.

Moscardo, G. (2009) 'Tourism and quality of life: towards a more critical approach'. *Tourism and Hospitality Research* 9(2): 159–170.

Moscardo, G. (In Press) 'Exploring mindfulness and stories in tourist experiences'. *International Journal of Culture, Tourism and Hospitality Research.*

Moscardo, G. and Ballantyne, R. (2008) 'Interpretation in tourist attractions'. In Fyall, A., Leask, A., and Wanhill, S. (ed.) *Managing Tourist Attractions (2nd ed.)*, 237–254. Oxford: Elsevier.

Moscardo, G., Ballantyne, R., and Hughes, K. (2007) *Designing Interpretive Signs: Principles in practice.* Denver: Fulcrum.

Moscardo, G. and Benckendorff, P. (2010) 'Mythbusting: Generation Y and Travel'. In Benckendorff, P., Moscardo, G., and Pendergast, D. (eds.) *Tourism and Generation Y*, 16–26. United Kingdom: CAB International.

Moscardo, G., Laws, E., and Faulkner, B. (2001) 'Tourism into the twenty first century: moving ahead and looking back'. In Faulkner, B., Moscardo, G., and Laws, E. (eds.) *Tourism into the Twenty First Century: Reflections on experience*, xviii–xxxii. London: Cassells Academic.

Moscardo, G., Morrison, A. M., and Pearce, P. L. (1996) 'Specialist accommodation and ecologically-sustainable tourism'. *Journal of Sustainable Tourism* 4(1): 29–52.

Moscardo, G., Murphy, L. M., and Benckendorff, P. (Eds.) (In Press) *Generation Y and Travel Futures.* Oxford: Goodfellow.

Moscardo, G. and Pearce, P. L. (2004) 'Life cycle, tourist motivation and transport: some consequences for the tourist experience'. In Lumsdon, L. and Page, S. J. (eds.) *Tourism and Transport: Issues and agenda for the new millennium*, 29–43. Oxford: Elsevier.

Mottiar, Z. (2006) 'Holiday home owners, a route to sustainable tourism development? An economic analysis of tourist expenditure data'. *Journal of Sustainable Tourism* 14(6): 582–599.

Mrnjavac, E. and Marsanic, R. (2007) 'Intelligent transportation systems in improving traffic flow in tourism destinations'. *Tourism and Hospitality Management* 13(3): 627–636.

Murphy, L., Moscardo, G., Benckendorff, P., and Pearce, P. L. (2008) 'Tourist Shopping Villages–Exploring Success and Failure In A Woodside and D Martin (eds) *Tourism Management: Analysis, behaviour and Strategy,* 405–423. Wallingford: CABI.

Murphy, L., Pearce, P., Benckendorff, P., and Moscardo, G. (2008) *Tourist shopping villages: challenges and issues in developing regional tourism.* Paper presented at the Tourism and Hospitality Research, Training and Practice: Where the Bloody Hell are We? Proceedings of the 18th Annual Council of Australian University Tourism and Hospitality CAUTHE Conference, Gold Coast, Australia, 11–14 February 2008.

Murphy, P. (2002) 'Sea-change: reinventing Rural and Regional Australia'. *Transformations* 2: 1–12.

Murphy, P. E. and Murphy, A. E. (2004) *Strategic Management for Tourism Communities.* Clevedon: Channel View.

Nagle, G. 1999. *Focus on Geography: Tourism, leisure and recreation, Cheltenham*, Nelson Thornes, pp. 54–56. Conference proceeding.

Nash, D. (2007) *The study of tourism: anthropological and sociological beginnings.* Amsterdam; Boston; London: Elsvier Science.

National Geographic (2009) *Greendex 2009: consumer choice and the environment- A world wide tracking report highlight report.* Available at: http://www.nationalgeographic.com/greendex/assets/Greendex_Highlights_Report_May09.pdf (May 2010).

New Zealand Tourism Board (2010) *Qualmark.* Available at: http://www.tourismnewzealand.com/delivering-the-promise/developing-the-tourism-industry/qualmark (31 May 2010).

Newby, H. (1979) *Green and Pleasant Land? Social Change in Rural England.* London: Hutchinson.

Ng, C. F. (2003) 'Satisfying shoppers' psychological needs: from public market to cyber-mall'. *Journal of Environmental Psychology* 23(4): 439–455.

Nickerson, N. P., Black, R. J., and McCool, S. F. (2001) 'Agritourism: motivations behind farm/ranch business diversification'. *Journal of Travel Research* 40(1): 19–26.

Nilsson, L. P. (2002) 'Staying on farms: an Ideological background'. *Annals of Tourism Research* 29(1): 7–24.

Nowak, D. J. and Dwyer, J. F. (2000) 'Understanding the benefits and costs of urban forest ecosystems'. In J. E. Kuser (ed.), *Handbook of Urban and Community Forestry in the Northeast*, 11–25. New York: Kluwer Academic, Plenum Publishers.

O'Connor, P. and Frew, A. (2002) 'The future of hotel electronic distribution: expert and industry perspectives'. *Cornell Hotel and Restaurant Administration Quarterly* 43(3): 33–45.

O'Toole, T. and Tarling, L. (2000) *Bread Winner: A Fresh Approach to Rising to the Top.* Melbourne: Information Australia.

Oh, J. Y.-J., Cheng, C.-K., Lehto, X. Y., and O'Leary, J. T. (2004) 'Predictors of tourists' shopping behaviour: examination of socio-demographic characteristics and trip typologies'. *Journal of Vacation Marketing* 10(4): 308–319.

Ollenburg, C. and Buckley, R. (2007) 'Stated economic and social motivations of farm tourism operators'. *Journal of Travel Research* 45(4): 444–452.

Ontario Ministry of Tourism (2007a) *Regional Tourism Profiles, 2005: Region 3: Niagara Region*. Toronto: Queen's Printer for Ontario.

Ontario Ministry of Tourism (2007b) *Shopping—An Analysis of the shopping segments from the Travel Activities and Motivations Survey (TAMS): The US and Ontario Markets.*

Ontario Ministry of Tourism (2007c) *Travel Activities and Motivations of Canadian Residents: An Overview* Ontario Ministry of Tourism.

Ontario Ministry of Tourism (2007d) *US Travel Market: Shopping and Dining While on Trips of One or More Nights.*

Otsuka, N. and Reeve, A. (2007) 'Town centre management and regeneration: the experience in four english cities'. *Journal of Urban Design* 12(3). 435–459.

Paddison, A. and Calderwood, E. (2007) 'Rural retailing: a sector in decline?'. *International Journal of Retail and Distribution Management* 35(2): 136–155.

Page, S. J. and Hardyman, R. (1996) 'Place marketing and town centre management: a new tool for urban revitalization'. *Cities* 13(3): 153–164.

Pal, J. and Sanders, E. (1997) 'Measuring the effectiveness of town centre management schemes: an exploratory framework'. *International Journal of Retail & Distribution Management* 25(2): 70–77.

Pang, M., Ying, N. H., and Qing, K. X. (2010) *Big Spenders, AsiaNews May 21—June 3, The Straits Times*. Available at: http://www.asianewsnet.net/epaper/pdf/AsiaNews%20May%2021-June%203.pdf (31 May 2010).

Papatheodorou, A., Rossello, J., and Xiao, H. (2010) 'Global economic crisis and tourism: consequences and perspectives'. *Journal of Travel Research* 49(1): 39–45.

Paraskevas, A. and Arendell, B. (2007) 'A strategic framework for terrorism prevention and mitigation in tourism destinations'. *Tourism Management* 28(6): 1560–1573.

Park, M. (2000) 'Social and cultural factors influencing tourists' souvenir-purchasing behavior: a comparative study on Japanese "Omiyage" and Korean "Sunmul"'. *Journal of Travel and Tourism Marketing* 9(1): 81–91.

Park, N. K. and Farr, C. A. (2007) 'The effects of lighting on consumers' emotions and behavioral intentions in a retail environment: a cross-cultural comparison'. *Journal of Interior Design* 33(1): 17–32.

Parolin, B. P. (2001) 'Structure of day trips in the Illawarra tourism region of New South Wales'. *Journal of Tourism Studies* 12(1): 11–27.

PATA (2009) *Visa and PATA Asia Pacific Travel Intentions Survey: Determining travel preferences for 2009 and Beyond* PATA.

Pe'er, A. and Vertinsky, I. (2008) 'Firm exits as a determinant of new entry: is there evidence of local creative destruction?'. *Journal of Business Venturing* 23(3): 280–306.

Pearce, P., Benckendorff, P., and Johnstone, S. (2001) 'Tourist attractions: evolution, analysis and prospects'. In Faulkner, B., Moscardo, G., and Laws, E. (eds.) *Tourism in the 21st Century: Lessons from experience*, 110–128. London: Continuum.

Pearce, P. L. (1990) 'Farm tourism in New Zealand: a social situation analysis'. *Annals of Tourism Research* 17(3): 337–352.

Pearce, P. L. (2004) 'The functions and planning of visitor centres in regional tourism'. *Journal of Tourism Studies* 15(1): 8–17.

Pearce, P. L. (2005) 'Professing tourism: tourism academics as educators, researchers and change leaders'. *Journal of Tourism Studies* 16(2): 21–33.

Pearce, P. L. (2007) 'Persisting with authenticity'. *Tourism Recreation Research* 32(2): 86–90.

Pearce, P. L. (2008) 'Studying tourism entertainment through micro-cases'. *Tourism Recreation Research* 32(2): 151–163.

Pearce, P. L., Morrison, A. M., and Moscardo, G. M. (2003) 'Individuals as tourist icons: a developmental and marketing analysis'. *Journal of Hospitality & Leisure Marketing* 10(1–2): 63–86.

Pearce, P. L. and Moscardo, G. M. (1992) *The Boutique/Specialist Accommodation Sector: Perceived Government Needs and Policy Initiatives.* Townsville, Queensland: James Cook University.

Pearce, P. L. and Thomas, M. (2010) 'Mapping the road; developing the cognitive mapping methodology for accessing road trip memories'. In Prideaux, B. and D.Carson (eds.) *Drive Tourism-trends and Emerging Markets.* Oxfordshire: Routledge.

Perdue, R. R. (1995) 'Traveler preferences for information center attributes and services'. *Journal of Travel Research* 33(4): 2–7.

Pérez, J. G. (2002) 'Ascertaining landscape perceptions and preferences with pairwise photographs: planning rural tourism in Extremadura, Spain'. *Landscape Research* 27(3): 297–308.

Pierssene, A. (1999) *Explaining our World: An approach to the art of environmental interpretation.* London: E & FN Spon.

Pine, B. J. and Gilmore, J. H. (1998) 'Welcome to the experience economy'. *Harvard Business Review* 76(4): 97–105.

Pine, B. J. and Gilmore, J. H. (1999) *The Experience Economy.* Boston: Harvard Business School Press.

Pine, B. J. and Gilmore, J. H. (2002) 'Differentiating hospitality operations via experiences: why selling services is not enough.'. *Cornell Hotel and Restaurant Administration Quarterly* 43(3): 87–96.

Pittman, R. H. and Culp, R. P. (1995) 'When does retail count as economic development?'. *Development Review* 13(2): 4–6.

Pizam, A. and Mansfeld, Y. (Eds.) (1996) *Tourism, Crime and International Security Issues.* New York: John Wiley & Sons.

Plummer, R., Telfer, D., Hashimoto, A., and Summers, R. (2005) 'Beer tourism in Canada along the Waterloo-Wellington Ale trail'. *Tourism Management* 26(3): 447–458.

Popcorn, F. and Hanft, A. (2001) *Dictionary of the Future.* New York: Hyperion.

Powe, N. and Shaw, T. I. M. (2003) 'Market towns: investigating the service role through visitor surveys'. *Planning Practice & Research* 18(1): 37–50.

Powe, N. A. (2006) 'Understanding urban attitudes towards country towns: considering their potential as visitor attractions'. *Journal of Retail and Leisure Property* 5(4): 255–269.

Prideaux, B., Laws, E., and Faulkner, B. (2003) 'Events in Indonesia; exploring the limits to formal tourism trends forecasting methods in complex crisis situations'. *Tourism Management* 24(4): 475–487.

Pullman, M. E. and Gross, M. A. (2004) 'Ability of experience deisgn elements to elicit emotions and loyalty behaviours'. *Decision Sciences* 35(3): 551–578.

Qualmark New Zealand (2010) *Qualmark—100% PURE Assurance.* Available at: http://www.newzealand.com/travel/trade/marketing-toolbox/qualmark/qualmark-quality-assurance.cfm (31 May 2010).

Rainey, D. L. (2006) *Sustainable Business Development.* Cambridge: Cambridge University Press.

Rayman-Bacchus, L. and Molina, A. (2001) 'Internet-based tourism services: business issues and trends'. *Futures* 33(7): 589–605.

Reader's Digest (1993) *Illustrated Guide to Australian Places.* Surry Hills, NSW: Reader's Digest.

Reeve, A. (2004) 'Town centre management: developing a research agenda in an emerging field'. *Urban Design International* 9(3): 133–150.

Reisinger, Y. and Turner, L. (2002) 'The determination of shopping satisfaction of Japanese tourists visiting Hawaii and the Gold Coast compared'. *Journal of Travel Research* 41(2): 167–176.

Richards, G. and Raymond, C., (2000) Creative tourism. *ATLAS News*, 23, 16–20.

Richards, G. and Wilson, J. (2006) 'Developing creativity in tourist experiences: a solution to the serial reproduction of culture?'. *Tourism Management* 27(5): 1209–1223.

Riganti, P. and Nijkamp, P. (2008) 'Congestion in popular tourist areas: a multi-attribute experimental choice analysis of willingness-to-wait in Amsterdam'. *Tourism Economics* 14(1): 25–44.

Ritchie, J., Molinar, A., Mario, C., and Frechtling, D. (2010) 'Impacts of the world recession and economic crisis on tourism: North America'. *Journal of Travel Research* 49(1): 5–15.

Rittichainuwat, B. N. and Chakraborty, G. (2009) 'Perceived travel risks regarding terrorism and disease: the case of Thailand'. *Tourism Management* 30(3): 410–418.

Ritzer, G. (1999) *Enchanting a Disenchanted World: Revolutionising the means of consumption.* Thousand Oaks: Pine Forge Press.

Ritzer, G. and Stillman, T. (2001) 'The postmodern ballpark as a leisure setting: enchantment and simulated dc-McDonalidization'. *Leisure Sciences* 23(2): 99–113.

Roberston, J. and Fennell, J. (2007) 'The economic effects of regional shopping centres'. *Journal of Retail and Leisure Property* 6(2): 149–170.

Rowe, M. (1991) 'B&Bs: how easy to ignore?'. *Lodging Hospitality* 47(February): 22–23.

Sayadi, S., Roa, M. C. G., and Requena, J. C. (2005) 'Ranking versus scale rating in conjoint analysis: evaluating landscapes in mountainous regions in southeastern Spain'. *Ecological Economics* 55(4): 539–550.

Schoenherr, S.E. (2006) Evolution of the shopping center.

Schumpeter, J. (1975) *Capitalism, Socialism and Democracy (2nd ed.)*. New York: Harper.

Schwartz, N. H. and Kulhavy, R. W. (1981) 'Map features and the recall of discourse'. *Contemporary Educational Psychology & Marketing* 6(2): 151–158.

Sedona Chamber of Commerce (2010) *Shopping in Sedona*. Available at: http://visitsedona.com/index.php?action=article&id=42 (31 May 2010).

Sen, S., Block, L. G., and Chandran, S. (2002) 'Window displays and consumer shopping decisions'. *Journal of Retailing and Consumer Services* 9(5): 277–290.

Sharpley, R. (2004) 'Tourism and the countryside'. In Lew, A., Hall, C. M., and Williams, A. (eds.) *A Companion to Tourism*, 374–386. Malden: Blackwell.

Sharpley, R. and Vass, A. (2006) 'Tourism, farming and diversification: An attitudinal study'. *Tourism Management* 27(5): 1040–1052.

Shaw, C. and Ivens, J. (2005) *Building Great Customer Experiences*. Basingstoke: Palgrave Macmillan.

Sheldon, P. and Dwyer, L. (2010) 'The global financial crisis and tourism: perspectives of the academy'. *Journal of Travel Research* 49(1): 3–4.

Singapore Tourism Board (2006) *Overview*. Available at: https://app.stb.gov.sg/asp/sq/sq01.asp (31 May 2010).

Singapore Tourism Board (2008) *Singapore Star Service e-Brochure*. Available at: http://www.servicestar.com.sg/doc/SingaporeStarService_eBrochure.zip (31 May 2010).

Smardon, R. C. (1988) 'Perception and aesthetics of the urban environment: review of the role of vegetation'. *Landscape and Urban Planning* 15(1–2): 85–106.

Smeral, E. (2010) 'Impacts of the world recession and economic crisis on tourism: forecasts and potential risks'. *Journal of Travel Research* 49(1): 31–38.

Smith, R. K. and Olson, L. S. (2001) 'Tourist shopping activities and development of travel sophistication'. *Visions in Leisure and Business* 20(10): 23–33.

Snepenger, D. J., Murphy, L., O'Connell, R., and Gregg, E. (2003) 'Tourists and residents use of a shopping space'. *Annals of Tourism Research* 30(3): 567–580.

Snepenger, D. J., Reiman, S., Johnson, J., and Snepenger, M. (1998) 'Is downtown mainly for tourists?'. *Journal of Travel Research* 36(3): 5–12.

Song, H. and Lin, S. (2010) 'Impacts of the financial and economic crisis on tourism in Asia'. *Journal of Travel Research* 49(1): 16–30.

Southworth, M. (1969) 'The sonic environment of cities'. *Environment and Behavior* 1(1): 49–69.

Southworth, M. and Southworth, S. (1982) *Maps: A visual survey and design guide*. Boston: Little, Brown & Company.

Spangenberg, E. R., Crowley, A. E., and Henderson, P. W. (1996) 'Improving the store environment: do olfactory cues affect evaluations and behaviors?'. *Journal of Marketing* 60(2): 67–80.

Stamboulis, Y. and Pantoleon, S. (2003) 'Innovation strategies and technology for experience-based tourism'. *Tourism Management* 24(1): 35–43.

Stipanuk, D. M. (1993) 'Tourism and technology: interactions and implications'. *Tourism Management* 14(4): 267–278.

Stone, I. and Stubbs, C. (2007) 'Enterprising expatriates: lifestyle migration and entrepreneurship in rural southern Europe'. *Entrepreneurship and Regional Development* 19(5): 433–450.

Sugiyama, M. S. (2001) 'Food, foragers, and folklore: the role of narrative in human subsistence'. *Evolution and Human Behavior* 22(4): 221–240.

Sullivan, M. (2002) 'The impact of pitch, volume and tempo on the atmospheric effects of music'. *International Journal of Retail & Distribution Management* 30(6): 323–330.

Swallow, L. (2009) *Green Business Practices for Dummies*. Hoboken: Wiley.

Talbot, J. F., Kaplan, R., Kuo, F. E., and Kaplan, S. (1993) 'Factors that enhance effectiveness of visitor maps'. *Environment and Behavior* 25(6): 743–760.

Tang, L., Morrison, A. M., Lehto, X. Y., Kline, S., and Pearce, P. L. (2009) 'Effectiveness criteria for icons as tourist attractions: a comparative study between the United States and China'. *Journal of Travel & Tourism Marketing* 26(3): 284–302.

Taplin, J. H. E. and McGinley, C. (2000) 'A linear program to model daily car touring choices '. *Annals of Tourism Research* 27(2): 451–467.

Tauber, E. (1995) 'Why do people shop?'. *Marketing Management* 4(2): 58–60.

Thayer, R. and Atwood, B. (1978) 'Plants, complexity, and pleasure in urban and suburban environments'. *Journal of Nonverbal Behavior* 3(2): 67–76.

Thomas, C. J. and Bromley, R. D. F. (2002) 'The changing competitive relationship between small town centres and out-of-town retailing: town revival in South Wales'. *Urban Studies* 39(4): 791–817.

Thomas, C. J. and Bromley, R. D. F. (2003) 'Retail revitalization and small town centres: the contribution of shopping linkages'. *Applied Geography* 23(1): 47–71.

Thomas, M. (1998) *The Image of Towns in Australia from the Perspective of Tourists, Residents and Local Leaders*. Townsville: James Cook University.

Tideswell, C. and Faulkner, B. (1999) 'Multidestination travel patters of international visitors to Queensland'. *Journal of Travel Research* 37(4): 364–374.

Tiefenbacher, J. P., Day, F. A., and Walton, J. A. (2000) 'Attributes of repeat visitors to small tourist-oriented communities'. *The Social Science Journal* 37(2): 299–308.

Tilden, F. (1977) *Interpreting Our Heritage (3rd ed.)*. Chapel Hill: University of North Carolina Press.

Times Research Group (2004) 'Outbound Tourism Potential from India Prepared for Royal Norwegian Embassy, New Delhi'. Available at: http://www.innovasjonnorge,no/upload/Kundeportal/filer/markedsmuligheter/Outbound%20tourism%20India.doc. (28 May 2010).

Timothy, D. (2005) *Shopping Tourism, Retailing and Leisure*. Clevedon: Channel View.

Timothy, D. (2006) 'Safety and security issues in tourism'. In Buhalis, B. and Costa, C. (eds.) *Tourism Management Dynamics*, 19–27. Oxford: Elsevier.

Timothy, D. and Butler, R. (1995) 'Cross-border shopping: a North American perspective'. *Annals of Tourism Research* 22(1): 16–34.

Todorova, A., Asakawa, S., and Aikoh, T. (2004) 'Preferences for and attitudes towards street flowers and trees in Sapporo, Japan'. *Landscape and Urban Planning* 69(4): 403–416.

Tonts, M. and Greive, S. (2002) 'Commodification and creative destruction in the Australian rural landscape: the case of Bridgetown, Western Australia'. *Australian Geographical Studies* 40(1): 58–70.

Tosun, C., Temizkan, S. P., Timothy, D. J., and Fyall, A. (2007) 'Tourist shopping experiences and satisfaction'. *International Journal of Tourism Research* 9(2): 87–102.

Touring Club Italiano (2010) *Bandiere Arancioni*. Available at: http://www.bandierearancioni.it/ (27 May 2010).

Tourism Emergency Response Network (2010). Statement on Air Traffic Disruption in European Airlines April 21, 2010. Madrid: United Nations World Tourism Organisation.

Tourism Intelligence International (2010) *Travel and Tourism's Top Ten Emerging Markets* Available at: http://www.tourism-intelligence.com/article.php?id=67 (May 2010).

Tourism Research Australia (2008) *Destination Visitor Survey: Hahndorf Visitor Profile and Satisfaction Survey.* Canberra: Tourism Research Australia.

Tourism Research Australia (2009a) *International Visitors in Australia: Quarterly Results of the International Visitor Survey, December 2009.* Available at: http://www.ret.gov.au/tourism/tra/Pages/default.aspx (31 May 2010).

Tourism Research Australia (2009b) *Travel by Australians: Quarterly Results of the National Visitor Survey, December 2009.* Available at: http://www.ret.gov.au/tourism/tra/Pages/default.aspx (31 May 2010).

Tourism Victoria (2006) *Goldfields Profile Year Ending June 2006.* Melbourne: Tourism Victoria.

Tourism Victoria (2008) *Goldfields Market Profile Year Ending December 2007.* Available at: http://www.tourism.vic.gov.au/images/stories/goldfields-market-profile-2007.pdf. (27 May 2010).

Travel Industry Association (2001) *The Shopping Traveller.* Available at: http://www.tia.org/pubs/pubs.asp?PublicationID=89 (July 2007).

Tse, T. S. M. (2006) 'Crisis management in tourism'. In Buhalis, D. and Costa, C. (eds.) *Tourism Management Dynamics*, 28–38. Oxford: Elsevier.

Turley, L. W. and Milliman, R. (2000) 'Atmospheric effects on shopping behaviour: a review of the experimental evidence'. *Journal of Business Research* 49(2): 193–211.

Turner, L. and Reisinger, Y. (2001) 'Shopping satisfaction for domestic tourists'. *Journal of Retailing and Consumer Services* 8(1): 15–27.

Ulrich, R. S. (1984) 'View through a window may influence recovery from surgery'. *Science* 224(4647): 420–421.

Ulrich, R. S. (1986) 'Human responses to vegetation and landscapes'. *Landscape and Urban Planning* 13: 29–44.

Underhill, P. (1999) *Why We Buy: The science of shopping.* New York: Simon & Schuster.

Underhill, P. (2004) *Call of the Mall.* New York: Simon & Schuster.

UNWTO (2010) *World Tourism Barometer, January 2010, 8(1).* United Nations World Tourism Organisation.

Uriely, N. (2005) 'The tourist experience: conceptual developments'. *Annals of Tourism Research* 32(1): 199–216.

Urry, J. (1990) *The Tourist Gaze: Leisure and travel in contemporary societies*. London: Sage.

Urry, J. (1995) *Consuming Places*. London: Sage.

Van der Wagen, L. and Davies, C. (1998) *Supervision and Leadership*. Melbourne: Hospitality Press.

Vanslembrouck, I., Huylenbroeck, G., and Meensel, J. (2005) 'Impact of agriculture on rural tourism: a hedonic pricing approach'. *Journal of Agricultural Economics* 56(1): 17–30.

Vaughan, L. (2006) 'Making connections: the case of Borehamwood'. *Built Environment* 32(3): 281–197.

Vermuri, A. W. and Costanza, R. (2006) 'The role of human, social, built and natural capital in explaining life satisfaction at the country level: toward a national well-being index'. *Ecological Economics* 58(1): 119–133.

Victorian Bushfire Royal Commission (2009) *Interim Report*. Available at: http://www.royalcommission.vic.gov.au/getdoc/a19c8100–3ae9–43bc-896f-57-cbe35ca680/Executive-summary (May 2010).

Visser, G. (2004) 'Second homes and local development: issues arising from Cape Town's De Waterkant'. *GeoJournal* 60(3): 259–271.

Vrechopoulos, A. P., O'Keefe, R. M., Doukidis, G. I., and Siomkos, G. J. (2004) 'Virtual store layout: an experimental comparison in the context of grocery retail'. *Journal of Retailing* 80(1): 13–22.

Wakefield, K. L. and Baker, J. (1998) 'Excitement at the mall: determinants and effects on shopping response'. *Journal of Retailing* 74(4): 515–539.

Wakefield, K. L. and Blodgett, J. G. (1994) 'The importance of servicescapes in leisure service settings'. *Journal of Services Marketing* 8(3): 66–76.

Wang, N. (1999) 'Rethinking Authenticity in Tourism Experience'. *Annals of Tourism Research,* 26(2): 349–370.

Ward, P., Davies, B., and Kooijman, D. (2007) 'Olfaction and the retail environment: examining the influence of ambient scent'. *Service Business* 1(4): 295–316.

Warnaby, G. (2008) 'Maps and the representation of urban shopping destinations'. *International Journal of Retail & Distribution Management* 36(3): 224–234.

Warnaby, G., Alexander, A., and Medway, D. (1998) 'Town centre management in the UK: a review, synthesis and research agenda'. *The International Review of Retail, Distribution and Consumer Research* 8(1): 15–31.

Warnaby, G., Bennison, D., and Davies, B. J. (2005) 'Marketing town centres: retailing and town centre management'. *Local Economy* 20(2): 183–204.

Warnick, R. B. and Klar, L. R. (1991) 'The bed and breakfast and small inn industry of the Commonwealth of Massachusetts: an exploratory survey'. *Journal of Travel Research* 29(3): 17–25.

Weaver, D. (2005) 'The distinctive dynamics of exurban tourism'. *International Journal of Tourism Research* 7(1): 23–33.

Weaver, D. B. and Fennell, D. A. (1997) 'The vacation farm sector in Saskatchewan: a profile of operations'. *Tourism Management* 18(6): 357–365.

Weaver, D. B. and Lawton, L. J. (2001) 'Resident perceptions in the urban-rural fringe'. *Annals of Tourism Research* 28(2): 439–458.

Webb, B. (2000) 'Shopping redefined: towards a new concept of retailing'. *International Journal of Retail and Distribution Management* 28(12): 503–507.

Wener, R. E. and Kaminoff, R. D. (1983) 'Improving environmental information: effects of signs on perceived crowding and behavior'. *Environment and Behavior* 15(1): 3–20.

West, B. (Ed.) (2005) *Down the Road: Exploring backpackers and independent travel* Perth: API Network.

Westwood, S. (2006) 'Shopping in sanitised and un-sanitised spaces: adding value to tourist experiences'. *Journal of Retail and Leisure Property* 5(4): 281–291.

Wight, P. A. (1998) 'Opening the door on market trends in ecotourism accommodation'. *Proceedings of the Ecotourism Association of Australia*. Conference prodeeding.

Wilkie, M. (1995) 'Scent of a market'. *American Demographics* 17(8): 40–47.

Williams, A. (2006) 'Tourism and hospitality marketing: fantasy, feeling and fun'. *International Journal of Contemporary Hospitality Management* 18(6): 482–495.

Wilson, L. (2007) 'The family farm business? Insights into family, business and ownership dimensions of open-farms leisure studies'. *Leisure Studies* 26(3): 357–374.

Wine Country Cooking School (2010) *Wine Country Cooking School*. Available at: http://www.winecountrycooking.com/ (31 May 2010).

Wineries of Niagara-on-the-Lake (2010) *Wineries of Niagara-on-the-Lake*. Available at: http://www.wineriesofniagaraonthelake.com/ (31 May 2010).

Wolf, K. L. (2005a) 'Business district streetscapes, trees, and consumer response'. *Journal of Forestry* 103(8): 396–400.

Wolf, K. L. (2005b) 'Trees in the small city retail business district: comparing resident and visitor perceptions'. *Journal of Forestry* 103(8): 390–395.

Wolff, P. (1999) *Hot Towns: The future of the fastest growing communities in America*. Piscataway: Rutgers University Press.

Wong, J. and Law, R. (2003) 'Difference in shopping satisfaction levels: a study of tourists in Hong Kong'. *Tourism Management* 24(4): 401–410.

Woodside, A. G., Cruickshank, B. F., and Dehuang, N. (2007) 'Stories visitors tell about Italian cities as destination icons'. *Tourism Management* 28(1): 162–174.

Woodside, A. G., Sood, S., and Miller, K. R. (2008) 'When consumers and brands talk: storytelling theory and research in psychology and marketing'. *Psychology and Marketing* 25(2): 97–145.

Xia, J., Arrowsmith, C., Jackson, M., and Cartwright, W. (2008) 'The wayfinding process relationships between decision-making and landmark utility'. *Tourism Management* 29(3): 445–457.

Xiang, Z. and Gretzel, U. (2010) 'Role of social media in online travel information search'. *Tourism Management* 31(2): 179–188.

Xiang, Z., Wober, K., and Fesenmaier, D. (2008) 'Representation of the online tourism domain in search engines'. *Journal of Travel Research* 47(2): 137–150.

Yalch, R. and Spangenberg, E. (1990) 'Effects of store music on shopping behavior'. *Journal of Consumer Marketing* 7(2): 55–63.

Yeung, S., Wong, J., and Ko, E. (2004) 'Preferred shopping destination: Hong Kong versus Singapore'. *International Journal of Tourism Research* 6(2): 85–96.

Young, M. (1999) 'Cognitive maps of nature based tourists'. *Annals of Tourism Research* 26(4): 817–839.

Yu, H. and Littrell, M. (2003) 'Product and process orientations to tourism shopping'. *Journal of Travel Research* 42(2): 140–150.

Yu, K. (1995) 'Cultural variations in landscape preference: comparisons among Chinese sub-groups and Western design experts'. *Landscape and Urban Planning* 32(2): 107–126.

Yüksel, A. (2004) 'Shopping Experience evaluation: a case of domestic and international visitors'. *Tourism Management* 25(6): 751–759.

Yüksel, A. (2007) 'Tourist shopping habitat: effects on emotions, shopping value and behaviours'. *Tourism Management* 28(1): 58–69.

Yüksel, A. and Yuksel, F. (2007) 'Shopping risk perceptions: effects of tourists' emotions, satisfaction and expressed loyalty intentions'. *Tourism Management* 28(3): 703–713.

Zaichkowsky, J. L. (1985) 'Measuring the involvement construct'. *Journal of Consumer Research* 12(3): 341–352.

About the Authors

Laurie Murphy has been an academic staff member in the School of Business at JCU since 1991 (part-time from 1998-2005). Her current research interests include destination branding and marketing particularly at a regional level, and tourist shopping villages. She has also published research on the backpacker travel market which influenced the development of a National Backpacker Tourism Strategy by the Australian Federal Government in 1995. Laurie is on the editorial board of the Journal of Travel and Tourism Marketing and the Journal of Travel Research.

Gianna Moscardo has been a member of the academic staff of the School of Business since February 2002. Before joining the School of Business she had been a Principal Research Fellow and project leader in tourism research in the Cooperative Research Centres for Reef and Rainforest for eight years managing a series of research and extension activities aimed at enhancing the sustainability of tourism activities in Northern Australia. To date she has authored or co-authored more than 150 refereed international research publications including 3 research books, and more than 45 articles in international academic journals. She was elected to the World Tourism Organization's International Academy for the Study of Tourism Scholars in 2005.

Pierre Benckendorff is a Senior Lecturer at University of Queensland and an adjunct Senior Lecturer in Tourism Management in the School of Business, James Cook University, Australia. His current research interests include visitor attraction management, urban and built tourism settings, entertainment, tourism technologies and tourism education and he has authored and co-authored a number of academic articles in these areas. He is a member of several international tourism organisations including the Council for Australian University Tourism and Hospitality Educators, the Asia Pacific Tourism Association and the PATA Young professionals.

Philip Pearce is the Foundation Professor of Tourism at James Cook University. His interests in tourism were developed during his doctoral studies at Oxford University where he analysed the behaviour of tourists on European package tours. He has a continuing interest in tourist behaviour and has written 7 books concerned with aspects of tourism including co-authoring the recent volume with Routledge Tourists Tourism and the Good Life. He is a founding member of the International Academy for the Study of Tourism and Honorary Professor at Xi'an International Studies University, Xi'an, China.

Author Index

Subject Index